KV-638-653

R.T.C. LETTERKENNY

e

One million poor?

The Challenge of Irish Inequality

Edited by Stanislaus Kennedy RSC

turoe
press

For assistance with the publication of this book the publishers gratefully acknowledge The Conference of Major Religious Superiors and the Society of St Vincent de Paul.

© J. Curry, B. Dillon, E. Fitzgerald, R. Gilligan, N. Kearney, S. Kennedy, M. Mernagh, S.M. Miller, J. O'Brien, L. O'Brien, D. O'Mahony, L. Ryan, A.D. Tussing, W. Walsh, and the Estate of P. Birch 1981. This collection© Turoe Press, 1981.

0 905223 30 6
Cover design by Hugh Donoghue
Typesetting by Kairos, Maynooth
Printed by The Leinster Leader, Naas

Published by Turoe Press Ltd., PO Box 1113
Baldoyle, Dublin 13, Ireland.

CONTENTS

Acknowledgements

To the authors for their willing response to my request for contributions to this book and for their co-operation throughout; to Mary Whelan for her advice and encouragement and to the publishers, Turoe Press, for   constant support during the preparation of the book.

Stanislaus Kennedy RSC
October, 1981

INTRODUCTION

Stanislaus Kennedy R.S.C.

Why a book about poverty? Simply because poverty still exists in a period of world recession and signs are that it is on the increase. For most people in Ireland poverty and low income are inextricably linked. Poverty is evident in bad housing, poor health and in educational under-achievement. Poverty is associated particularly with groups such as the unemployed, the illiterate and those who are chronically ill or economically dependent, small farmers, one parent families, travellers, the homeless, people in institutional care. This is essentially because these groups are unable to make themselves heard in a world of competing interest groups such as employers, farmers, professionals, trade unionists and others.

Despite the fact that individuals and groups have been researching and writing in specialist journals on the subject of poverty in Ireland over the years, particularly since the late '60s, their insights have not been brought together in one volume until now. People have a desire and a right to know the extent of poverty and the ways in which it can be eliminated.

At the beginning of this year a group of people with a range of expertise and a variety of approaches in the area of poverty and inequality were asked to contribute to this volume. The method of eliciting contributions was selective and the book does not, therefore, highlight all aspects of poverty or all groups suffering from poverty or working with the poor in Ireland, neither does it address itself to the question of wealth nor to the groups and individuals who possess wealth. It has little to say directly about poverty on a world scale or about the vital need for a developed country like Ireland to have a commitment to redressing the balance of power, status and prosperity between the developed and underdeveloped worlds. These are issues which those of us concerned with this book would see as needing full treatment in a separate volume. Such a realis-

7

ation however must not blind us to the reality and challenge of poverty in Ireland.

The Definition of Poverty

What does poverty mean? Until recent times poverty was defined in *absolute* terms. Among the early studies of poverty the work of Seebohm Rowntree is most important. Rowntree saw poverty as affecting those 'whose total earnings were insufficient to obtain the minimum necessities for the maintenance of merely physical efficiency' *(Poverty: A Study of Town Life, London, 1901)*. In more recent times social science has been putting emphasis on a definition which would place poverty in *relative* terms, culturally determined by particular societies. According to Peter Townsend:

> Individuals, families and groups in a population can be said to be in poverty when they lack the resources to obtain the type of diet, participate in the activities and have the living conditions and amenities which are customary or are at least widely encouraged and approved in the society to which they belong. Their resources are so seriously below those commanded by the average individual or family that they are, in effect, excluded from ordinary living patterns, customs and activities (*Poverty in the United Kingdom, A Summary of Household Resources and Standards of Living, London 1979*).

The Irish Reality

While any fixed measure of absolute poverty or of a poverty line is necessarily subjective, it can, however, be a useful indicator of poverty at any given time. This book opens with the assumption that most people's perception of what it means to be poor in Ireland today corresponds with the standard of living attainable on statutory social welfare payments.

Nearly one million people receive a social welfare payment each week and about 700,000 people, which is 20% of our population, depend on social welfare for their only or main long-term source of income. In fact, taking together all the up-to date informational available, it can be concluded that 30% of all households in Ireland today are living in poverty. The elderly and families where the breadwinner is out of work through sickness or unemployment make up a substantial proportion of

8

those who are poor. But there is also a significant minority of families with a parent at work who are in the poorest group and here the incidence of poverty is directly related to family size. While only one in ten families with one child are poor, one in three families with four or more children is in the poorest group.

That about one million of our population suffer deprivations associated with poverty, makes the fact that little information is available on the subject all the more surprising. We in Ireland have been very close to the experience of poverty both in time and context. Yet we have not analysed or conceptualised or synthesised it in any objective and unified manner as other countries have done. We tend to work on the assumption that people understand what poverty is and where it exists. But do we? It is clear from the contents of this book that low income is only one aspect of poverty. Many people continue to disciminate between the 'deserving' and the 'undeserving' poor.

This is bad enough. What is worse is to relegate into the latter category those superficially dubbed 'feckless', 'lacking in moral fibre' or legally dubbed 'vagrants' because they do not conform to the values of our society. For example, we regularly criminalise and imprison the single homeless for not having homes even though one of the most glaring inequalities in our society is the exclusion of the single homeless from the right to a house or a home.

The book shows that emphasis on providing shelter and the incrementalist responses from successive governments have done little to redress the serious inequalities which still persist in our housing system. It highlights our failure to honour our commitment to cherishing people equally by not completely appraising our housing situation so that each and every citizen has decent living conditions. It points to how our old people are being more and more distanced from whatever economic and social development is taking place in our society. It describes the poverty of rural Ireland which is as degrading and isolating as urban poverty. It examines the different perspectives and theories of urbanism and urban poverty and argues that these have not been brought together in such a way as to lead to a coherent approach to the solution to poverty.

The Challenge

The book examines the policies, activities and strategies of both private and public institutions in tackling poverty. It challenges the churches to have the courage to work towards creating a more just and caring society in which individuals are prepared to make personal sacrifices for the less well off. It questions the commitment of successive governments to the eradication of poverty and argues that as poverty has never been a central political issue it has largely been left to committed pressure groups together with a few politicians to fight the battle of the poor. It analyses the impact of our health, education and housing policies on the poor and puts forward constructive proposals as to how these policies could be implemented more equitably and to the benefit of the poor. It challenges the legal system to act as a double-edged weapon in fighting poverty through legislation and adequate legal services. Tracing the history of social work in Ireland it asserts that since social work has grown as a profession there seems to be a tendency on the part of social workers to distance themselves from the problems of poverty. It asks whether those involved in social work and community work could have more influence on social policy in order to eliminate poverty. It highlights the role which pilot schemes can play in fighting poverty. Drawing attention to the innovative work carried out in the Irish programme of Pilot Schemes to Combat Poverty from 1974 to 1980 it challenges the government to transfer the lessons of these pilot schemes into national policies to combat poverty, and to learn from the experiences of other countries.

It is obvious from the book that there is no simple, static, unchanging solution to the problem of poverty.

Immediately at least, some of the disadvantages which poor people suffer could be removed quickly but we must not lose sight of the long-term change which the elimination of poverty will require. The consensus which emerges from the contributions to this book is that although there have been efforts to alleviate poverty such efforts have been piecemeal and have not been planned in any coherent way. Neither has there been any commitment by successive governments to the long term change needed in order to eliminate poverty and injustice. One of the contentions of the book is that it is the inescapable duty of government to carry out a continual analysis of the problem of poverty and to develop a social policy to meet changing needs. No government should be permitted to evade that duty. This policy must recognise that *how* poverty is eliminated is no less important than *it be* eliminated. It must see the poor as full participants in their future development. To achieve that there must be public education about the extent and nature of poverty, inequality and injustice in Ireland.

It is important to recognise that if there is a tiny element of injustice in a society it is an unjust society because it tolerates injustice. If we live in an unjust society no one is unaffected; the effects of injustice are insidious. If we continue to define poverty in terms of personal inadequacy of the poor or continue to focus on the poor in isolation and not in the context of the whole of society then we will continue to deal with symptoms and results rather than causes. While no one could deny the need for services to ease the burden of poverty and to discriminate in favour of the poor too exclusive a concern for the alleviation of poverty can easily lend legitimacy to a social system in which glaring disparities in income, wealth, status and power are accepted as unimportant all in the name of meeting basic needs.

* Poverty will be eliminated if and when those who have the resources in this country and the power which resources give — whether it is political, social, economic or professional power — are prepared to share it with the powerless and voiceless in our society.*This will require not only a redistribution from the rich to the poor but also distribution from those who are not so rich to the less well off. Who, for example, is to pay the cost of the economic difficulties facing us at present? Must the main burden be borne by the poor and those who lose their employment? To what extent will you and I be prepared to bear the cost? Who, for example, is going to give the lead and say I have enough in order that those who do not have enough might get more and what are the constraints which prevent an individual or group from taking that stand? Ultimately a more equitable society can only come about when individuals and groups are prepared to make personal sacrifices. The task is daunting. It will require firm commitment and courageous leadership. But what also emerges from this book is a note of hope — hope based on clear insight into our society, its needs and its potential for change. *One Million Poor*? will, it is hoped, provoke discussion on the issue of poverty and social justice, serve as an impetus for immediate reforms and help towards the formulation of planning necessary for the elimination of poverty and inequality in Ireland.

PART I

The Extent of Poverty in Ireland

Eithne Fitzgerald

Many people and families in Ireland today still experience poverty in their daily lives. Almost a million people receive social welfare payments each week — for very many, these benefits, hardly too generous, are their only main long-term source of income. Many workers also experience poverty, particularly those trying to bring up a large family, and a sizeable minority of workers have a standard of living below that of an old age pensioner. While our growing towns and cities show a surface prosperity, we have our visible signs of poverty also — the living conditions of the travelling people, the decaying inner city areas, areas of rural depopulation and decline, and institutions and homes in urgent need of modernisation or replacement.

Irish society still knows deprivation and inequality. We have inequality in education and life chances, in access to and security of employment, in housing and living conditions, in income and wealth. Loneliness, bereavement, and family problems add their own dimension of poverty. How widespread is poverty in Ireland? There is no single simple answer to this question, but to try to answer it as best as possible it is necessary to take a closer look at what we mean by poverty.

With the growth in incomes and in living standards in the Western world, our concept of what it means to be poor has changed. It is clear that in depth and in scale poverty in Ireland is in most cases removed from the type of poverty experienced in the Third World. Yet poverty here is very real. We recognise as poor not only those who can barely feed and clothe themselves, but also the many whose incomes and living conditions fall below the accepted minimum norms of our society. While actual hunger and malnutrition are now thankfully rare in this country, many people find themselves hard pressed to provide for the other basic needs — shelter, fuel, clothes, transport. Many families lack a home of their own, a secure centre for family life, and must share one with another family in grossly overcrowded conditions. Many people, particularly the elderly, live in housing which is sub-standard and lacking in what are today looked on as the essential amenities of running water and an indoor bathroom and WC.

Poverty does not only consist of low income and poor housing and living conditions. We find other areas like educational under-achievement, illiteracy, crime and vandalism are closely related to poverty and bad living conditions. While different aspects of poverty are explored in the contributions to this book, this chapter examines the extent of poverty measured mainly in terms of low income. Although it is recognised that concentrating on income data alone does not give the whole picture, low income is nevertheless the crucial test of poverty.

Where Do We Draw The Poverty Line?

There is no uniquely accepted definition of poverty, and the debate goes on between those who believe that poverty is an absolute condition, and those who believe that poverty is relative and that what constitutes poverty varies over time and place. Whichever view is taken of the nature of poverty, it is not possible to select a definition of poverty which is not largely subjective.

For those who regard poverty as absolute, there is no fully satisfactory way of defining an absolute poverty standard. Early researchers constructed detailed minimum family budgets, based on subsistence purchases of a wide range of goods, from food to clothing and housing. There is obviously a strong subjective element in agreeing what items should be included in such a subsistence budget — is a TV or a car still a luxury? and then in assuming that rational purchases on the lines specified in the budget are actually made by poor families. A subsistence income that does not allow for the odd lapse to buy a pint is not very realistic.

Some researchers have argued that the level of welfare rates defines an objective standard of poverty, being society's conssensus view of the minimum needed to live on.[1] While it is hardly realistic to think that welfare rates represent society's considered judgement on a minimum basic standard of living, benefit rates do provide an easily available scale which many people find close to their own perceptions of a poverty income. If benefit scales are used over time to measure the poverty line, however, the more that benefits improve, the faster will the numbers in poverty appear to grow.

The official USA approach to constructing a poverty line has been to look at subsistence food budgets for different types of family, and to multiply the various budgets by about three to get an appropriate poverty line for each family size.[2] This somewhat arbitrary procedure is based on the observation that poor families in the USA spent about a third of their income on food.

Those who argue that poverty is relative say that poverty occurs where people have too low an income to participate in normal life of their community. Some people then go to define a poverty income by relating it to 'normal' incomes in the community. One such approach is to relate a poverty line to average earnings, e.g. by setting it at a rate of say two-thirds of average earnings. Others consider that the lowest slice of the income distribution are living in poverty, and may choose a proportion ranging from the lowest 10 per cent up to the lowest 30 per cent of the income distributions as constituting the poverty group. If this purely relative view of poverty is taken, that the lowest say 30 per cent of the income distribution is poor, improvements in the standard of living generally will be seen as leaving the problem of poverty unchanged — the poor will always be with us.

Whichever view is taken, and wherever the line is drawn, it must be recognised that the choice of a poverty line is a subjective one. It is also important to bear in mind that in most cases, society does not divide neatly into those who are well off and those who are poor. There is very little difference in real living standards between families who are marginally above a 'poverty line' and those marginally below it. Some account must be taken of the different needs of families of varying size and composition in drawing up a poverty line. An income of £60 a week could mean relative comfort for a single person, but poverty for someone with six children.

While recognising the difficulties involved in defining a poverty line for the purpose of looking at the extent of poverty in Ireland, the standard of living attainable on social welfare seems to offer a reasonable working definition of what it means to be poor in Ireland today. As the benefit rates (Oct. 1981) quoted in Table 1 show, the kind of living standard which can be achieved on these incomes is low, and the view that these living standards constitute poverty is one which has a wide acceptance.[3] These levels do not form an absolute poverty line, but

15

are a rough guideline to be followed in examining the issue of poverty.

TABLE 1
Examples of Basic Social Welfare Incomes, Oct. 1981

	Contributory benefit £ per week	Means-tested benefit £ per week
Unemployed couple, 4 children	66.20	57.35
Widow or deserted wife, 2 children	46.00	42.55
— supplementary welfare	—	32.25
Pensioner, living alone	33.85	29.20

Counting The Poor

There are a number of sources from which to build up a picture of poverty and low income in Ireland — the Household Budget Surveys, social welfare records, reports of the Revenue Commissioners, Farm Management Surveys, and others. Each source has its drawbacks and limitations, and none of the sources dovetails exactly to provide a fully comprehensive and up-to-date picture.

The first real attempt at counting the poor in Ireland was Seamus O'Cinneide's paper to the Kilkenny Poverty Conference in 1971.[4] Using the data then available, he estimated how many adults and children were below the poverty standard he chose, and he calculated that one person in four was living at or below the poverty standard of £300 a year for a single person, £500 for a couple, with another £100 for each child.

Updating this estimate using O'Cinneide's methodology is not easy, because the method relied on detailed Census figures, and there has not been a full census since 1971. However, since 1971, many more sources of information on low incomes have become available, and can be used to establish the numbers of people with low incomes.

The last full-scale national survey of household incomes was the Household Budget Survey of 1973.[5] Smaller scale surveys covering urban areas have been published up to 1978. However, the principal reason for using the 1973 data is because it is the only data on household incomes which we can compare the living standards of families of differing size and composition, at different levels of income. The Central Statistics Office provided access to the raw data on each household in the computer files of the survey, and each household was weighted according to the number of 'equivalent adults' it contained, to reduce the different households to a common base of comparison.[6]

Studies of family spending have shown a consistent pattern in the levels of spending by families of different sizes. Studies in the UK have calculated the relative costs of children, of single people living alone, and of married couples. Based on this research and taking a married couple as the unit, an 'equivalence scale' of .6 for a single person, .25 for each child and .5 for each additional adult was used to convert each household to a common basis of comparison. With each household standardised like this, income per unit was calculated. Taking the married couple as the unit, it was worked out what income each household would require to keep its existing standard of living unchanged if each household were to consist only of a married couple, instead of the different sizes and shapes of families which actually exist. For example, a couple and five children would have a weight of 2.25; in other words they need two and a quarter times the income of a married couple on their own in order to maintain an equivalent standard of living. Such a family with an income of £225 a week would be deemed to have an 'equivalent income', in terms of the unit married couple, of £100 a week.

The distribution of income for 1973, on this 'equivalent income' basis was then calculated. The results show that 20 per cent of households had disposable incomes which in terms of the living costs of a married couple were at or below £11.20 a week. Adjusting that to current (August 1981) money values gives a living standard at or below £37.50 a week. In other words, one in five households in 1973 had a living standard at or below that attainable today by a married couple on an income of £37.50 a week.

The poorest 30 per cent of families in 1973 had disposable incomes at or below the equivalent of £13.60 for a married couple. That works out as £45.50 at today's money values. The comparative level of these incomes can be judged by noting that today a pensioner couple gets £46 a week. About 30 per cent

17

of all private households in 1973 had living standards below those of today's old age pensioners. One in five households had living standards which were *three-quarters or less* of those of today's pensioners.

The standard of living obtainable on social welfare pensions today corresponds roughly to our current perception of what it means to be poor. By that definition about 30 per cent of households in 1973 could be regarded as poor.

Who Are The Poor?

The elderly and the unemployed feature strongly among the poorest households. But there are also many families where the bread-winner is working, particularly where there is a large family. These poor households where there is a parent in work account for between a fifth and a sixth of those in poverty. While one in ten families who have one child are poor, one in three families with four or more children are poor. Poverty is widespread in old age. About two-thirds of households headed by an elderly person are poor. Tables 2 and 3 give the details.

TABLE 2

Households in the Lower Income Groups, 1973

	Lowest 20%	Lowest 30%
Married couple and children, working parent	15½	20
Married couple and children, parent out of work	9	6
One-parent families	1½	2
Other families with children	12½	14
Elderly — 1 person (65 and over)	16	15
— couple	10	10
Other households with children	34½	32
Total	100	100

18608141

TABLE 3

Percentage of Households of Each Type in the Upper and Lower Income Groups, 1973

	Upper 70% %	Lower 30% %
Households with children		
(a) with a working parent		
couple, 1 child	89	11
couple, 2 children	90	10
couple, 3 children	83	17
couple, 4 or more children	67	33
(b) parent out of work		
couple and children	13	87
(c) one-parent families	73	27
(d) other families with children	72	28
Elderly		
living alone	29	71
couple	39	61
Other households, no children	75	25
Overall	70	30

This data relates to families living in private households and permanent homes.

Continuing Poverty: The Up-To-Date Data

Poverty for many individuals and families is the outlook supported by the most up-to-date information of incomes, since the last overall national survey in 1973. There is a continuing problem of low income among families with a parent earning. The latest report of the Revenue Commissioners shows that in 1977/78 there were 42,000 families with children in the tax net with income below £2,500 a year (under £4,350 at today's prices).

The sharp rise in unemployment, the growing number of one-

19

parent families, and the fact that State income support for working families (i.e. children's allowances plus the cash value of income tax allowances for children) have continued to decline in real terms, all confirm the picture of continuing poverty among families.

Farm Poverty

Low incomes in farming have been highlighted in successive Farm Management Surveys. Quite aside from the dramatic 50 per cent fall in average farm incomes over the last two years being experienced in the current recession in agriculture, these surveys have over the years catalogued the extremely low incomes received on small uneconomic farm holdings, and indeed they have forecast as a result the disappearance of hill farming as a way of life.

In 1977, 26 per cent of full-time farms had a family farm income of under £2,000 and 11 per cent of these had incomes of less than £1,000. In 1978 the number of full-time farms below £2,000 dropped slightly to 24 per cent, but the onset of the farm recession in 1979 saw it rise to 31 per cent. That means in 1979 about 40,000 full-time farmers had family farm incomes of less than £2,000. The continuing farm problems in 1980 and 1981 would raise that number even higher.

The poorest farms are found predominantly in the west of Ireland and are closely associated with small farm size, poor land, as well as an ageing population. The persistence of the problem of poverty in these areas, in good farming years and in bad, points to the need for deeper structural reform. (John Curry in Chapter 2 explores the issue of rural poverty in greater depth).

Farm prosperity in the early and mid-seventies brought little benefit to many farmers whose holdings were scarcely economic. To these farmers where poverty has always been an issue, we must add today many farmers on medium-sized holdings whose experience in the recession has reduced them to a bare subsistence standard of living.

People Depending on Social Welfare

Almost a million people — individuals and their dependants — are at the receiving end of social welfare and health board allowances each week. For very many, the level of social welfare benefit sets their living standard over the long term. Despite improvements over the years in the real value of benefits, the increases have come from a very low base, and poverty or near-poverty is still the norm for most who depend on these benefits.

To illustrate this it is useful to look at the latest returns from the urban Household Budget Survey for the lowest income group, mainly elderly people. In 1978, 7 per cent of all urban households had incomes of under £20 a week, most of them elderly people living alone. A further 6 per cent, mainly elderly couples, had incomes of between £20 and £30 a week. At today's prices, average income per head for the first group is £18 a week, and for the second, under £30. These low-income elderly families spend about 40 per cent of their budget on food alone, and despite subsidy and fuel voucher schemes, a further 12 per cent goes on fuel. While improvements have taken place in pensions, the general view is still one of widespread continuing poverty. And while the pension in 1973 was 22.4 per cent of the disposable income of the average worker, by 1980 the ratio was little improved at 23.7 per cent.

Means-Tested Payments

About 380,000 individuals and their families receive a means-tested payment each week. The biggest group are old age pensioners, followed by those on unemployment assistance — most of them being long-term unemployed. Other categories catered for are the disabled, widows and others bringing up a family on their own, and elderly single women. About 17,000 people with 20,000 dependants draw Supplementary Welfare Allowance, most of them to supplement income from other welfare payments which has been inadequate for their needs. For most people on means-tested payments, these payments are meeting a long-term financial need, not just a temporary interruption of income. Eighty per cent means-tested benefits are paid at the maximum rate, indicating that the bulk of recipients have little or no means of their own. For recipients who have other sources of income, the rule that any means (or any means over £6 in the case of pensioners and one-parent families) must be offset against benefits paid, effectively limits their total income to broadly the level set by the benefit rate. So virtually all those receiving means-tested payments rely on incomes at or just slightly above the level set by the benefit rate, and for most of them this sets their long-term standard of living.

Contributory Benefits

While some of those receiving contributory benefits which are not means-tested may be able to top up their benefit by income from other sources, for very many there is little or no extra income to stretch out the benefit.

The only area where there is extensive supplementation of social insurance benefits is in the case of disability benefit, where many employees also get sick pay from their jobs. However, 20 per cent of those on disability benefit have been sick for thirty weeks or longer, and it is safe to assume that this proportion of the total depend mainly on their disability benefit cheques.

Redundancy payments and pay-related benefit can cushion the financial impact in the early months of unemployment. However, about three-quarters of those receiving unemployment benefit have worked for under six months in the preceding twelve, and have therefore to rely mainly on their welfare payments.

While between a third and a half of widows aged under 65 have a job, over two-thirds of widows are aged over 65 and too old to work. For most of these, the only other income they are likely to have comes from small savings and occupational pensions. Some old age and retirement pensioners also have pensions from their jobs with which to stretch out their State pensions. But as the Green Paper on a national income-related pension scheme pointed out, outside the public sector, occupational pensions have to date been limited, and particularly so for manual workers. Where retired people or their widows are entitled to such pensions, the principal drawback is the fact that outside the public sector, these pensions do not keep up with inflation. With the very high inflation rates we have seen over the last number of years, after the first couple of years the level of help given by these pensions dwindles away. With about two-thirds of elderly households below the 'poverty line', and with many wives of contributory pensioners qualifying on a means test for pensions in their own names, it seems clear that only a minority of pensioners have any significant income over and above their State pensions.

Table 4 gives details of individuals and families receiving

social welfare payments. Table 5 attempts to estimate how many of those depend chiefly on social welfare in the long term. All means-tested recipients, and roughly half of insurance-based recipients, are included to cover the likely extent of other income for different categories. Taken together, the total shows that about 700,000 people or about one in five of the total population — now depend on social welfare as a main long-term source of income.

This proportion has risen with the steep rise in unemployment in the last year. As can be seen from the tables, the retired, the unemployed, and the widowed make up the greater part of the total. One in six of all children live in these families which rely heavily on social welfare.

Other Dimensions of Poverty

So far we have looked at data on low incomes. Other aspects of the experience of poverty, such as poorly equipped homes, homelessness itself and educational under-achievement, will now be touched upon, and a brief glance taken at the many facets of poverty experienced by particularly deprived groups — one-parent families, travellers, people living in institutions.

Household Amenities

A considerable proportion of households lack amenities and facilities which are now regarded as basic.

Lack of basic housing amenities is concentrated in rural areas. The 1971 census showed half of all households in rural areas lacked an indoor water supply. Only one third had a bath or shower compared to nearly 80 per cent of urban households. Only 42 per cent of homes in rural areas had a flush toilet. While there have been improvements in many cases since 1971, the latest data, for 1978 (urban areas only) shows a sizeable minority without basic amenities. 14 per cent of urban households have no bath/shower, 9 per cent have no hot water, and 8 per cent have no indoor toilet. Elderly households in particular are likely to lack these amenities. The recent Society of St Vincent de Paul survey, *Old and Alone in Ireland*, showed over half the elderly living alone in Ireland have no bath or shower, and a third possess no kitchen sink. Three-fifths have no hot water supply, and less than half the elderly living alone have an indoor flush toilet. The improvements in housing in

TABLE 4

Recipients of Weekly Social Welfare Payments and Their Dependants, 1980

Payment	Recipients	Adult dependents	Child dependents	Total
Contributory benefits				
Disability benefit	67,292	23,710	50,342	141,344
Invalidity pension	15,953	7,014	10,272	33,239
Maternity allowance	1,722	—	—	1,722
Old age (con) pensions	65,111	18,000	3,413	86,524
Retirement pensions	31,734	15,134	3,733	50,601
Unemployment benefit	67,154	28,634	62,403	158,191
Widow's (con) pensions	69,457	—	21,200	90,657
Orphan's (con) allowance	819	—	—	819
Deserted wife's benefit	2,787	—	4,894	7,861
Total, contributory benefits	322,029	92,492	156,257	570,778

24

Means-tested payments

Old age (non-con) pensions	130,860	9,618	4,033	144,511
Unemployment assistance (Excluding smallholders)	50,178	23,430	64,932	138,540
Widow's (non-con) pensions	11,242	—	6,500	17,742
Orphans allowance	172	—	—	172
Deserted wife's allowance	2,834	—	3,912	6,746
Unmarried mother's allowance	5,290	—	5,736	11,026
Prisoner's wife's allowance	182	—	540	722
Single women's allowance	3,100	—	—	3,100
Supplementary welfare allowance (not receiving other benefit)	5,170	1,000	8,600	14,700
Disabled person's maintenance allowance	23,000	6,900	12,200	42,100
Infectious diseases maintenance allowance	284	101	178	563
Total, means-tested benefits	232,312	41,049	106,631	379,992
Overall Total	554,341	133,541	262,888	950,770

Source:— Parliamentary questions 11 November 1980; Unemployment figures, January 1981; the number of dependents on DPMA, and the net numbers drawing supplementary welfare who are not drawing other benefits have been estimated by the author.

TABLE 5

Estimated Number Depending on Social Welfare as Main Long-Term Income, 1980

Benefit received	Recipients	Adult dependants	Child dependants
Contributory benefits			
Disability benefit	13,458	4,742	10,068
Invalidity pension	15,953	7,014	10,272
Old age pension	45,578	12,600	2,390
Retirement pension	22,214	10,594	46,800
Unemployment benefit	50,365	21,476	5,300
Deserted wife's benefit	2,787	—	4,894
Means-tested benefits			
Old age pensions	130,869	9,618	4,033
Unemployment assistance	50,178	23,430	64,932
Widow's pensions	11,242	—	6,500
Deserted wife's allowance	2,834	—	3,912

Prisoner's wife's allowance	182	—	540
Unmarried mother's allowance	5,290	—	5,736
Single women's allowance	3,100	—	—
Supplementary welfare allowance	5,170	1,000	8,600
DPMA	23,000	6,900	12,200
IDMA	284	101	178
Total	**420,615**	**97,475**	**188,968**

Total Recipients and Dependants:

707,058 (21 per cent of total population)

N.B. This table is based on the data in Table 4. It is assumed that all recipients of means-tested benefits depend on those benefits as their main source of income. In the case of contributory benefits we have taken 20 per cent of DB recipients (those on DB for 30 weeks or longer); 75 per cent of UB recipients (those with less than six months' employment in the previous twelve months); 70 per cent of contributory pensioners (assuming that those outside the previously calculated 'poverty group' are likely to have reasonable pensions form their jobs; it is assumed that 15,000 of the 20,000 working widows get contributory pensions, and these are excluded, included are 70 per cent of the remainder — mainly elderly widows — on the same basis as old age pensioners.

rural areas seem to have passed the elderly by.

Turning to appliances, the table below shows the proportion of homes which lack particular appliances. Those least likely to possess them are again the elderly, those living in rural areas, and low income families and the families of unskilled workers.

TABLE 6

Percentage of Homes Lacking Various Appliances

	1973 urban %	1973 rural %	1973 Total %	1978 urban %
Fridge	36	60	46	15
Washing machine	48	65	55	35
Telephone	72	89	80	64
Car	52	45	50	48

Source: Household Budget Surveys

Education

The numbers who cut their education short usually signifies family poverty or problems of some description. About 5 per cent, or 4,000 of so, leave school before the official school-leaving age of 15; a further 19 per cent of the age-cohort leave when they are 15. Literacy studies, notably by Dr Desmond Swan, have indicated there is a sizeable minority of teenagers with literacy problems.

Under-achievement in education is usually a symptom of poverty and bad living conditions, and of course makes it more likely that the under-achievers in their turn face only low-paid jobs, and further poverty for their own families in the future.

Poverty and Housing Costs

In looking at poverty, it is not enough to consider just family income; we must also examine family spending. One major area where the costs faced by different families are very variable is in relation to housing. A family who bought an ordinary semi-detached house ten years ago may be paying about £50 a month in repayments, a family who are now trying to rent or

28

buy the same house can be paying four times that amount for a home for themselves. The same income, depending on the housing costs which are faced, can mean a comfortable living standard for one family, and near penury for another. Many young couples find they are simply unable to find a home to buy or rent for themselves at a price they can afford. Many young families live with in-laws in conditions of appalling over-crowding while they wait for a home from the local authority. There are around 35,000 families, most of them without any separate home of their own, on council waiting-lists around the country. About 8,000 families are on waiting-lists in the greater Dublin area, and the majority of these have been assess-ed as living in grossly overcrowded conditions. If we look simply at their income, some of these families would not be assessed as poor, but their inability to provide a home of their own means they experience poverty in their day-to-day living conditions.

Particular Groups in Poverty

It will now be useful to examine the extent of poverty among a few specific groups.

One-Parent Families

Although relatively few one-parent families showed up in the statistics of poverty taken from the Household Budget Survey, it is clear that very many one-parent families are living in poverty and finding great difficulty in coping single-handedly on an in-adequate income. One in twenty children is being reared by one parent only. Many depend on social welfare benefits which range, for a mother with two children, from £32.25 a week if she is on Supplementary Welfare, to £46 if she has a con-tributory widow's pension. Many separated mothers must de-pend on maintenance payments which are both inadequate and erratic. The Royal Commission on Income and Wealth in the UK found that nearly 60 per cent of one-parent families were in poverty, compared to 14 per cent of two-parent families.[9] In Ireland, where fewer mothers coping alone can take a job to supplement their welfare benefits, the numbers in poverty may be even higher.

The majority of parents coping alone are widows, but growing numbers of separated wives and single mothers keep their babies. They share common problems — financial worry, trying to fulfil the role of two parents, anxiety and loneliness.

Single mothers in particular find the cost and the quality of available housing a great problem. The rent of a single bed-sitter in Dublin is now from £15 to £20 a week, and managing this on an income of £34.80 is impossible. Where she has such a place of her own, the single mother finds that bringing up a child on her own in a bed-sitter is no easy task. Some find the difficulties of managing alone on an inadequate income overwhelming, and increasing numbers of children are coming into care from single mothers who feel they can no longer cope.

Many parents on their own need to go out to work to supplement their income. While only 14 per cent of married women in the 30 to 44 age-group have a job outside the home, 44 per cent of widows in the same age-group are working. Arranging suitable care for their children is a constant problem. All children need continuity, and these children in particular, yet many mothers have to make do with a succession of different child-minders because there is no alternative. Financially, the working widow or single parent finds herself at a disadvantage. Her outgoings are rarely significantly less than those of a married couple, particularly where she is paying for child care, yet her tax allowances and tax bands are less than those of a couple. Most who do work find they are confined by lack of training and experience to the lower-paid categories — 'women's work'.

Parents drawing the means-tested pensions or social assistance allowances forfeit these allowances if their incomes exceed the benefit rates. For example, an unmarried mother with earnings of £35 a week or over forfeits her whole allowance. Many women find they are caught in a poverty trap; they either live on their allowance and manage as best they can, or else if they take a job they find after a full day's work, and after paying for child care, bus fares, etc., that they take home little more than their allowance anyhow.

The double difficulties of coping alone, and coping on inadequate incomes, adds up to poverty for most of Ireland's one-parent families.

Travellers

Travellers are probably the most visibly poor of all groups in Ireland today. There are now about 2,000 travelling families representing 13,500 people, over half of them children. Very many are living on unapproved sites, in deplorable living conditions. In the Dublin area there are now 570 families, 310 on unapproved sites.[10] Caravans and trailers are usually damp and overcrowded, and there is no water or sewerage on unapproved roadside sites. The regular tragedies of fire deaths among travelling children underlines their appalling living conditions.

Most adult travellers are illiterate. Their traditional skills have become irrelevant in today's world. Only about half the travelling children attend school on a regular basis.

Nearly 60 per cent of travellers are under 15 years of age. This reflects not only the very large families and the early marriage age, but also the low life-expectancy of travellers. It also points to a future population explosion among the travellers when these children marry and have families of their own.

Travellers are generally regarded as outcasts by the settled community. Those on unapproved sites are constantly aware that they are likely to be forcibly moved on. The strong opposition which emerges whenever there are proposals to site a halt for travelling families emphasises the hostility with which they are viewed by many of the settled community.

The policy of settlement is still slow, relative to the growing numbers of travelling families. Integration has hardly begun. If those who decry the supposedly large incomes earned by trading travellers examine closely the living conditions of their families, and the prospects which face their children, there can be little doubt that, whatever their incomes, poverty is their daily lot.

People in Institutional Care

About 14,000 people are in-patients of psychiatric hospitals, three quarters of them being long-stay patients. There have been many criticisms of the standard of our psychiatric hospitals, most of them nineteenth-century buildings far removed from present day requirements. Many of the buildings have been poorly maintained over the years. Many long-term patients receive only one or two visits during the year from friends or relatives. For very many people whose life is in these institutions, life is a grim experience indeed.

Our psychiatric hospitals still house a number of mentally handicapped and geriatric patients, although it is policy to provide these patients with places more suited to their own needs.

About 13,000 elderly people are living in geriatric hospitals and welfare homes. A further number live as long-term patients in district hospitals, and even mental hospitals. As with psychiatric hospitals, a lot of the accommodation for the elderly is inadequate and in need of replacement. There is a shortage of good quality geriatric and welfare home places, and a queue for what is available. While there are very many dedicated people working in the geriatric services, many elderly people live in institutions where there are few day-time activities, where accommodation is poor and privacy limited. Institutional regimes in many homes can be depersonalising, and elderly people living in homes and hospitals are often more or less forgotten by relatives and friends.

Money too can be a problem. The old age pension plus the limited Health Board subvention do not in many cases meet the full costs of care in a private institution. Many elderly people are limited by cash as to where they can go to spend their declining years. Old age pensions are paid directly to the hospitals or homes, leaving limited pocket money for the elderly person.

Institutional care has been the poor relation of the health services. Resources have been directed towards the more popular areas like acute hospitals, while even basic maintenance, let alone replacement, of older institutions, has slipped farther down the list of spending priorities.

Tackling the problems in our long-stay institutions, for instance, will be a slow and expensive task. But we must deal with what has been one of the hidden areas of poverty.

Conclusion

The challenge of poverty in Ireland today is still substantial. The latest comprehensive data suggests that more than one in four in Ireland experiences poverty in their daily lives. The elderly, the unemployed, and the larger families, are those most likely to be poor.

The most up-to-date information highlights the continued persistence of the problem of poverty among urban workers supporting a family, in depressed farming areas, among pensioners, and those out of work. Nearly a million people receive a social welfare payment each week. About 700,000 — just 20 per cent of the whole population — depend on social welfare for their principal long-term source of income. One in six of all children is in a family which so depends on social welfare.

Many families lack amenities we now regard as basic. Three

out of every five old people living alone lack the basic water amenities of hot water, flush toilet, and bath or shower. Poverty shows its face in bad housing and in educational deprivation, as well as low income. The problems faced by one-parent families, by travellers, by people living in long-stay institutions, all illustrate the different dimensions of poverty.

We are often complacent about poverty in our midst. The argument is frequently put that with general growth and development in Western economies, the rising tide will lift all boats. The continued prevalence and persistence of poverty in Irish society illustrates that this is not the case. We need a commitment to tackle not just its symptoms, but the fundamental causes. We need a real commitment to redistribution of resources in Irish society.

The figures presented in this chapter show how substantial the challenge of poverty is. As a society we must be prepared to meet that challenge.

REFERENCES

1. Eg. Abel-Smith and Townsend, *The Poor and the Poorest.*

2. Cf. Mollie Orshansky, 'Counting the Poor', (Us Dept. of Labour).

3. See NESC Report 47, 'Alternative Strategies for Family Income Support', Chapter 2 and appendix, for data on the spending patterns of families on social welfare.

4. *Social Studies* (Maynooth, August 1972).

5. The Household Budget Survey is primarily an expenditure survey, although it collects useful data on incomes. However, as is usual in such expenditure surveys, the income figures are known to be under-estimated.

6. This re-weighting exercise was carried out as part of the background work for NESC Report 'Alternative Strategies for Family Income Support'. Chapters 2 and 3 of that report give details of this work on the 1975 HBS data, and of the methodology of equivalence scales.

7. The Parliamentary Question, 11 November 1980.

8. B. Power, *Old and Alone in Ireland*, report of a survey on old people living alone (Dublin 1980).

9. Royal Commission on Income and Wealth, Vol. VI, *Lower Incomes.*

10. Dublin census of travelling people, October 1980, as reported to Dublin County Council.

Urban Poverty

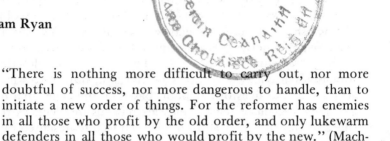

Liam Ryan

"There is nothing more difficult to carry out, nor more doubtful of success, nor more dangerous to handle, than to initiate a new order of things. For the reformer has enemies in all those who profit by the old order, and only lukewarm defenders in all those who would profit by the new." (Machiavelli—

In 1851 Henry Mayhew, one of the founders of *Punch,* in publishing his staggering picture of Victorian poverty, *London Labour and the London Poor,* stated that it "surely may be considered curious as being the first attempt to publish the history of a people, from the lips of the people themselves, giving a literal description of their labour, their earnings, their trials, and their sufferings, in their own 'unvarnished' language; and to portray the condition of their homes and their families by personal observation of the places and direct communion with the individuals."[1] Until Mayhew, very few writers had dared shock or offend their contemporaries by telling the truth about such matters.

Since then the truth about the plight of the urban poor has been told in many ways. The poor have been measured, surveyed and sorted into all sorts of categories, but in the end the diversity of the poor overwhelms any simple attempt to describe them. As the 1969 American Commission on Income Maintenance Programs put it: "What may be said simply is that millions of our fellow citizens are living in severe poverty, with few prospects for a better life, and often with little hope for the future . . . To the poor, poverty is no statistical or sociological matter. Their condition exists as a daily fight for survival. This Commission has found their deprivation to be real, not a trick or rhetoric or statistics. And for many of the poor, their poverty is not a temporary situation but an enduring fact of life."[2]

Five Traditional Perspectives

Over the past century attempts to define and measure poverty have proved as elusive as attempts to eradicate it. Invariably in the voluminous but inconsistent literature on the subject, the concept of poverty becomes limited by the purpose which is to be served by the definition. However, it is possible to distinguish five traditional perspectives, all of which have made their own distinctive contribution to theories of urban poverty.

One tradition is that of Mayhew — the descriptive, sometimes literary, sometimes journalistic, but always moving account of the lives of the poor, based on the belief that man's emotions are more readily moved than his intellect. In recent times in Ireland this tradition has been well represented by two comprehensive reports in the current affairs monthly magazines, *Nusight* (Nov. 1969) and *Magill* (April 1980). In the latter report, authors Brian Trench and Pat Brennan conclude: "One million people in the Republic of Ireland live in poverty. Poverty is endemic to Irish society and extends not just to the unemployed, the travellers, and the slum-dwellers, but reaches right into the middle classes. In Ireland, social inequality is greater than in any other E.E.C. country . . . The 300,000 at the top of the pile receive six times the income which goes to the 500,000 at the bottom."[3]

Another tradition is the polemical, probably best exemplified by Frederic Engel's *The Condition of the Working Class in England,* and carried on in more recent times in the critical works of George Orwell.[4] The best example of this tradition in Ireland is to be found in the writings of James Connolly, who, in advocating a socialist solution to poverty and inequality, once declared to his friends in the Gaelic movement: "You cannot teach starving men Gaelic."[5] Connolly's philosophy has been re-echoed in more recent times in a 1973 report prepared by the Labour Party entitled *Poverty in Ireland.* This report, which is significant in being the only policy document on poverty issued by any of the major political parties, concludes: "Poverty is an indictment of our nation because we as a people have placed our trust in a social system which is inherently divisive and unjust. No amount of quantitative growth in the capitalist system will eradicate poverty. Fifteen years of steady economic development since 1958 have not reduced the numbers unemployed nor, indeed, increased the total number at work. Capitalism — and its political proponents — have failed the Irish people and the poor most of all. The

Labour Party asserts that political action can and, with the support of the people, will eradicate poverty by fundamental and total reform of the socio-economic system. Policies for people must replace policies for profit and property."[6]

A third tradition is the official commission of enquiry, ranging, for example, from the Poor Inquiry of the early 1830's to the 1963 Report of the Commission on Itinerancy. Many such nineteenth century official enquiries produced reports that exhibit considerable sociological skill both in collecting data and in channelling it into practical policy recommendations. For instance, the Commissioners appointed by King William IV in 1833 to Inquire into the State of the Poorer Classes in Ireland not only took oral evidence but also widely circulated questionnaires, and within three years published the evidence and findings in several volumes of reports and appendices. Over the past century in Britain, the official enquiry has been one of the favourite methods of formulating social policy and has successfully produced such formidable instruments of social reconstruction as the Royal Commission on the Poor Laws of 1905-9, the Beveridge Committee on Social Insurance and Allied Services 1941-2, and the various education committees of the early 1960's. Despite these and many other achievements, however, this method of policy formulation has come in for considerable criticism in the late 1970's accused of generating conservative rather than radical policies, of providing 'administrative' rather than 'structural' solutions, and generally of offering middle-class remedies to working-class problems.[7]

A fourth tradition is the scientific research survey. Ever since Charles Booth's monumental study on *The Life and Labour of the People of London* researchers have sought to measure poverty in a scientific way and to use such measurement to establish a Plimsoll-line for income, a minimum below which no household should fall. Booth, and especially Rowntree, provided a working model for a vast series of surveys in the twentieth century, each researcher adding a slight variation to the original broad definition. But as poverty persisted despite the best efforts of the 'safety-net' of welfare state legislation, researchers and policy-makers were forced to look to newer and more sophisticated methods and hypotheses. While writers like Michael Harrington[8] in America popularised the 'two-nations' theory of the poor and the rich — a term coined by Disraeli a century earlier — and helped inaugurate vast new programmes, in Britain Peter Townsend was leading the survey research tradition in replacing concepts of 'absolute', 'minimum' or 'subsistence' with notions of relative deprivation, plimsoll-line incomes with lack of resources of all kinds, individual inadequacy with structural defects, and ultimately replacing poverty with inequality. Meanwhile, of course, the poor themselves were no longer grateful for the crumbs which fell from the rich man's table; they had a right to be seated at the board and were beginning to demand it. Yet, if one accepts the evidence of Townsend's 1979 *Poverty in the United Kingdom,* not merely are the seats at table fewer but the very crumbs themselves also.[9]

One of the few attempts in Ireland to survey poverty in the classic British tradition was a pioneering effort undertaken by a group in University College, Cork, in 1944, under the direction of President, Alfred O'Rahilly, and Professor of Economics, John Busteed. Following Rowntree's 'human needs standard', a minimum level of need based on requirements of food, shelter, clothes, light and fuel was established, costed, and adapted to local consumer habits. The survey then sought to measure the standard of living of each family living in Corporation Housing in Cork City by comparing its income with its needs. The survey showed that over 45 percent of households were living in poverty, but for a variety of reasons a final report was never published.

The fifth tradition, Action Research, is more recent in origin. From the mid-1960's there was a growing disillusionment with the survey research tradition because, apart from other short-comings, it was clear that an improvement in the condition of the poor rarely results from the presentation of facts to publics or governments. The research tradition had emphasised the guar-enteeing of a minimum standard of living; now the emphasis has switched to education, opportunity, job programmes, and mobility through participation and self-help. In short, what has been described as a 'doors' approach has replaced the older 'floors' approach.[10] There were obvious attractions in the doors approach. As Joan Higgins of Southampton University puts it: "The floors approach implied a long-term and increas-ing commitment to the poor. The doors approach was a short-term strategy designed to get people off welfare. It involved the poor doing things for themselves rather than passively accepting a State hand-out. It had an aura of dynamism and progress about it . . . The floors approach seemed like money poured down a bottomless pit of need. The floors approach, some argued, had been tried and failed, the time had come for new strategies in the fight against poverty."[11]

The new strategy of Action Research had as its main focus the elimination of 'pockets of poverty' especially in urban areas. Its most important features became the designation of particular areas, the maximum feasible participation of the poor in the programmes, the belief that social change is brought about not by implementing some preordained plan but by responding to situations as they arose, and the hope that through reflective action the means of social reform could best be discovered, and appropriate social policy would follow. The better known examples of action research (with year of commencement) are: in America, the Community Action Program (1964) in which more than one thousand communities took part, and the Model Cities Program (1966) which covered one hundred and fifty areas; and in Britain, the five areas under the Educational Priority Area (1968) programme and the twelve communities which took part in the Community Development Project (1969).

In Ireland, the twelve projects of Combat Poverty (1974)[12] embodied much of the community action approach, and its findings parallel closely those of the British and American programmes. The projects which set realistic and local objectives, which used strategies that had some hope of attaining them, and which confined their horizons to problems that were soluble with available resources were the most successful. Far less effective were those which attempted to deal with broad national issues and confront problems which had their roots in national policy. The truth remains that community action is successful only to the extent that the causes of poverty come from within the individual, the family or community and not from without. For those who believe that the causes lie in the structure of the economy or of society, community action can be a frustrating and unproductive experience. It is easy to fall into the trap of believing that 'nothing can be done until everything is done' and to become disillusioned when initiatives from below are not immediately translated into dramatic changes in public policy.

Is Urban Poverty Really Urban?

As the changing pattern of poverty unfolds, it becomes clear that poverty is not exclusively an urban problem nor is it generated by the nature of cities. The problem belongs not in urban sociology but in the sociology of complex societies. As Anthony Giddens[13] and others have shown, poverty is generated by modern industrial society and to understand it, whether urban or rural, we must understand also the middle and dominant groups in the system, and how they relate to each other. Similarly, as many anthropologists have noted for American society,[14] problems such as poverty, racism, and sexism are fundamental characteristics of the larger social system and not merely aspects of urban localities.

Consequently, if one adds an urban dimension at all then it would be essential to study the effects of the urban setting on the poverty population. By and large, this remains to be done because sociological research has concentrated on the poorer segment of urban populations rather than on the urban characteristics of poorer people. No social unit, however large or small, is autonomous and independent. To study poverty by focussing entirely upon the poor is to disregard the continuous interactive process which continually recreates poverty.

Selecting an inner-city slum, a minority ethnic or racial group, a squatter settlement or shanty town, or a deprived new housing-estate as a unit in which to study poverty is a misleading approach. Basically, it creates the impression that because problems are to be found in the slum the solution to these problems must be found there. It also runs the danger, now well recognised in many criticisms of Oscar Lewis' culture of poverty theory, of viewing poverty as a self-perpetuating subcultural system. However, to be fair to Lewis, he did explicitly recognise that the evolution of a culture of poverty is a consequence of modern industrial capitalist society rather than the urban environment.

If one takes a worldwide perspective, it is immediately evident that urban poverty is, for the most part, rural poverty relocated and refashioned within the city area. Since the early nineteenth century, all sorts of people have been on the move. These migrations have reflected changes in technology, in political organisation, and in the world economy. They have uprooted vast populations, many of which have become urban dwellers for the first time. These streams of humanity have included peasants attracted by the promise of new jobs, immigrants lured by the promise of new worlds, and refugees fleeing from old worlds of famine, persecution and genocide. As a result migration literature and poverty literature have become intertwined in many instances. In fact, even two hundred years since these migrations began, urban squatter settlements are today the fastest growing and most widespread forms of poverty. Whether known as *barriadas* (Peru), favelas (Brazil), *villas miserias* (Argentina), *colonias proletarias* (Mexico), *bustees* (India), or *bidonvilles* (French Africa), these are the present-day counterpart of the Victorian slums created by massive rural migration in nineteenth century Britain.

Significantly, it is one form of urban poverty which Irish cities have almost escaped. The mass migration of impoverished rural-dwellers from the Irish countryside, both in this century and in the last, was not to Irish cities but to Britain and America where they helped swell the ranks of the urban poor. Indeed, in his description of conditions in Manchester in 1844, Frederick Engels drew a horrifying portrait of 'Little Ireland', a slum which was a disgrace even for the Manchester of those days.[15] By and large, rural migrants to Irish cities seldom enter the urban arena at the bottom, so that urban Ireland over the past one hundred years is almost unique in that the bulk of its poverty is found among an indigenous rather than a migrant population.

In addition to the migrant, cities too act as magnets for the marginal. Among these are those considered deviant by the larger society such as criminals and delinquents; or those thought to be a little 'odd' such as artists, radicals, and intellectuals; or those looking for *the geographical cure,* who come with problems — personal or otherwise — and who believe that if only they could get a new start in fresh surrounding all would be well. Inevitably, cities become places littered with bits of humanity, so that the inscription on the pedestal of the Statue of Liberty could well be the motto of all cities: "Give me your tired, your poor/ your huddled masses yearning to breathe free/ the wretched refuse of your teeming shore/send these the home-less tempest-tossed to me." Only, of course, the city continues to toss them to less than the tempest simply because the geographical cure rarely works. The real tempest is often inside themselves, and for many each fresh move is only a fresh mistake. The plight of the vagrant poor is one of the most desperate of all urban groups. Fundamentally, they are alienates due to a set of personal inadequacies and bad luck which leaves them unable to cope with the social, psychological or emotional aspects of their situation. Because of economic disadvantage,

41

they are forced to live among others similarly situated — individuals who, they soon discover, may be dangerous, difficult and out to exploit them in petty or significant ways.

The Urban Factor

Granted, then, that much of urban poverty does not originate in the city, and that the main causes and explanations of poverty must be found at the level of the total social system, in what way does an urban setting produce additional effects on the poorer segment of the population? Here, too, we can understand the effects of urbanism on the poor only if we first understand the general consequences of urbanism.

The urban influence may be explained in two ways. Either one accepts that the urban environment is different from other social environments and produces, because of its own essential unique features, changes in social personality and in social structure; or one believes that urbanism does not produce major socio-psychological consequences, that its influence is insignificant, and that the dynamics of social life are best explained in terms of nonecological factors such as social class, ethnicity, and stages in the life-cycle. Both propositions are difficult to prove. The former commends itself to social geographers, the latter to urban anthropologists, while sociologists have sought to compromise by synthesising the two approaches.

One such synthesis is proposed by American sociologist, Claude Fischer,[16] in *The Urban Experience.* He identifies three main theories of urbanism:

1. *Determinist theory* (or *Wirthian* theory) argues that urbanism increases social and personality disorders over those found in rural places.

2. *Compositional* (or *nonecological*) theory denies such effects of urbanism; it attributes differences between urban and rural behaviour to the composition of the different populations.

3. *Subcultural theory* adopts the basic orientation of the compositional school but holds that urbanism does have certain effects on the people of the city, with consequences much like the ones determinists see as evidence of social disorganisation.

42

The determinist theory finds its fullest exposition in Louis Wirth's 1938 essay,[17] "Urbanism as a Way of Life", in which he sought to identify the forms of social behaviour and organisation which appear in urban settlements: social bonds are weakened; influence of family, friend and neighbours declines; stress, alienation, individualism and social disruption follow; people are left unsupported to suffer their difficulties alone; and they are unrestrained by social rules from committing all sorts of acts from the simply odd to the dangerously criminal.

In contrast to determinists, compositional theorists such as Herbert Gans[18] and Oscar Lewis[19] believe that behaviour is largely influenced by intimate social groups based on kinship, neighbourhood, occupation, economic position, life-style, cultural characteristics and similar personal attributes. The essence of the compositional argument is that these private milieus endure even in the midst of large cities. It is these attributes, not the size, shape, or density of the community, that shape social and psychological experience. It was in this context that Lewis elaborated his much-criticised 'culture of poverty' concept. Lewis began his career by attacking Robert Redfield's deterministic folk-urban dichotomy, and it is important to note that Lewis does not imply that the nature of the city influences the development of the culture of poverty. Rather, he is attempting to show the manner in which attitudes and behaviour patterns, that initially developed in response to deprivation, are passed on to subsequent generations through socialisation. Again, it is the intimate primary group and not the urban influence which is emphasised. Many commentators wrongly assumed that because his work was done in urban areas, he was implying that poverty and the culture of poverty were urban phenomena.

The third approach, *subcultural theory*, as presented by Fischer, contends that urbanism independently affects social life — not, however, by destroying social groups as determinism suggests, but instead by helping to create and strengthen them. The most significant social consequence of urban size is the promotion of diverse *subcultures* (culturally distinct groups such as college students or Chinese-Americans). Like compositional theory, subculture theory maintains that intimate social groups persist in the urban environment and have a profound influence on human behaviour. But in contrast to compositional analysis, which discounts any effects of urbanism, it argues that these groups are affected directly by urbanism, particularly by the effects of 'critical mass'. Urbanism has unique consequences, including the production of deviance, not because it destroys social worlds — as determinism argues — but because it more often creates them.

Fischer argues that urbanism both creates and intensifies subcultures through the process of critical mass. By this he means that a population size emerges, large enough to permit what would otherwise be only a small group of individuals to become a vital, active subculture. Sufficient numbers allow them to support activities and institutions that serve the group; allow them to have a visible and affirmed identity, to act together in their own behalf, and to interact intensively with each other. As Fischer puts it: "Let us suppose that one in every thousand persons is intensely interested in modern dance. In a small town of 5,000 that means there would be, on average, five such persons, enough to do little else than engage in conversation about dance. But in a city of one million, there would be a thousand — enough to support studios, occasional ballet performances, local meeting places, and a special social milieu. Their activity would probably draw other people beyond the original thousand into the subculture. The same general process of critical mass operates for artists, academics, bohemians, corporate executives, criminals, as well as for ethnic and racial minorities."[20]

Fischer does not mention poverty-groups among his subcultures, but it is clear that his theory can readily be applied to them. Urban life may or may not generate poverty but the process of *critical mass* operates effectively through shared behaviour patterns to identify, isolate, intensify, and perhaps stigmatise all kinds of groups of poor people — slums and ghettos, inner-city deprivation, skid-row, shanty towns, and difficult housing estates. In all of these, a population size of similarly situated individuals becomes sufficiently large to generate a set of social conditions which is over and above the sum total of individual deprivation, and which in a very real sense creates deprived areas as well as deprived individuals. As the British Department of the Environment 1977 *Policy for the Inner Cities* puts it: "The Inner Area Studies have shown that there is a collective deprivation in some inner areas which affects all the residents, even though individually the majority of people may have satisfactory homes and worthwhile jobs. It arises from a pervasive sense of decay and neglect which affects the whole area. This collective deprivation amounts to *more than the sum* of all the individual disadvantages with which people have to contend."[21] This factor of critical mass and its consequence is precisely what is *urban* about urban poverty.

To summarise, if we are to interpret urban poverty in the light of our three theories of urbanism, some prior distinctions must be made. Firstly, it is clear that because problems occur within cities, they are not necessarily urban problems. Secondly, we must distinguish problems *in the city* which appear to be urban because of the population concentration from problems *of the city* which are created by the pattern of population concentration. And thirdly, we must make a distinction between causation and exacerbation.

Determinists hold that most urban problems, including poverty, are problems *of the city,* whereas compositionalists argue that these are problems *in the city* whose causes must be sought elsewhere. Following subcultural theory, we have argued that poverty is both in and of the city; it is largely the offspring of modern industrial society with its dual effect of simultaneous enrichment and impoverishment but it is greatly intensified and exacerbated by the nature of cities. Similarly with cities, area-based exacerbation of social problems is much more likely than area-based causation, so that programmes of positive discrimination on an area basis are unlikely to be ever totally successful. The comment of Davidoff and Gould on American poverty programmes is likely to have universal validity: "What these programmes have in common is an underlying strategy based on a false assumption — the assumption that because the problems of race and poverty are found in the ghettos the solution to these problems must also be found there."[22]

The New Ghetto: The Inner City

The urban community is subject to constant transformation and reconstruction but the results of change and growth are not uniformly distributed. Some areas develop, other decay. The inner city with all its contradictions — affluence and poverty, renewal and decay, luxury hotels and miserable tenements — has strategic importance in the urban social system. It is the area of intense competition for land, living space, property and power, but today in almost all major cities it is in 'crisis' due to a multiplicity of problems, social and economic, political and administrative, environmental and aesthetic. In many cases the inner city has become a disaster area containing the dropouts from the contest for jobs, education, and housing – those who tried and failed or never had a chance.

Although the problems of Irish cities are similar to those of most older cities in the western world, the relatively small scale of the problem should make their solution easier, with the possible exception of Dublin. In *Dublin Old And New*, written in the 1930's, Stephen Gwynn stated: "There is no use ignoring it: Dublin has always been a city of the miserably poor, and the misery was worst when Dublin had wealth and used it ostentatiously. Before the War a wise Benedictine said to me that he had never anywhere seen such display of extreme poverty except in Naples. And in Naples they have the sun."[23] Perhaps the most powerful pictures of Dublin slum life are those found in the plays of Sean O'Casey who tended to view his native place as a city of worthless men held together by valiant women.

Dublin's poverty problem dates back to the mid-19th century when the decline in commercial enterprise coupled with the inability of Irish manufacturers to compete with more advanced industrial products of England, created vast unemployment among the Dublin working class. By 1879 there were nearly 10,000 tenement houses in the city centre occupied by about 117,000 people (about 45 percent of the city's population) of whom 30,000 were estimated to be living in dwellings unfit for human habitation.[24] The situation had only marginally improved by 1935 when a report on slum clearance stated: "Dublin has some 33,000 families living in 5,357 tenements. It is calculated that some 90,000 of these people live in one-room tenements. More serious still, 8,000 families are living in tenements which have been condemned as unfit for human habitation, and 1,440 families are occupying unfit basements."[25]

Between 1936 and 1971, the population of the Inner City was reduced by half as municipal housing estates in the suburbs replaced the slum. While this greatly improved the physical living conditions, the lack of adequate services in the new and extensive estates, the planning ideology which sometimes favoured high-density residential tower blocks, and the uprooting of existing communities, initially frequently exacerbated the problems they sought to solve. Meanwhile in the city centre, the tenements have all but gone but not the problem of poverty. By very definition the people who remain belong to the lowest economic groups; the respectably employed have gone to the semi-detached suburbs; the more elite poor have gone to the housing estates; and the really poor and under-priviliged are increasingly concentrated in the inner city area. Industry has followed the workers to the suburbs, the employ-ment structure of the city centre has become increasingly white-collar, and the only semi- or unskilled jobs that remain for inner city residents are irregular and intermittent.

Not just in Dublin but in many British and American cities, programmes of slum clearance and urban renewal have con-centrated the poorest sections of the population and produced what American sociologist, Lee Rainwater, has called a "tangle of pathology" — a multiplicity of social problems which arise in areas of extreme deprivation. Rainwater gives a list of the be-haviour patterns which middle-class people generally think of as hallmarks of this tangle of pathology:

1. High rates of school dropouts
2. Poor school accomplishment for those who stay on
3. Difficulties in establishing stable work habits on the part of those who get jobs
4. High rate of dropping out of the labour force
5. Apathy and passive resistance in contact with people who are 'trying to help' (social workers, teachers and so on)
6. Hostility and distrust toward neighbours
7. Poor consumer skills — carelessness or ignorance in the use of money
8. High rates of mental illness
9. Marital disruptions and women as heads of homes
10. Illegitimacy
11. Cruelty to children or indifference to children's welfare
12. Property and personal crimes
13. Drug addiction, alcoholism
14. Destructiveness and carelessness toward property, one's own and other people's.

He concludes: "All these behaviour patterns greatly d'
middle-class people, and most of them are even mo_
to the lower class people who must live wi*
lower class families engage in even som_
all lower class people live in an en_
ability of either participating in such
the victim of it, is much higher than _
In epidemic terms, this is a high risk pop

Suburbs and Housing Estates

The most dramatic sociological contribution of the modern city to poverty has been its crystallisation of the class society created by the industrial revolution. To drive a car through a middle-class suburb and then through a city slum is for many people an everyday experience. As seen from the car the basic difference is one of housing, the attractive suburban homes contrasting with the run-down and congested inner-city blocks. There may be many more profound differences between social classes, but segregation on the basis of type and ownership of house has become the supreme symbol for a class conscious populace. The striking contrast between the semi-detached of the private sector and the inferior terraces of the public sector is remarkable in an age which adopts a public policy of equality in education, in health, in social security, and in many other areas of social provision. Undoubtedly, some day equality of housing provision will become a major aspect of public concern — perhaps in the twenty-first century. If so, then Ireland has certainly sown the seeds of conflict with policies of segregating urban populations into large single-class housing estates.

The social worlds thus created enable the process of critical mass to operate all the more strongly. These social worlds do sometimes touch and interact, but they rub against one another only to recoil. A common reaction is to embrace one's own social world all the more firmly, thus adding to the segregation and further intensification of one's class differences.

As we have seen, this process also increases social problems as — sometimes in slums, sometimes in new housing estates — the city condenses into a single neighbourhood all the problems of poverty and minorities, and all the indolence, impotence, indifference and hostility with which our cities have so far dealt with these problems.

The worldwide North/South dualism highlighted in the Brandt Report is parallelled in every city of the world by a sort of *urban dualism* wherein the deprivation of slums and the poverty of large municipal housing estates contrast with the relative affluence of middle-class suburbs.

The poor, then, stand on the brink of two worlds, the world which they must live and the world of middle-class attitudes values which forms the basis of the wider society. They do ave a separate system of values, nor do they reject the class values to which they are constantly exposed from the media, from teachers, from pulpit and platform. But often, their whole experience of life teaches them that it is impossible to cope with day-to-day living or to achieve any real self-esteem in terms of those values. When they turn to styles of life or behaviour patterns other than the conventional, these are pursued not because they are seen as intrinsically desirable but because there is no other choice if one wants to survive in a grim and hostile world. They are not confused between how they must live and how they would like to live if things were different. Very often their whole life is given over to learning patterns of adaptation and survival, patterns which often interfere with adapting to a different world if such a world becomes available.

Strategies of Survival

It is not uncommon to hear the dominant members of society continue to make the Victorian distinction between the 'deserving' and the 'undeserving' poor. The former accept the norms and values of the dominant group and accept their own subordinate place in society. The undeserving reject these norms, are therefore characterised as immoral or lazy, and should be coerced into reform or isolated from the rest of the community. Oscar Wilde was one Victorian who saw it somewhat differently. He claimed: "To recommend thrift to the poor is both grotesque and insulting. It is like advising a man who is starving to eat less. Man should not be ready to show that he can live like a badly fed animal. No: a poor man (should be) ungrateful, unthrifty, discontented and rebellious . . . As for the virtuous poor, one can pity them, of course, but one cannot possibly admire them. They have made private terms with the enemy, and sold their birthright for very bad pottage."[28]

The basic choice for the poor is one of acquiescence or rebellion, or to put it more politically, the choice is whether to turn to John Kenneth Galbraith or to Karl Marx for a solution to their problems.

However, for the poor who are either unable or unwilling to derive gratification from the existing social system, there appear to be four broad categories of survival strategy.

One, the *bohemian* strategy. For an individual who gets little reward from a job or unemployment, whose talents are unappreciated by family, community or wider society, who has failed to impress either teachers or employers, there is a certain attraction in seeking success by casting off many of the more conventional forms and adopting a life style that is expressive and challenging, perhaps even bizarre. This adaptive process has given western society the teddy-boy and the skin-head, the mods and the rockers, the mini-skirt and punk-rock. In its more benign forms, the resulting behaviour is often taken up by working -class and middle-class generally, though the older generations of the latter are more likely to dismiss it as shiftless or immoral. Needless to say, this is a survival strategy which is particularly attractive to youth.

Those who lack the talent to impress, and whose frustration finds no safety-value in exhibitionsim, are more likely to resort to the *rebellious* strategy in which, through crime or violence, one takes what others will not give. Violence is never far distant from the urban slum; within the home both wives and children are likely to experience totally unpredictable beatings, on the streets gang warfare among boys, fights among girls, and pavements full of frustrated unemployed who inevitably clash either with one another or with the police. The growing crime-rate, muggings and purse-snatching, soccor violence on the terraces, and the increasing danger of city streets by day or night, are ample evidence that the rebellious strategy is growing in popularity. Once it was neither popular nor calculated but more a form of spontaneous teenage recreation, something akin to a group of rural youths robbing an orchard. Today, however, it appears as a more deliberate and mature response, more a way of life, a strategy of survival in a depressing situation.

For those who through age or infirmity cannot fight against the condition of poverty, there remains either the escapist or the depressive response. The *escapist* strategy is particularly favoured by those who resort to drink or drugs, or by all who need a cushioning defence from the reality of their situation. It is the one particularly associated with the vagrant and the dosser. He needs something pretty powerful to form a curtain between him and the reality of his situation. Some use alcohol, others who don't drink have the mental defence of withdrawal from reality. Life can become quite pleasant because one is living a new life inside one's head and not the reality of one's actual situation. Judgment becomes supressed or distorted so that the tragedy of the situation is not nearly so bad for the person to whom it is happening as it is to the person observing it. And so the dossers sit and drink and dream and their dreams in which they engage in delusions of grandeur, of success, of what they would do with a million pounds. To the ordinary person, this might seem just a bit of fanciful imagining, but taken a few steps further coupled with increased withdrawal from the reality of the situation and it becomes insanity.

Finally, there is the *depressive* strategy, the one most likely to be adopted by the housewife or the unemployed. This is the strategy of retreat and self-isolation, of an increasing constricting of goals to the minimum required for physical survival. Apathy replaces anger; there is no despair because there is no ambition, no disillusionment because there is no promise, no prospect because to plan for tomorrow is merely to unnecessarily increase one's misery. Instead, there is simply the squalor and decay of a life that lacks expectation.

It must be emphasised, of course, that almost every poor person at one time or another adopts the more conventional strategy of working within the existing social system and using whatever opportunities it offers either to improve one's lot or to develop a satisfactory lifestyle where one is. However, among the poor, the young especially show increasing signs of being either unable or unwilling to settle for a conventional deprived lifestyle.

Postscript on Policies

There are two basic explanations of poverty. One is that opportunities do exist whereby the poor can improve their lot, but that because of certain attitudes and values which they hold — deriving either from their present poverty or from their cultural heritage — they are unable or unwilling or too apathetic to seize them. The second explanation is that among the poor the will to achieve exists but the opportunities do not. Depending on which proposition one believes, one seeks to change the poor or to change society. While these changes can be attempted in a wide variety of ways, there appear to have been four broad types of solution depending on whether the policies advocated were inspired by humanitarian, psychological, sociological, or political consideration.

Charity based on compassion for the poor, inspired either by Christian or humanitarian motives, has been the oldest form of welfare. Indeed, Lloyd George saw his package of State social reforms in the early years of this century as a natural extension of private collective charity. He was, he said, carried forward on a tide of social pity that was only wanting expression: "The individual demands it, the State needs it, humanity cries for it, religion insists upon it." In more recent times, however, the altruistic virtues are accused of being an obstacle rather than a solution. It is said that charity degrades and demoralises; that just as the worst slave-owners were those who were kind to their slaves, and so prevented the horror of the system being realised by those who suffered from it, so today the people who do the most harm are those who try to do the most good. Put more politically, this argument reads that it is immoral to use private property to alleviate the evils that result from the institution of private property.

These arguments are pernicious. They would have validity only if a utopian solution to social problems were immediately possible by political action. But meanwhile mankind, including the poor, must live in the real world. No matter what political system humanity adopts, there will always be 'those who don't fit in'. There will always be a need for individuals and organisations who help alleviate the plight of the needy without making the reform of the recipient or of society a necessary condition of such aid.

As social work replaced charity in the 1940's and 1950's, so the influence of psychology replaced atruism as the basis for social policy. Poverty was seen as resulting from deep-rooted personal or cultural traits which required outside help to remedy. This led to a case-model approach which tended as a theory of poverty to convert characteristics of the poor into causes. In his significantly titled *The Affluent Society* (1958) Galbraith stated that poverty in America is no longer "a massive affliction, more nearly an afterthought." He argued that the poor have dwindled to two hard-core categories. One is 'insular poverty' or regional pockets of poverty especially in rural areas. The second category is 'case poverty' which Galbraith says is "commonly and properly related to characteristics of individuals so afflicted as mental deficiency, bad health, inability to adapt to the discipline of modern economic life, excessive procreation, alcohol, insufficent education." He reasons that such poverty must be due to individual defects, since "nearly everyone else has mastered his environment; this proves that it is not intractable." Others, such as Lewis, add attitudinal characteristics to the list and emphasise the 'culture of poverty'.

The case-model approach tended to adopt a 'services strategy' in programmes for the poor. Some of these services aimed at helping the poor earn a better income (such as Job Corps and other training programmes), or at rescuing the next generation (as in 'Head Start' and other pre-school education projects), or to provide poor people with consumer education programmes, home management skills, or special health programmes. Many of these were based on the assumption that if the poor learned better skills and adopted a different mentality, they would then be able to accomplish tasks which would do away with their poverty. Here, however, we are back in the same old vicious circle: whatever characteristics the poor have which prevent them moving out of poverty, they have because they are poor. Attitudes will not change until one's economic situation changes.

The general lack of success of the services strategy in the early poverty programmes in Britain and America, coupled with the reawakened interest of sociologists in the problem, led in the 1960's to structural rather than cultural explanations and to a 'generic-model' of poverty which emphasised that the problem results from general defects in the structure of the economy and of society. In short, to do anything about poverty one must first do something about wealth. Peter Townsend, for instance, sees the class structure of Britain as the key factor, enabling the rich to preserve and enhance their wealth and deny it to others. This they do through a variety of institutional mechanisms. The result is that certain sections of the population are denied access to a proportionate share of resources and thus have to adopt lifestyles which further cut them off from the rest of society.

The implications of the structuralist explanation are enormous: piecemeal reform which does not drastically change the distribution of resources will be ineffective; excessive wealth and income must be abolished; there must be an end to unemployment, and a total reorganisation of community services. But the real question remains, how? Townsend admits that it would be wrong to suggest that any of his remedies are easy or even likely. There are two comments that must be made on the radical nature of his solutions. The first is that to continue to focus on poverty measurement which defines 25 percent of the population as living in poverty is unlikely to lead to political policy changes; the problem seems so vast that if one cannot do anything until one does everything, then the plight of the very poor, the bottom five or ten percent, is neglected. The second comment is that in one sense his solution is too easy: it is easy to find the answer in a utopian socialist world which does not exist. rather than face the more difficult task of resolving the problem in the actual existing situation of a limited capitalist democracy. Is the structuralist radicalism really cursing the darkness rather than lighting a candle? The radical reformer must meet the objection that the resources which the socialist wishes to divide more equitably are the product of the capitalist system, and to change the system is to run the risk of eliminating the resources along with the inequalities. The Eastern European experience is a reminder that while poverty may enslave a section of the community, it is not a solution to propose resolving it by enslaving the entire community.

Much of the sociological research into poverty has been inspired by the belief that society has not eliminated poverty because it has lacked the information on which to base realistic policy. For a growing number of reformers, however, poverty persists not because we do not know how to eradicate it but because we do not wish to do so. What society needs is, therefore, not further research but a political will to initiate reforms. What these reforms might be varies with the political philosophy of the commentator. For the more impatient Marxist, if the system is unable or unwilling to reform then it must be destroyed; for others, the hope still survives that a just society can be fashioned without revolutionary change. A major influence in the development of a political perspective on poverty was the appearance of Piven and Cloward's *Regulating the Poor* in 1972.[29] Their thesis, which has come to be known as the Conspiracy Theory, is that social policy does not evolve out of compassion or humanitarianism, nor out of the presentation of research findings to governments, but as a response by dominant groups in society to threats to social stability. Ruling elites respond only to whatever threatens their interest, more particularly to violence or threats of violence. Consequently, they make concessions to the poor only when they feel threatened by the poor, and Piven and Cloward take examples from America and Britain to show that over the centuries poor relief has always been a response to threats of confrontation.

Conspiracy theory has been criticised as overstating the rationality of policy-makers and attributing greater powers of foresight, strategy, planning and efficiency to them than seems reasonable. However, it remains a popular theory among those who have grown weary of the lack of success of poverty programmes, who argue that the only remaining policy is that of confrontation.

The truth is, of course, that all four approaches — the humanitarian, the psychological, the sociological, and the political — have validity. There is scope for all four simultaneously, and poverty writers have done a great disservice by presenting these as if they were mutually exclusive and in total oppostion to one another. Poverty is a human problem, not an abstract one. It is not like a puzzle or mathematical problem: there is no absolute definitive answer at the back of the book. There is no single answer to it which is simply and totally right. Its solution remains provisional, tentative and imperfect; it is something we grope towards in uncertainty, perhaps depending as astrologers and awaiting our Copernicus.

FOOTNOTES

1. Henry Mayhew, *London Labour and the London Poor,* 3 vols., London 1851.

2. *Poverty Amid Plenty: The American Paradox,* The Report of the President's Commission on Income Maintenance Programs, 1969, p. 13.

3. *Magill,* April 1980, p. 10

4. F. Engels, *The Condition of the Working Class in England,* Panther Books, 1969 (first published 1845). George Orwell, *The Road to Wigan Pier,* Penguin, 1962.

5. James Connolly, "The Language Movement" in *Socialism and Nationalsim,* Sign of the Three Candles, Dublin, 1948 p. 58 (first published in *The Workers Republic,* 1899)

6. *Poverty In Ireland: A Report Prepared by the Labour Party,* Dublin, 1973, p. 36.

7. See, for example, K. Coates and R. Silburn, *Poverty: The Forgotten Englishmen,* Penguin, 1970; and J.C. Kincaid, *Poverty and Equality in Britain,* Penguin.

8. Michael Harrington, *The Other America: Poverty in the United States,* Macmillan, 1962; Penguin, 1963.

9. P. Townsend, *Poverty in the United Kingdom,* Penguin, 1979.

10. S.M. Millar, "The Great Society's Poor Law", *Annuals of the American Academy* of Political and Social Science, September, 1969.

11. Joan Higgins, *The Poverty Business: Britain and America,* Basil Blackwell, Oxford, 1978, p. 108.

12. *Final Report: Pilot Schemes to Combat Poverty in Ireland, 1974-80,* Dublin, 1981.

13. A. Giddens, *The Class Structure of the Advanced Societies,* Hutchinson, 1973.

14. See G. Gmelch and W.P. Zenner, *Urban Life: Readings in Urban Anthropology,* St. Martin's Press, New York, 1980, p. 278.

15. F. Engels, "The Condition of the British Working Class in 1844" in *Marx Engels on Britain,* Lawrence and Wishart, 1953, p. 94.

16. C. Fischer, *The Urban Experience,* Harcourt Brace Jovanovich Inc., 1976.

17. Louis Wirth, "Urbanism as a Way of Life", *American Journal of Sociology*, 44 (1938), pp. 3-24.

18. Herbert Gans, *The Urban Villagers*, Free Press, New York, 1962.

19. Oscar Lewis, *Five Families: Mexican Studies in the Culture of Poverty*, Basic Books, New York, 1959.

20. C. Fischer, "Theories of Urbanism" in G. Gmelch and W.P. Zenner, *Urban Life*, St. Martin's Press, New York, 1980, p. 67.

21. Department of the Environment, *1977 Policy for the Inner Cities*, H.M.S.O., London, p. 4.

22. Davidoff, P. and Gould, J., "Suburban Action", *Journal of the American Institute* of Planners, January, 1970 (quoted in Higgins, *The Poverty Business*, 115).

23. Stephen Gwynn, *Dublin Old and New*, Browne and Nolan, Dublin.

24. Cf. Deirdre O'Connor, *Housing in Dublin's Inner City*, School of Architecture, University College Dublin, 1979, p. 7.

25. Citizens Housing Council, *Report on Slum Clearance in Dublin*, Dublin 1938, p. 9.

26. Lee Rainwater, "The City Poor", *New Society*, 23 November 1967.

27. *Ibid.*, p. 741.

28. Oscar Wilde, "The Soul of Man Under Socialism" in *The Works of Oscar Wilde*, Collins, London and Glasgow, 1948, p. 1020.

29. Frances Fox Piven and Richard Cloward, *Regulating the Poor*, Tavistock, London, 1974.

Poverty and Housing

Brian Dillon, Lancelot O'Brien, Donal O'Mahony

At first sight the links between housing and poverty may appear to be simple and direct, and research has indeed pinpointed many statistical relationships between poor housing and some negative aspects of individual and community life.[1] Such relationships, however, have been shown by other researchers to be highly complex and it has been contended that the evidence produced is to a certain extent inconclusive. Nevertheless, despite the lack of solid evidence, not many researchers would go so far as to deny that links between bad housing and individual and social problems do exist. Such links comprise the areas of health, attitudes, educational and employment opportunities, and the general quality of life, amongst others. The view that inequalities in housing provision are somehow manifested in health conditions, in educational and economic opportunities and in criminal tendencies, has been used historically to justify government intervention in our housing market. The aim of this intervention has been the improvement of housing provision above what it would be under unfettered market conditions, particularly for lower income groups.[2]

In more recent times government policies in areas such as health and education have somewhat eased the problems of access to these and other necessary services. At the same time, if not as a consequence, State intervention in housing has come to be justified more in terms of the need to compensate for inequality in the distribution of income. So the principal motivation for intervention in the housing market now is not so much to break the links between poor housing and major health problems, for example — although such links are still significant in certain areas and amongst certain sections of our population — but rather to break the link between poor housing and low income.

In a free market, the degree to which housing need will be satisfied depends upon the population's ability to pay and its preferences, and hence the relationship between the level and distribution of income and the cost of housing. In our society the high cost of housing, coupled with the unequal distribution of income, has meant that significant sections of our population would have been incapable, without help, of meeting the full economic cost of accommodation of a reasonable standard. Accordingly, if left unrestrained, the private housing market would produce a very unreal distribution of housing resources, with the poor ending up in the lowest quality dwellings, assuming they could manage to gain access to dwellings at all.

Despite the long history of government involvement in our housing system, designed to solve this and other problems, a wide range of serious housing problems still persist and affect significant numbers of Ireland's population.[3] The people thus affected we refer to as the 'housing poor', and during the course of this chapter we will argue that this group will continue to represent a significant, if not growing, section of our population for as long as the present piecemeal approach to problem-solving is maintained as part of government housing policy. We see the need for a major shift in society's approach to housing, a shift which, among other aspects, would involve a real recognition of the 'right to housing' and the reduction of the present large-scale inequalities which lie at the base of most of our housing problems.

Among the many other aspects of the 'right to housing' which could be analysed, we shall briefly refer here to the issue of 'choice'. The question of choice can be considered as one of the most important elements in the individual right to housing. The real significance of this is that it can give expression to the elementary human right to organise one's immediate surroundings in accordance with one's needs and wishes, and it also provides a safeguard against the tendency to standardise housing and divest it of any individual features.

Some Aspects of Housing Poverty

For the moment, however, we shall describe some of the more significant aspects of our housing system which we consider to be indicators of housing poverty. In doing so we shall draw heavily on the experience of Threshold[4] and concentrate mostly on the urban housing scene, since Threshold's work has been mainly in the urban environment and also since the problems of poor housing are more concentrated and visible in our cities. We begin by referring to a typical Threshold case, not, unfortunately, an isolated one, but an all-to-common example of the type of problem dealt with on a daily basis since we first opened more than three years ago.

Before coming to Threshold Joe and Mary S. had 'lived in a single room with their two young children on the south side of Dublin for eleven months — it was their third 'flat' since they were married four years ago. They had been paying £16 per week for this room and for the use of a bathroom which they shared with three other flats. When the heating system failed and they were left with no hot water, Joe began to make representation to the non-resident landlord to have the situation rectified. After three weeks he got a response — a notice to quit. When Joe and Mary came to Threshold their options were very limited. They knew better than anyone the stress involved in getting another flat — the days lost at work, the mental strain, the 'sorry no children' response from most landlords. They realised that trying to secure a loan to buy their own home was a lost cause; the Local Authority loan scheme offered little prospect — the couple had not been able to save enough for even a small deposit because of the high rents they had had to pay over the years. With the support of Threshold, an eviction from the private-rented sector gave them priority standing with Dublin Corporation as a homeless family. This 'secured' for them a flat on the tenth floor of a corporation block miles removed from Joe's place of work. The S. family now 'live' on this tenth floor. The lift very often does not work and Mary finds the whole existence a constant strain. What keeps them going is the prospect of saving enough money to place a deposit on a small house, and securing a loan from the Local Authority. They will probably succeed in this after two years. Joe and Mary are lucky — their period of purgatory may only be a brief one.

Just as poverty has traditionally been measured in terms of income levels alone, poor housing conditions have been closely associated with the physical characteristics of our housing stock. The above example is intended to illustrate that the 'housing poor' today are a much broader and more diverse group than those who simply have to endure poor physical conditions.

Housing poverty must be seen in a much broader context — embracing social, economic and institutional factors. Such factors tend to be ignored in official pronouncements on housing need, presumably because they are not as amenable to measurement and remedy as physical housing indicators.

Studies of housing need in the past couple of decades have measured the need for provision of houses. These measurements have been based on well-researched indicators of rates of obsolescence, age of dwellings, provision of basic amenities, occupancy rates, population projections and other factors important in setting building and improvement targets.[5] Unsatisfactory housing, however, is a problem of which unfitness, lack of amenities, and even overcrowding are no more than symptoms.

Measured against these indicators alone, we can see from Table 1 that considerable progress has been made in tackling all these symptoms.

TABLE 1

Indicators of Improvements in Housing Quality
1946 – 1971

	1946 %	1961 %	1971 %
Dwellings erected pre 1919	–	57.9	44.8
Households with piped water inside	38.7	51.0	73.8
Households with sanitary facilities inside	23.1	42.7	62.9
Persons in households with more than two persons per room	17.6	11.5	9.3
Average persons per room	1.01	0.90	0.86

Source: Census of Population 1946 (Vol. iv) and 1971 (Vol. vi)

Furthermore, we can assume that progress in these areas has continued since 1971 (although significant numbers in certain areas are still badly affected) judging by the fact that between 1971 and 1975 more than 45,000 dwellings were reconstructed with State aid and that almost 63,000 grants were paid for the installation of water and sewerage facilities in the same period.[6]

Despite the undeniable progress which is being made, and of which we are constantly being reminded in statistical terms, there exist other indicators of housing poverty in Ireland which merit increasing cause for concern and immediate action. It is in these other less palpable and measurable areas that progress had been minimal and in some instances negligible, lending credence to the contention that the numbers of housing poor are actually increasing. As examples of these less apparent processes, we will touch on three areas of our housing system which we see as maintaining rather than combatting housing poverty: lack of choice, insecurity and lack of comprehensive planning.

(i) Lack of Choice

For many individuals and families in Ireland today housing choice is severely restricted, partly because of inadequate income but also partly for institutional reasons. It would be fair to assume, however, that institutional barriers to choice in housing are most severely felt by lower income groups.

The main barriers facing an individual or family wishing to own their own home are primarily related to income, but the size of income is not the only barrier. For example, building societies, upon which most potential owner-occupiers rely to enable them to purchase a dwelling, also take into account factors such as income stability, occupation and status. The Local Authority mortgage scheme (SDA), which is the main alternative source of mortgage finance, also presents difficulties for those seeking entry into the owner-occupied sector. Firstly, the limit on the maximum size loan which can be granted (currently £14,000) means that a sizeable deposit must be accumulated by the potential purchaser to secure even the most modest accommodation at current prices. Secondly, the limitation on income level (currently £7000 p.a.) means that many young couples, particularly those who find it increasingly difficult to meet rents in the private rented sector, fail to qualify for the Local Authority loan because they are earning too much. Finally, the scheme is open only to family units, and single people are not eligible to apply.

Barriers such as these, which severely limit choice for many people, are the main reasons for the strong relationships between owner-occupation, income and social class which persist in our housing system. In 1973, for example, the Household Budget Survey showed that some 76 per cent of households with professional and managerial heads were owner-occupiers (either outright or mortgaged) compared with only 49 per cent of skilled manual and 33 per cent of semi-skilled and unskilled manual heads of households. Reference to Table 2 shows the link which exists between tenure and household income.

TABLE 2

Household Income 1965–1966 and 1973 by Tenure

	1965–1966 Average Weekly Direct Income	1973 Average Weekly Disposable Income
Owned outright	£20.40	£33.10
Owned with mortgage	£24.92	£46.80
Rented from L.A.	£15.18	£33.90
Rented from private owner	£16.58	£32.10
All households	£18.94	£36.20

Source: Household Budget Surveys 1965/66 and 1973.

Barriers to choice also exist in the public sector, with initial access or transfer depending upon the availability of housing and the numbers requiring housing at any given time, as well as upon the prevailing transfer or allocation policy.

At present (April, 1981), for example, there are more than 8000 families or elderly people on the waiting list for Local Authority housing in Dublin alone, while there are plans for the completion of only 1500 new dwellings in the Dublin Corporation area for the period 1981/2.

Given this alarming supply/demand position, it is only those who are in extremely grave housing circumstances who can realistically expect to be housed and, even for these families, the choice of area and type of accommodation is becoming more and more restricted. Single people under the age of 60 years will not be considered at all except on special medical grounds.

Inadequate supply coupled with unfettered exposure to market forces restrict choice in the private rented sector. Without any control on rents in the vast majority of tenancies, and a great demand for what little accommodation exists, the individual or family's 'choice' is generally governed solely by what they can get at a rent they can afford. Obviously the same factors are at work in inhibiting mobility within the sector, and the high cost of other dwellings often means that great difficulty is experienced in moving into owner-occupation.

We have examined the significant restrictions on choice as they affect those trying to buy their own homes, those seeking access to Local Authority accommodation and those who must attempt to rent accommodation from private landlords. Without doubt, however, the most severe consequence of the lack of choice afforded by our housing system is felt by those who inevitably finish up at the bottom of the heap in the scramble for housing — the homeless. The result of a recent survey of Dublin hostels undertaken by the 'Campaign for the Homeless', [7] for example, confirms that no hostel in the city offers shelter to an entire family unit — husband, wife and children. The 'choice' open to these unfortunate families is between splitting up in order to secure accommodation or spending the night on the street.

(ii) Insecurity

While, in our view, lack of choice is an important indicator of poverty in housing, the security of tenure afforded once an individual or family has gained entry into a dwelling is equally important.

It is in this respect that people relying on private rented accommodation have least cause for joy. In a two-year period Threshold dealt with more than 1000 threatened or actual evictions from private rented accommodation. In the uncontrolled part of this sector (which covers the vast majority of tenancies) the landlord does not have to have an apparently rational reason for evicting a tenant. Thirty-one per cent of the Threshold eviction cases, for example, arose out of the fact that the landlord considered that the occupants were no longer 'suitable tenants', and a further 31 per cent because the property was being sold. Only 8 per cent faced eviction because of non-payment of rent.[8]

The landlord will inevitably succeed in gaining possession, except in very unusual circumstances, even if the tenant seeks legal protection. Leases are the exception rather than the rule, and those that do exist rarely exceed three years.

The owner-occupied sector is the most frequently associated with a high level of security of tenure. This is true if security is defined in terms of protection from eviction alone. A very real type of insecurity is widespread in this sector, however, when we consider that this protection depends ultimately on the ability of the household to meet the costs of home ownership. This can exert a considerable strain on family life, especially amongst lower income groups, when the ultimate penalty for failing to meet the cost of ownership is the loss of one's home. The securing of a mortgage then does not necessarily protect a family from deprivation, since very often the price they pay is that they cannot 'afford' to be sick, have more children or lose their employment. Adverting to the fact that the rate of home ownership in Ireland, at 75 per cent, is perhaps the highest in Europe[9] often hides this very real and disturbing form of insecurity.

The potential for such disaster in Local Authority accommodation is less of a threat, mainly because of the fact that rents are, or can become, related to the income of the tenant and because of the reluctance of the authorities to seek evictions save in very exceptional circumstances. Tenants in central urban areas have less security in this respect, however, as widespread redevelopment can mean compulsory relocation for families in 'designated' areas. A recent example of such redevelopment is the Sean McDermott Street area of Dublin.

(iii) Lack of Comprehensive Planning

The redevelopment of inner-city areas is one indication of a much broader problem which contributes directly to housing poverty. We have contended that statistics on physical housing conditions cannot be evaluated apart from institutional constraints on lack of choice and security of tenure. Neither can the statistics represent progress in the housing field unless they are augmented by evidence of how existing planning policy places people with regard to the basic economic, political, recreational and integrational needs. In other words, real planning must address itself to social and community needs as well as to economic prerogatives.[10]

As yet very little research has been addressed directly to the problem of social segregation in Irish housing policy. Increased concern has been expressed through the media recently as more and more problems have become associated with certain housing areas (particularly the more recent Local Authority developments in urban locations). These problems range from high levels of unemployment to an increase in the incidence of street violence involving young people.[10]

There is, we believe, a pressing need to re-examine the planning policies which currently operate with the intention of assessing how they contribute to the grouping of social problems, thus creating the ghetto situation, the stigma of an address and the attendant need for increasing supplies of police, social workers and Valium.

In economic terms alone, as one commentator has put it, the price we pay is a heavy one:

> To the extent that ill-health, crime and lack of opportunity are associated with poor housing, together with the effect on the household concerned, poor housing imposes direct costs on society at large in the form of greater public spending on, for example, medical services and crime prevention.[11]

Minimum acceptable living standards in Ireland must be determined in the light of the typical living conditions enjoyed by the majority of our population. Should we be surprised, therefore, that those who must live in ghetto conditions should perceive their living standards as falling well below this norm and should be vulnerable to feelings of demoralisation, powerlessness and anger?

Joe and Mary S., to whom we referred earlier, are not only amongst the ranks of the housing poor because they live in bad physical housing conditions. They are also victims of a housing policy which offers them the minimum of choice and security in planning for a normal life, and of a planning system which caters for their housing needs in isolation from basic community necessities.

The Housing Poor: Who Are Affected Most?

The indicators of housing poverty which we have examined are not distributed equally between all sections of our population or all areas of our country. When we identify those who suffer most in these areas we can immediately see that we are dealing with people who are already disadvantaged in other areas of life also. They include many newly married couples, young single people living in flats, the elderly in whatever housing sector and, of course, those who suffer the terrible stigma of outright homelessness.

As regards married couples, the most apparent casualty is the couple who are not yet eligible for Public Authority housing. They cannot buy their own home without over-reaching themselves financially by borrowing to get a deposit, possibly taking out insurance policies for collateral and subsequently facing mortgage repayments for their home, all of which leaves them virtually below the breadline. The consequences of such strained living have disastrous implications for healthy family life. From our own experience and from contact with a broad range of voluntary organisations, it would appear as if the problems arising from this source have now reached grave proportions.

Yet such couples are often looked upon as being more fortunate than those who are forced to rely on private rented accommodation. For while the couple in the private rented sector may have all the financial strains of the house-purchasing couple, they face additional problems in that more often than not they must endure poor living conditions and, worst of all, they have no security of tenure. (Of the 600 couples married less than five years and living in the private rented sector who approached Threshold, 202 were facing eviction).[12]

The elderly living alone are often silent sufferers of housing poverty. A recent report compiled by the Society of St Vincent de Paul[13] revealed that 59 per cent of elderly people living alone in the Republic of Ireland have no provision for hot water and that 57 per cent have no bath or shower. Even such a basic requirement as a wash-hand basin is a luxury that only 48 per cent of the elderly living alone can claim, and one in every three has no flush toilet. More than half of these people are living in dwellings erected before 1919 and very acute hardship is widespread, whatever the housing sector they belong to.

A category of people not often associated with housing poverty, but who certainly suffer in this respect, is the young boy or girl from the country who comes to work or study in the city. Many of these young people not only undergo a kind of culture shock in an environment quite different from what they are accustomed to, but they discover very quickly, in the houses which are converted into flats, overcrowding with all its attendant problems. They can also be exposed to trespassing and harassment by landlords, evictions — both legal and illegal — and exorbitant rent increases. (470 young single people reported rent increases to Threshold over a two-year period: 40 per cent of these were increases of more than 30 per cent at a time).[14]

One must highlight the single mother living in a private flat as the person who is often in the most tragic position of all. Emotional, financial and social insecurity is topped off by the basic insecurity of living in her 'home' on a week-to-week basis with prospects of finding alternative accommodation minimal if she is 'asked' to leave. (The greatest single problem amongst single parents who came to Threshold was outright homelessness).[15]

It is precisely in this problem of homelessness that housing poverty in our society is most starkly illustrated — the number of men, women and children who have to live in hostels or who are living on the side of the road in tents or caravans. Amongst such people one not only discovers the 'wino' and the 'drop out' — although their rights must be protected too — but young 'intelligent' people who for one reason or another did not just make it in our highly competitive society. From Threshold experience the likelihood of becoming homeless is closely associated with level of income. During the period April 1978 to July 1980, 55 per cent of the homeless people who sought our help had incomes of less than £57 per week and less than 10 per cent of these were single persons.)[16]

For young married couples, the elderly people living alone, the young flat dwellers and hostel dwellers, the attainment of decent living conditions is a constant struggle, and for those in low income groups, often no more than a pipe dream. Given current levels of unemployment, the prediction of a continually increasing population and a piecemeal approach to tackling housing problems, and prospects for the 1980s don't offer these groups a lot of hope.

Role of Housing Policy

Due to the serious social and economic effects of bad housing and the consequences of major inequalities in housing provision, Irish housing policy has the stated objective of trying to ensure a minimum level of housing provision for every family, independently of income.

As stated already, the free market would fail to supply accommodation of a reasonable standard to low-income households; so successive governments have intervened in the operation of the housing market in a variety of ways in order to try and realise the above stated objective. Policies devised include rent control, the provision of public sector housing at subsidised rents, and the provision of rent assistance in special cases. As a result of these and other measures, it is fair to say that the poor are less concentrated in the poorer end of the housing spectrum than might otherwise have been the case.

Nevertheless, despite certain improvements, various pieces of evidence show that the poor, on average, live in inferior accommodation — that those with the lowest incomes are also often those with the poorest housing. This is not altogether surprising in view of the fact that we have come nowhere near attaining equality of access to housing which would allow for relatively free choice, regardless of income. Income, and the immobility of institutional factors, still play major roles in influencing the distribution of housing resources, and the right to adequate housing is still not a socially accepted right.

In fact, many analysts of our housing situation point out that the objective of providing a minimum standard is the one which has predominantly influenced our housing legislation down the years.

For example, Pfretzschner has stated that

> There is implicit in almost all of the Irish housing laws. . . an awareness that a large proportion of Irish families lack a large enough income to enable them to purchase or rent shelter which is sufficient to their needs.[17]

With such an emphasis on providing basic shelter down through the years, the trend towards equality in housing opportunity has been severely subsumed in housing policy.

Furthermore, even the most recent elaborations of housing policy objectives comprehend family needs only, while the needs of single people receive no mention at all. This also manifests itself in many aspects of policy practice — the most glaring being the exclusion of almost all single people from gaining access to Local Authority dwellings.

The legislative framework governs the structure of the housing system, but the other major vehicle for the influence of public policy on the housing system is public finance. Very large sums of money flow from the exchequer into the system through various channels, while certain forms of taxation are closely related to housing. Naturally, these two-way flows affect the overall level of equality pertaining in the system.

Of these flows of funds, the one we wish to touch on in general terms here is the payment of subsidies, actual or implicit, which reduces the cost of occupation for various segments of the population.

It seems reasonable to suggest that some of our existing housing subsidies at least have been perpetuated by governments because of inertia and political pressures. Such subsidies have done little to aid the poor and new entrants to gain access to all sectors of the housing market, or to foster mobility of households. A report undertaken by the National Economic and Social Council, for example, has estimated that in 1975 the aggregate subsidisation of owner-occupiers exceeded that of Local Authority tenants, despite the fact that the highest average income was in the former sector.[18] Such subsidies have also, amongst other problems, led to serious under-occupation.

A final area of comment on the role of public policy relates to the private-rented sector. This is down-graded both in terms of subsidy flows and in terms of legislation to control it. The only serious area of legislative intervention, through the Rent Restriction Acts, has led to disastrous results in the controlled part of the sector and has probably had repercussions in the sector as a whole.[19]

The lack of proper legislation has meant that standards in general are extremely low and overcrowding and sharing of facilities are quite common occurrences. The net result of the concentration on provision of family — type dwellings in the owner-occupied and Local Authority sectors has been to leave the private rented sector to stagnate.

What is Needed?

In the space of a few short pages we have attempted to paint a very broad canvas of housing poverty in Ireland. The words 'problem' and 'crisis' often appear in relation to Irish housing. Yet in most of these instances commentators are referring to *a* particular problem or *one* specific crisis — the number of people living in slums, the high levels of rent in private-rented accommodation, the numbers on Local Authority waiting lists, the difficulties in securing home loans, and many more. Our present housing system reflects the response of successive governments who have tended to react to one particular crisis at a time. As noted by Baker and O'Brien, 'The Irish housing system reflects the mixed and pragmatic nature of Irish social organisation as a whole.'[20]

We would argue that, just as the problem of housing poverty is greater than even the combination of these 'symptoms', ways of solving it must be comprehensive, well-informed and co-ordinated. We do not see this as the place, therefore, to put forward incremental recommendations directed at the issues that have been raised. Such an approach would, we believe, lend credence to the idea that the approach to housing is basically 'sound' and that particular 'problem areas' can be tackled in isolation. This has been the hallmark of response from successive governments.

A more realistic approach to tackling poverty in housing, therefore, depends upon the fulfilling of three more fundamental needs: the need for a wider identification of the problem itself; the need for information and research; the need for alternative strategies.

Identification of Problem

This we feel is a prerequisite to success in any of the other areas mentioned. In attempting to assess the dimensions of housing poverty we must, firstly, address the problem *of* housing rather than problems *in* housing. There exists a basic human and social need for housing which offers security, proper living conditions and a degree of choice, and does not pre-empt such a high proportion of income that the provision of other basic human needs is impaired.

The State should recognise this as an unambiguous right in constitutional terms. While our existing Constitution implies this right[21], contradictions are apparent in decisions taken almost daily. While the various debates on public spending single out areas in need of financial assistance, we tend to lose sight of the system of priorities we are constructing for ourselves; if we are serious about our constitutional commitment on housing as both a basic human need and an inalienable social right, then it must be examined in the light of all other decisions made. How do we measure the need for proper housing against, for example, the need for urban motorways? While our existing Constitution contains the implied right that everyone must enjoy a dwelling of acceptable standards, a direct statement of such a right in clear unambiguous terms is called for, followed by the necessary legal provisions defining the extent of such a right and ensuring that the standards set are maintained in succeeding years.

The causes and effects of poor housing have ramifications well beyond the provision of housing units and any meaningful approach to the problem involves, in the first instance, seeing it as a complex and serious problem rather than as a series of issues. We need to realise the importance of *planning* for housing, while departing from the continuous array of crisis measures which typifies our present approach.

We should not look initially to government for the development of a more comprehensive approach. In the past, successive governments have tampered with sectors of the housing market in isolation because presure had been exerted by specialised interest groups. Specialised interest groups themselves have campaigned on behalf of one sector of housing or one section of the population. Their demands have often conflicted with other interest groups equally committed and genuine. Changes in attitudes towards housing, therefore, should begin with a social awareness and lead to the demand for better housing by all and for all.

Research/Information

The value of an up-to-date, accurate and meaningful compilation of data about the housing inventory of a nation would appear to be as obvious as the maintenance of a current industrial inventory to any productive corporation.[22]

Perhaps the most striking indicator of how seriously the problem of housing deprivation is taken is the poverty of information on the issue. The most detailed data available on the national housing stock is nine years out of date and even this (1971 Census) falls far short of giving us a complete picture of housing need. Having realised the complexity of the processes which create housing poverty, and the widespread nature of its harmful effects in individual, social and economic terms, then the need for research becomes as obvious as Pfretzschner states. In order to tackle effectively the problem of housing poverty we need to plan for a better quality and more equitable housing system. We cannot do this at present because *we don't know enough.*

The Development of Alternatives

It is only when given a more comprehensive and widespread awareness of the housing problem, and the need for information on it, that more meaningful policies and strategies can emerge. It is only then also that traditional means of alleviating housing stress can be effectively questioned. We see the promotion of voluntary and co-operative involvement in housing in Ireland as being important in all three areas mentioned.[23]

Any real attack on housing poverty, then, depends firstly on the will to grasp the severity of the problem in all its aspects, and secondly, on the will to formulate and implement well-researched policies aimed at the problem and not its varied symptoms. This type of commitment can only emerge if our whole approach is coloured by the idea of housing as a fundamental right. Should we continue in our present piecemeal attack on the symptoms, then not only will the housing poor always be with us, they will inevitably form an increasingly large, deprived and demoralised section of Irish society.

Note
The authors of this chapter wish to acknowledge the help of the Threshold committee, staff and volunteers, who by their constant commitment to the work of assisting the homeless and the flat-dweller made our contribution possible. In particular, we thank committee member, Paul Byrne, OMI, former director of SHACK who was awarded OBE for his work on housing in Britain.

REFERENCES

1. For example, S. Lansley, *Housing and Public Policy*, Croom Helm, London, 1979.

2. See P.J. Meghan, *Housing in Ireland* (Dublin, 1965).

3. T.J. Baker and L.M. O'Brien, 'The Irish Housing System — A Critical Overview', ESRI Broadsheet No. 17 (Dublin, 1979).

4. Threshold is a voluntary organisation offering information and advice to those experiencing housing difficulties. Pax Christi provided the initial support and it was grant-aided by the National Committee on Pilot Schemes to Combat Poverty for two years but is now completely dependent for finance on a fund-raising committee. The majority of the more than five thousand cases dealt with since it began in 1978 originated in the private rented sector. Threshold is now a limited company with a management council and a number of sub-committees, three full-time staff members and twenty volunteers. The principal office is at the Capuchin Franciscan Friary, Church Street in Dublin, with a second office at 52 Lower Rathmines Road. Threshold is also committed to a research programme, using the information gathered in its case work to highlight the major housing problems and to find ways to tackle the causes of homelessness.

5. Examples of these studies include 'Population Projections 1971-86: The Implications for Social Planning — Dwelling Needs', NESC Report No. 14 (Stationery Office, Dublin, 1976); 'Housing Forecasting and Planning' (Dublin, 1978), a Department of Environment monograph, 'Housing Stastics', a Department of Environment quarterly bulletin.

6. NESC, op. cit.

7. Campaign for the Homeless, *A Directory of Hostel Provision in Dublin* (Dublin, 1981 — forthcoming).

8. Threshold, *Private-Rented — The Forgotten Sector* (Dublin, 1981).

9. P. Duffy, 'Housing Needs: The Prospects for the 1980s'. Paper presented to the Annual Conference of the Irish Branch of The Regional Studies Association, Dublin, 1981.

10. See, for example, 'Two Tales of a City', *The Irish Times*, 20 March 1981; 'Bleeding to Death in Sherrif Street', *Hibernia*, 29 May 1980; 'Today Tonight', RTE feature on Fatima Mansions, January 1981.

11. Lansley, op. cit.

12. Threshold, op. cit.

13. B. Power, *Old and Alone in Ireland* (Dublin, 1980).

14. Threshold, op. cit.

15. Ibid.

16. Ibid.

17. P. A Pfretzchner, *The Dynamics of Irish Housing* (Dublin, 1965).

18. 'Housing Subsidies', NESC Report No. 23 (Dublin, 1977).

19. Threshold, 'The Present Crisis in Rent-Controlled Accommodation (1980 — unpublished).

20. Baker and O'Brien, op. cit.

21. Bunreacht na hEireann, Article 41 (1 and 2).

22. Pfretzchner, op. cit.

23. D. O'Mahony, 'Housing by Voluntary Bodies'. Threshold paper presented at a Seminar for Local Authority Officials having responsibility for Local Housing Information Centres, organized by the Institute of Public Administration in conjunction with the Department of the Environment, Dublin 1981.

Poverty and Homelessness

Justin O'Brien

The single homeless is a recent term used to describe and identify a group of people who may be said to be without a settled way of life. They have more often been described as vagrants, vagabonds, tramps, down and outs, dossers, skid row people, destitues — all names which imply stigma and prejudice and deny a central feature of their condition, namely, being homeless. As a group they are usually readily identifiable in the public consciousness and are publicly visible by reason of their poor clothing and attire, their unkempt appearance and perhaps by the commital of anti-social acts such as begging and drunkeness, attracting a mixture of sympathy, indignation and rejection from the public. They are one of the most obvious examples of the existence of poverty and destitution in Irish society, despite its growing prosperity and the expansion of the State's Welfare and Social Services.

The single homeless, or skid row inhabitants as they are known in the USA, have attracted considerable attention and research there, but here in Ireland and the UK they have merited little attention or research. The American researchers have described their condition in three inter-related ways, referring to the social and economic characteristics of the men who use the institutions on skid row, a particular culture common to a particular group which separates its inhabitants from society, and finally to a distinct geographical area in the centre of cities where they live. Bahr neatly sums up these three strands:

> The skidrow people live on skidrow territory, the others do not. In terms of the ecology of the city, the concentration of institutions and persons with homeless characteristics create a neighbourhood, a context which is different from the other regions of the city both in terms of symbolic nature (how people think about it, treat its residents and relate to it) and in terms of the population composition. Skidrow may also reflect a place of mind, but it is also a place or

area of the city and those who frequent it are aware of its distinctive identity.[1]

Most researchers view a person being on skidrow as being a manifestation of individual and social pathology which are explained by various social and psychological theories. It is because of the individual's personal and social inadequacies that he or she is homeless and dependent on skidrow's institutions. These institutions are the voluntary hostels and government reception centres, the penal institutions and the psychiatric hospitals. Indeed most research would seem to validate these theories by reason of the high rates of alcoholism, mental illness, unemployment and criminality that the single homeless population have. It is only recently that researchers have looked at skidrow from its inhabitants' viewpoint and how they try to adapt to the problems of chronic poverty, deprivation, illness, addiction and homelessness. Thus 'it is the socialisation of man into a permanent state of homelessness rather than any evidence of undersocialisation before arrival on skidrow that becomes the primary object of the study'.[2] No one doubts that the single homeless are at the very end, the dregs of a society.

Conditions Homelessness

Here in Ireland there are no exact or specific references to the single homeless in our legislation. The Minister of Health has stated:

Health Boards are required under Section 54 of the Health Act 1953 to provide such institutional assistance to persons who are unable to provide shelter and maintenance for themselves or their dependents, as appears to the Health Board to be necessary and proper in each particular case. Accommodation can be provided in Health Board Homes, or similar institutions or institutions such as hostels which are financially assisted by Health Boards. Under Section 12 of the Housing Act 1966, housing authorities can make financial assistance available to voluntary housing organisations which provide accommodation to needy persons including those who are homeless. Single homeless people can avail themselves of such health and social service benefits provided by the Health Boards and the Department of Social Welfare as may be appropriate to their need or entitlements.[3]

In effect this means that a single homeless person has no statutory right to a home. All that he is entitled to is shelter or accommodation in a county home or hostel.

Homelessness is usually perceived as a person or family being without a home and having to sleep on the streets. Once that need has been met by a person living and sleeping in overcrowded conditions with relations or in poor sub-standard conditions with a lack of amenities, there would be considerable disagreement as to whether this constituted homelessness. The general public and the persons who run the voluntary hostels and casual wards see the provision of a bed and shelter as the solution to a person's homelessness. But is this perception correct? The following represents a more realistic summation of the problem: 'Homelessness does not alone mean the absence of a roof, it means the absence of all the other things we associate with home, a place that is ours, where we are free from being pushed around, where there is love, where there is affection and where we too can express our affection.'[4] It also entails a lack of privacy, a place to have personal possessions, it means an isolation from our family, friends and the local community. A person living in a hostel or casual ward is subjected to all the above.

Throughout the eight Health Board regions there are twenty-five voluntary hostels and thirteen Health Board institutions providing emergency accommodation for homeless people. The Health Board institutions are usually the casual wards of the county homes and the psychiatric hospitals. The hostels are managed by voluntary groups such as The Legion of Mary, The St Vincent de Paul Society, the Salvation Army and the Simon Community. Six of the hostels are specifically for women, the rest for men, though the county homes may provide accommodation for members of either sex. The largest hostel in the country can accommodate up to 400 persons while the smaller ones take no more than eight to twelve persons. The average city hostel accommodates about eighty persons while the county hostels and county homes take considerably fewer. Overall, it may be estimated that there are over 2000 bed places available for homeless persons with most of these beds occupied each night. The major urban centres of Dublin, Cork and Limerick have the majority of the hostels between them, while the casual wards in the county homes and the smaller hostels are dispersed in the medium- and small-sized towns such as Kilkenny, Castlebar, Waterford, Killarney and Ennis. Only one Health Board region, the North Western, has no overnight emergency accommodation available. There has been a reduction of the number of bed places available as it is current Health Board policy to change the function of the old county homes to that of hospitals, as well as welfare homes with a permanent group of residents, and they no longer have overnight accommodation facilities. There would also seem to be some confusion as to who should provide such accommodation and shelter. One Heath Board official has said, 'The obligation on the Health Board was more traditional than legal.'[5] The Health Board also appears to be experiencing difficulties in the management of the county homes, with their dual functions of being a welfare home and having accommodation for a homeless person. Thus, they may have closed the casual wards because of these difficulties and because of the reduced number of migrant labourers travelling and seeking work in the rural areas.

The policy and regimes of the various hostels and casual wards may vary considerably but one can broadly state that they entail sharing a dormitory with other homeless persons or else paying extra for a small cubicle room. Management policy determines entry and exit from the place and in practically all hostels everyone has to leave by 9 a.m. in the morning, while some require entry by 7 p.m. in the evening. The hostels are usually crowded, with the obvious lack of privacy and storage for personal possessions. Some hostels allow persons to stay there every night, others only allow a person to stay there three consecutive nights in a week. The hostels are impersonal and are not social service orientated, seeing their function primarily as that of providing shelter. Some regimes demand that the homeless person conforms to certain patterns of behaviour such as being in on time, being clean and tidy, and being sober. Failure to comply to these norms means expulsion, more especially if a person is disorderly or aggressive. Because of the lack of freedom or self-determination accorded to the single homeless person, some choose to sleep rough or find 'skippers' in unused and derelict buildings and empty cars in preference to the strictures of the hostels and casual wards. Other homeless persons, especially the most deprived such as the wine alcoholics, may have no choice in the matter. On average, each night the Dublin Simon Community soup-run visits up to twenty persons sleeping rough, but there are many more who are safely hidden from them and the public.

79

Demographic Features

Because of the lack of study and research of the single home-less in Ireland, there is a paucity of information about their social, economic, medical and psychological conditions. The main research has been that of O'Cinneide's survey of Dublin hostel dwellers and Hart's study of the Dublin Simon Commun-ity.[6] The other data available is from the work of Trust, a special medical and social service for homeless persons in Dublin.[7] As stated, there are an estimated 2000 bed places available for the single homeless in Ireland, with most of these beds being occupied each night. The research of O'Cinneide, Hart and Trust indicate that the vast majority of the single homeless population is male, being 92 per cent, 87 per cent and 86 per cent respectively in each survey group. As regards mari-tal status, some 65 per cent of the Trust, O'Cinneide groups were single, and Hart has a lower percentage, 49 per cent, of unmarried persons, but a higher proportion 38 per cent, of separated persons.

The ages of the homeless cover a wide scale, from 16 to 65 years and upwards. The available evidence is not conclusive on this aspect but it suggests that 75 per cent of the home-less group are aged 30 years and older, indicating that com-pared to some USA research there are fewer in the older age group of 60 years onwards, but more in the under-30 age group.

The existence of a separate night shelter for homeless child-ren in Dublin is itself indicative of the number of young home-less.[8]

Income

In contrast to the USA skidrow population, Ireland's single homeless are nearly all unemployed. Hart, in his survey of the Irish Simon communities, established an unemployment rate of 95 percent, while none of those on Trust's records were in employment.[9] Most homeless persons have been unemployed for lengthy periods of time. Few come from professional or skilled occupational groups, and the vast majority have only been employed as unskilled workers. The only work that a homeless person can usually get is of a casual type such as kitchen portering, some construction and demolition work, potato and vegetable picking and harvesting. This casual work has been reduced dramatically because of improved technology, the expansion of the consumer market, the shift to factory-centred production and the unionisation of labour. There is no longer the need in our society for a pool of unskilled labour, often highly mobile, to be engaged in agricultural harvesting and construction work.

The main source of income for the single homeless are the State welfare benefits such an unemployment benefit, unemployment assistance, disability benefit, and supplementary welfare allowance. The respective rates of payment for the first three are as follows: £24.55, £20.40 and £24.55 weekly. Additional payments may be made to persons depending on their particular needs under the supplementary welfare allowance scheme. The vast majority of the single homeless rely upon the Unemployment Assistance or supplementary Welfare Allowance; an insignificant minority are entitled to Unemployment Benefit, indicating their lack of insurable employment and their unemployment over lengthy periods of time. Perhaps even more significant, when one considers their general medical condition, is the small number of the single homeless who benefit from the Disabled Persons Maintenance Allowance.

Medical Care

Because of their homelessness and their lack of a community base, few of the single homeless avail of the community services, particularly in the field of medical and social work care. Though entitled to medical cards and the services of a specific doctor, the single homeless appear to be reluctant to avail of the service for a variety of reasons such as the lack of permanent address and the waywardness of their life style, some stigma and a rejection of them by some medical practitioners. Accordingly they present themselves at the casualty wards of hospitals with their medical needs. They also attempt to use the casualty wards as a place to rest for a while. The hospital staff usually view them as being a nuisance and not very amenable to proper medical treatment.[10] The main medical problems of the single homeless are respiratory conditions, skin diseases and minor trauma, medical conditions which are linked to their life-style. Hart, discovered that 'no less than 82% of the overall sample from the four Irish communities suffered from some mental or physical disability such as depression, alcoholism, physical ill health or old age or a com-

81

bination of such disabilities'.[11] In the light of these conditions the small percentage of persons who actually avail of the Disabled Persons Maintenance Allowance would appear to be remarkably low.

Likewise, few of the single homeless avail of the services of the community-based social workers. This again is because of their lack of a permanent address and the waywardness of their lives, but also because the services they seek from social workers are usually of a material nature — money, clothes, shoes, food — rather than the case-work type of service which social workers usually provide. There is also a low priority assigned to them in terms of the field social worker's work load. Accordingly, it is left to the voluntary organisations to provide a social work type service.

Other notable features of the client group of homeless persons who used a specific medical service for homeless persons were that some 46 percent had a severe drink problem, 33 percent a history of long-term institutional care and 14 percent had been in prison more than once.

Institutions: Psychiatric Hospitals

Archard has commented quite correctly that 'The state has three formal and direct methods of responding to the problem presented by the single homeless. These are exercised by the institutions of criminal law, mental health and social welfare.[12] The institutions of criminal law and mental health play a major role in the single homeless configuration.

The available statistics from the Socio-Medical Board show that in 1974 some 489 persons of no fixed abode were admitted to the Irish psychiatric hospitals.[13]

These figures indicate that the single homeless has a considerably higher percentage of its members hospitalised and diagnosed as suffering from schizophrenia, alcoholism and alcoholic psychosis than the national average, while having a considerably lower proportion of its members diagnosed and treated for manic-depressive psychosis. Some 67 percent of all homeless admissions were from the St Brendan complex of hospitals in Dublin, reflecting the fact that it is the only complex that classifies and has a specific unit for persons of no fixed abode. It is most probable that many more homeless persons are admitted to the psychiatric hospitals, but they are not classified as homeless, their hostel addresses being accepted as places of permanent residence. Data from the Camberwell Reception Centre in London indicates that some 65 percent of the Centre's users were suffering from mental illness, but only 29 percent has been admitted to psychiatric hospitals.[14] The available Irish statistics show that a large proportion, some 25 percent at a minimum, of the single homeless population avail of and are in need of psychiatric care. As in the general hospital, homeless people often sign themselves in and out of the psychiatric hospital and do not complete their treatment programmes.

Table 1

National Admissions of All Homeless: Ireland 1974

	Male	Female	Total	%	National %
Schizophrenia	163	24	187	38.2	24.4
Manic-depressive psychosis	33	14	47	9.6	22.8
Other phychosis	21	10	31	6.3	10.4
Neurosis & personality disorder	49	24	73	14.9	16.4
Alcoholism & alcoholic psychosis	121	9	130	26.5	21.4
Mental handicap	11	6	17	3.4	2.7
Unspecified	4	0	4	0.8	1.5
Total	402	87	489	100	100

Source: Irish Psychiatric Hospitals and Units 1973/74 (Medical Social Research Board)

Hence they are viewed as being a nuisance as well as being a very difficult and incurable clientele. A major problem here is that there is no evident policy or special service for them in the institutions and more especially no special service for them on their discharge from hospital into the community. Likewise, the policy of discharging long-term psychiatric patients within the hospitals into the community has added to the numbers of single homeless living in the hostels. Though a large proportion of the single homeless suffer from psychiatric illnesses such as alcoholism and schizophrenia, the public usually have little sympathy for these individual personal problems, rather these illnesses merely confirm their defectiveness and their deviancy.

Prison

Trust is a voluntary organisation which provides a socio-medical service for the single homeless in Dublin. The Trust records showed that some 14 percent of the people it met had been imprisoned more than once. The commital of down and outs or single homeless persons to prison has been known as a revolving-door process, that is, arrest, a court appearance, imprisonment, release and re-arrest, the cycle repeating itself endlessly. The criminal acts the homeless usually commit are offences such as vagrancy, begging, drunkenness and drunk and disorderly. These crimes relate particularly to their life-style and the social conditions within which they are forced to live. Two laws in particular affect them, namely, Section 4 of the Vagrancy Act of 1824 and Section 12 of the Licensing Act of 1872.

The Vagrancy Act is an outmoded piece of legislation originally dating back to 1349 when the feudal lords attempted to lower the wages of the serfs and stop the free movement of labour. Chambliss[15] and Steele[16] show clearly how illegitimacy, criminality and stigma were attached to an unsettled way of life and how the power of the Vagrancy Acts were expanded in the changing social conditions of sixteenth-century England. The Acts were also amended and applied in conjunction with Poor Law relief, making its distinctions between able-bodied beggars and beggars unable to work, the deserving and the undeserving poor. Section 4 of the 1824 Vagrancy Act remains on our statute books and any person found guilty under this Act is deemed to be 'a rogue and a vagabond'. Two categories of vagrancy offences are of special relevance to the homeless, namely, vagrancy simple and its four begging offences.

Vagrancy simple is defined as 'wandering abroad and lodging in any barn or outhouse, and not having means of subsistence and not giving a good account of himself or herself'. In effect this means that any poor, unemployed homeless person may be arrested and convicted. The begging offences may be as follows: 'wandering abroad and endeavouring by the exposure of wounds and deformities to obtain or gather alms'. If a person is found guilty of any of the vagrancy offences they may be fined up to £2 and or sent to prison. Until it was recently declared unconstitutional, the section of the act known as 'loitering with intent' was applied also against the homeless. Chambliss accurately asserts that 'the lack of change in the vagrancy acts can be seen as a reflection of society's perception of a continuing need to control some of its 'suspicious' or 'undesirable' members'.[17]

For committing such offences, a person, if convicted, may be fined, and in default of payment be imprisoned for a period of no more than a month. A law which particularly pertains to the single homeless is Section 12 of the Licensing Act 1872. There are two sub-sections within it, namely, 'drunkenness simple' and 'drunkenness with aggravation'. Simple drunkenness is 'being found drunk in a highway or other public place, whether a building or not, or on a licensed premises', while 'drunkenness with aggravation' is 'being guilty while drunk of riotous or disorderly behaviour in a highway or other public place whether a building or not'. In effect, drunkenness in the privacy of one's home is not an offence while public drunkenness is. For committing these offences a person may be fined £2 and may be send to prison for thirty days whether in default of payment or not.

The life-style of the single homeless condemns them to frequent contact with the law enforcement agencies. Because of their homelessness and the absence of day centres they are forced to wander the streets and public places, always being liable to arrest for offences under the Vagrancy Act. The other aspect of the Act which militates against them is the offences relating to begging. Because of their lack of employment and the inadequate State Welfare benefits, some choose to beg from the public to supplement their income and so they may be arrested. Also if they are drinking or are drunk or drunk and disorderly in public they are likely to be arrested. The homeless person, because of his disaffiliation and demeanour, can be readily identified and be seen as a public nuisance. Particularly when drunk, they may commit a breach of the peace, use threatening language, beg from the public or just lie in the streets. This may be seen as detracting from public amenities such as a bus or railway station, public libraries, parks and churches. Alternatively, traders and shop-keepers may complain about their presence in the street and look for them to be moved on. Sometimes the Gardai, with altruistic feelings, arrest a homeless person in the belief that a period in prison may be of benefit to him by giving him a break from his self-destructive life-style. Alternatively, the process of arrest may reflect common social prejudice towards the single homeless from which the Gardai cannot be exempt.

Upon arrest, the homeless person is usually held overnight in a police cell and then brought to court the following day. The following case from a Dublin District Court is quite typical.

'I arrested the two defendants between 11 and 12 midnight last night', the Garda told District Justice Johnston in Dublin District Court 4. They were drunk and were fighting on the public highway. The Garda rested his case.

'Do you wish to ask the Garda anything? inquired the Justice.

'No,' said one of the defendants.

'Are you pleading?' asked the Justice.

'I am guilty, yes,' said the same defendant.

'Two pounds fine against each defendant, payable forthwith or seven days in default,' said the Justice.

'Ah, excuse me' said the defendant. 'I am working at present and I could give you money on Friday if you give me a chance.'

'You have no fixed abode,' said the judge.

'I have,' said the defendant.

'He gave me an address but I don't think he has stayed there for quite some time now,' said the Garda.

'He tells me he works four days a week for the Redemptoriests Brothers.'

86

'I won't change my orders,' said the Justice, as he rose and left the court.18

The most striking aspect of the above is the brevity of the administration of the case and the *fait-accompli* nature of it. A homeless person is rarely legally represented in court and equally rarely does anyone give evidence on his behalf or even a character reference. Practically all their cases are dealt with in the lower courts. In the above case, accepting that the two defendants were guilty, they were effectively imprisoned because of their homelessness and their poverty. Homeless people do not normally get bail, probation or suspended sentences. The fines of £2 to £5 which are imposed upon them are well within the financial capabilities of the ordinary citizen who is fined for such offences, but not so for the homeless. Consequently they are usually imprisoned upon conviction.

The prison reports give no indication of the number of single homeless who are imprisoned annually. One can only estimate the figure by the number who are committed for the offences of begging, drunkenness and vagrancy. In the past fifteen years the numbers convicted have ranged from 165 to 350 persons or, as a percentage of the prison population, from 7 to 20 percent. Drunkenness forms the major compenent of the numbers, with begging offences next. Vagrancy simple forms only a minute portion of the prison population and in recent years no one has been imprisoned for this offence. Women convicted of these three offences have always formed a major proportion of the offenders in the Women's Prison, ranging from 19 to 64 percent. The percentage has been reduced considerably because of the increased number of females currently imprisoned for other offences. These figures and percentages do not give an accurate estimation of the real numbers of homeless persons imprisoned as they will include members of the travelling community and exclude 'down and outs' who are convicted on other criminal offences. Most homeless offenders are imprisoned for short periods of time. Research in the UK by the Home Office shows clearly the correlation between homelessness and recidivism where it was discovered that by the time a person has collected twenty-one or more convictions he has a 77 percent chance of being homeless, and being homeless he has a 67 percent chance of being reconvicted.19 Their needs have been recognised but unfortunately no special provision has been made for them. In the USA, the UK and Sweden the futility of the revolving-door process has been recognised by the authorities. Specific provision has been created for the skidrow alcoholics with the decriminalisation of the drunkenness offences and the alternative detoxification centres instead of imprisonment. The fact that the homeless and the public may view our prisons as being essential institutions and rest homes for them is no justification for their imprisonment; rather, it is a sad indication of the lack of community-based facilities.

Ultimately, however, the cycle of arrest and inprisonment represents Irish society's deep rejection of the single homeless and their criminalisation and punishment for being homeless, for having a disease — alcoholism — and for being in poverty.

Public Attitudes

Townsend has ascribed the following characteristics to social minority: 'They have some characteristics in common which marks them off from "ordinary" people and which prevents them from having access to, or being accorded certain rights which are available to others and who are therefore less likely to receive certain kinds or amounts of resources.[20] It is clearly evident that the single homeless population are denied their rights and access to resources in all facets of their life — housing, employment, income, benefits, medical and psychiatric care. Their characteristics as identified by the public are entirely negative, being the antithesis of the values that our society espouses.

The homeless are seen as being dirty, unkempt and ragged, they are workless, lazy, unemployable individuals who refuse to work if given this opportunity: they are incurable, hopeless drug addicts, drunks, alcoholics and winos. They are seen as being criminal and deviant.

McGreil has commented that:

the problem with the 'down and out' who seek help from Simon is that they probably carry the stigma of 'unemployed', 'heavy drinker', 'alcoholic', 'drug addict' and in some people's mind that of 'criminal' and 'the dosser' is a composite social category of four or five of the most disliked categories in our society.[21]

The intense hostility in the past few years of local residents in Dublin and Limerick to the planned housing of single home-

88

less people in their areas indicates the degree of prejudice and stigma that is attached to them. Perhaps the major prejudice and hence the greater fear the residents had regarding the single homeless was sexual deviancy: 'the mothers could not feel safe letting their children out to play'.[22] 'the problems they were creating went beyond the hospital. They had been 'unsavoury incidents involving children'.[23] Also the single homeless are popularly perceived as being a homogeneous group of drunks: 'These people at the hostel are creating a very bad impression. They are often found lying on the streets with bottles and using foul filthy language.'[24] Except when attempts are made to house them, then single homeless as a group are barely recognised in Irish society.

Conclusion

Contrary to the popular perception, the single homeless population is in fact composed of many sub-groups, each with its own special needs. Ages vary from adolescents to old age pensioners. There are casual and itinerant labourers, the mentally ill and psychiatric patients, released prisoners and recidivists, mentally handicapped and physically disabled people, alcoholics and unsocial winos, and old age pensioners with no family ties. The population is not entirely stable either, as some manage to move on by perhaps finding employment and better accommodation, by returning home to their families for temporary periods, by emigrating to the UK. Others fall within it because of unemployment, family discord, alcoholism and psychiatric illness.

However, all the different sub-groups within the hostel population are confined within the limiting perimeters of the institutions which effectively segregate its members from conventional society. They have to sleep in crowded and impersonal circumstances (this is not to deny the care of the hostel staff). They usually have to leave the hostels by 9 a.m. in the morning and may not return till the evening. So they wander the streets in search of employment, a bed for the coming night, food, warmth, shelter. Day centres which offer food and shelter are scarce; there are only two in Dublin with a population of over 1000 hostel dwellers, and none in the other urban and rural centres. The penny dinners provided by religious and voluntary groups are the mainstay of their diet. One hostel costs as much as £3.00 per night, others are free of charge. They have little money to buy food or clothes. They can rarely afford cheap rented accommodation as it would easily account for a half of their welfare money. Some adapt to their situation by begging, by becoming dependent on alcohol, others rest anonymously in the shadows. They are all usually lonely and isolated individuals with personal sufferings, none were born into this situation and none made a conscious decision about entering it either. That suffering is most obviously seen on the impoverished and scarred faces of the alcoholics who excite the greatest antipathy from the settled community. Here they are a marginal group excluded from society, and once they have entered the hostel network it is extremely difficult to re-enter the settled community and participate fully in its social and economic activities.

The hostels and the casual wards that Irish society provides for its down and outs are a relic of the Poor Law and its casual wards for the undeserving poor. Within some of the hostels the nineteenth-century idea of moral defectiveness is still attached to the single homeless. They are the undeserving poor who should be offered only a minimum of assistance, for it is the individual's own weaknesses that has him where he is. The single homeless have been the object of moral reform, punishment and deterrence, and now more recently the socio-medical treatment medal.

During the twentieth century the subsistence and minimum rights concept of poverty has emerged, with the State expanding its welfare services by policies of redistributive taxation and universal benefits in cash and health services. The Department or Minister for Health and Irish society assumes that the granting of such benefits along with institutional assistance will be sufficient to alleviate the poverty of the single homeless. Their continued existence is merely further confirmation of their weaknesses and inadequacies, so further stigma and deviancy are attached to them. Despite the fact that there are high incidences of mental and physical illness, old age, alcoholism and physical handicap among the single homeless, the community-based services that they are entitled to are not granted to them. Accordingly, rather than psychiatric aftercare hostels, probation hostels, sheltered housing and domiciliary services for the aged, the hostels and casual wards suffice. Thus the various voluntary organisations are left to provide for this group, while the State's responsibility is split between the various departments — Environment, Justice, Health and

Social Welfare — with each one allocating responsibility to the other. Until the State on behalf of Irish society undertakes to provide suitable homes for the single homeless, they will always be publicly visible. When this primary need is met, only then can the more personal needs be treated. Otherwise this marginal group, stigmatised and rejected by our society, will continue to shock us in their attempts to survive and adapt to chronic poverty, illness and homelessness.

REFERENCES

1. H. Bahr. *Skid Row: An introduction to Disaffiliation* (Oxford, 1973).

2. Peter Archard, *'Vagrancy, Alcoholism and Social Control* (London, 1979).

3. Simon Ireland Newsletter, May 1978. A reply by the then Minister of Health, Mr Haughey, to a written parliamentary question by Deputy John O'Connell on who is responsible for the provision of services for homeless people.

4. Simon Ireland Newsletter, April 1978, from a talk by Mr Fred Donoghue, Director of Community Care in the Eastern Health Board Region, to a National Simon Conference in 1978.

5. A comment by the South-Eastern Health Board, CEO, at a Kilkenny Health Committee, about the difficulties the staff of a casual ward were experiencing. *The Kilkenny People*, 26 September 1980.

6. Seamus O'Cinneide, *A Survey of Dublin Hostel Dwellers* (The Medical Social Research Board, 1971): Ian Hart, 'Dublin Simon Community 1971-76, An Exploration, ESRI Broadsheet No. 15, Dublin 1978.

7. Information on clients who availed of medical and social aid in an eighteen-month period from 3 July 1976 to 7 October 1977 where, in all, a total of 749 persons had record charts opened.

8. The HOPE Annual General Report 1978/9. HOPE accommodated eighty-five children in the year, the majority of whom were aged over 12 years.

9. Hart, op. cit.

10. Alice Leahy, *Medical Care for the Vagrant in Ireland*, A Simon Ireland Publication, Dublin 1974.

11. Hart, op. cit.

12. Archard, op. cit.

13. Aileen O'Hare, 'Mental Illness and the Homeless', paper presented to the National Conference of the Irish Simon Communities, February 1978.

14. D. Tidmarsh and S. Wood, Psychiatric Aspects of Destitution: A study of Camberwell Reception Centre, in evaluating a community psychiatric service.

15. William J. Chambliss, 'The Law of Vagrancy' in *Crime and the Legal Process* by W.J. Chambliss (ed.) (New York 1969).

16. Dan W. Steele, '*Vagrancy — Social Origins and Response*', FARE Publications Study Paper No.1.

17. Chambliss, op. cit.

18. Nell McCafferty, 'In the Eye of the Law', *The Irish Times*, 19 December 1974.

19. Susan Fairhead and Tony P. Marshall, '*Dealing with the Petty Persistent Offender*'.

20. Peter Townsend, '*Poverty in the United Kingdom — A Survey of Household Resources and Standards of Living*', (Harmondsworth, 1979).

21. Michael McGreil, '*Attitudes towards the Socially Disadvantaged*', Paper read at the National Conference of the Irish Simon Communities, 1979.

22. Comment by one of the Chapelizod residents, opposing the proposed Simon Community House there, *Evening Herald*, 6 February 1976.

23. Comment by a member of the Kilkenny Health Committee, *The Kilkenny People*, 26 September 1980.

24. Comment by a Limerick City councillor in a debate in the city corporation over the proposed housing of homeless men, *The Irish Times*, 13 April 1977.

Rural Poverty [1]

John Curry

Professor John F. Jones, speaking at a conference on 'Social Development in Times of Economic Uncertainty' held in Hong Kong in July 1980, stated:

It should be remembered that most of the world's poverty is rural. The urban poverty of Calcutta or Rio de Janeiro is dramatic and apparent but for all its drama it is probably less terrible and certainly less pervasive than the rural poverty of Bangladesh or Chad. A good 70 percent of the poor in Asia or Africa live in the countryside, a fact often overlooked in national planning for such social services as health care, education, housing or indeed the most basic items like water.[2]

There is certainly a general tendency, as Jones indicates, to focus attention almost exclusively on poverty in urban areas while ignoring the fact that considerable deprivation may exist in rural areas. Furthermore, many existing social services have evolved in response to the problems arising from industrialisation and urbanisation. The problems and needs of the urban population have considerably influenced the setting of priorities in social policy and social legislation.

Even in Ireland, which by any definition has a considerable population living in rural areas, the nature of the deprivation which exists in many areas of the main urban centres is often highlighted while the problems of rural areas receive less attention.

Donnison has suggested that urban-rural and inter-regional inequalities constitute one of the five main types or patterns of inequality in Irish society.[3] He refers to the fact that economic development is never distributed evenly across the map and that young people in particular are attracted to the centres of new growth. Even the introduction of new jobs in growth industries in rural areas will not necessarily benefit the entire community and the older and less adaptable may gain little from such developments, he argues. Furthermore if jobs cannot be found for both men and women, and for a wide range of skills, and if local services are poor, the younger people will continue to leave rural areas. In most countries, according to Donnison, government programmes for dealing with urban-rural and inter-regional inequalities are less well developed and often less successful than those for dealing with other patterns of in-equality.

The main focus in this chapter will be on inequalities between rural and urban areas and within rural areas. In particular, the emphasis will be on the availability of and access to social services. Before examining these issues, however, some distinguishing features of rural areas are outlined.

Rural Areas

At the outset it is important to note that rural areas are not uniform or socially homogeneous. Some are characterised by small farms and poor soil quality while others contain some of the most productive pasture or arable land in Western Europe. Similarly, some have experienced persistently high out mig-ration while others have experienced an increase in population, in recent decades at least. The latter are likely to be those areas adjacent to relatively large urban centres. The population of such areas may be at a considerable disadvantage in relation to non-farm job-opportunities and services by comparison with populations in more remote areas. The rural population itself is, in many instances, no longer predominantly composed of farmers and the non-farming rural population is increasing. In general, the most serious socio-economic problems of rural areas tend to be concentrated in certain parts of the country, principally the western region.

For Census purposes the term 'urban' is applied to population centres of 1,500 inhabitants or more. Smaller centres of population as well as open countryside constitute the 'rural' areas. On this basis the 'rural' population in Ireland in 1971 accounted for less than half (47.8 percent) of the total population as compared with 71.7 percent in 1901.[4] The dominant position of the Dublin area in relation to the country's demographic position, however, distorts the picture somewhat. If the population of Dublin is excluded, then about 70 percent of the population lived in rural areas in 1971.

94

Some Demographic Features

Here only some of the salient demographic features of rural areas are examined. They are more fully described elsewhere.[5]

During the 1960s the national population increased for the first time since the mid-nineteenth century. This increase continued into the 1970s. The demographic transformation at national level conceals the fact that some rural areas continued to experience population decline in the 1960s and to a lesser extent in the 1970s. The pattern of decline in rural areas has changed considerably over the past few decades. By comparison with the 1950s, for example, the decline in population in rural areas is no longer as high nor as widespread in geographic terms. Stability or growth in population has now been achieved on a scale which would scarcely have been imagined in the 1950s.

Even within centres which over the last two decades have begun to achieve overall stability or growth in population, disparities can occur. In County Clare, considerable investment was made in the creation of industrial jobs especially at Shannon and during the latter half of the 1960s the county recorded an increase in population for the first time since the mid-nineteenth century. Yet the rural districts of Meelick and Ennis in the hinterland of the Limerick-Shannon-Ennis industrial complex were the only ones to record increases in population during the second half of the 1960s and throughout the 1970s Those rural districts located at a distance from the centres of growth continued to experience population decline (Table 1).

Despite recent changes, however, the effects of prolonged and persistently high out migration from rural areas in the past still pose considerable problems in many rural areas.

As a result of selective outmigration among young adults over a period of time, many rural communities contain disproportionate numbers of elderly persons. In 1971 13.2 percent of the population in rural areas was aged 65 or over as compared with 9.1 percent in urban areas. In general, counties in the western region (the least urbanised region of the country) tend to have proportionately more elderly persons. In 1979, for example, 17.3 percent of the population of Leitrim was aged over 65 or over.

The effects of out-migration are also associated with and reflected in household composition. In 1971 approximately one-quarter of households in rural areas contained non-family units (households with one person only and households with two or more persons not constituting a family unit) as compared with one-fifth in urban areas.

A further demographic feature of rural areas is the low density of population. In 1979 the density of persons per square mile ranged from 47 in Leitrim to 2,764 in Dublin County and County Borough. In general, counties in the western region have the lowest density of population. Some rural districts in Clare, Kerry, Galway, Mayo and Cavan had population densities of 30 or less persons per square mile.

These features have important implications for the provision of social services. High proportions of elderly or dependent persons will inevitably demand a response from certain statutory services but the problems in providing such services may often be accentuated by distance from centralised services in urban

Table 1

Population Change in Urban and Rural Districts of County Clare 1966-71, 1971-79

	1966-71	1971-79
Urban Districts		
Ennis	+ 2.4	+ 5.1
Kilrush	- 2.3	+ 4
Rural Districts		
Ballyvaughan	- 5.7	- 1.4
Corofin	- 3.2	+ 3.6
Ennis	+ 20.3	+ 44.1
Ennistymon	- 6.2	- 5.4
Kildysart	- 3.8	- 1.3
Kilrush	- 7.1	- 7.6
Meelick	+ 10.3	+ 48.3
Scariff	- 0.1	+ 7.6
Tulla	- 3.7	- 0.3
County Clare	+ 3.7	+ 13.2

Source: Census of Population 1971, 1979.

centres. The density of population also has important implications for the provision and delivery of services; the lower the density, the more difficult it becomes to achieve economies of scale.

Farming and Farmers

It has already been noted that the rural population is not homogeneous but the farming population is the most important single occupational group living in rural areas. The farming population itself is not homogeneous either and considerable differences occur, for example, in relation to farming systems, farming practices, farm size and farm income.

As with the rural population in general, the farming population has, until recently at least, been characterised by persistent decline. But the pattern of this decline has varied. The decline has been greatest on the smaller farms (under 50 acres). By comparison with other occupations, the farming population contains a very high proportion of elderly single farmers for whom the prospect of marriage is remote.[6]

Gardiner has pointed out that many of the problems, such as low farm income, in rural areas are influenced by the nature of the soils in any area and that this influence is strongest where an imbalance exists between soil resources and population density.[7] It has been estimated that marginal land occupies 45 percent of the total land area, with intermediate and good land occupying 11 percent and 43 percent respectively.[8] In general the counties with the highest proportions of their land area occupied by marginal land are in the western region.

The level and distribution of incomes in the farming community have implications for the provision of services, e.g. income maintenance services and eligibility for other services such as health care. Once again considerable differences exist between farmers in relation to income. This arises from a number of factors related to soil quality, size of farm and demographic features.

Prior to Ireland's entry into the EEC, farm incomes in general were lower than non-farm incomes. What has occurred since then is that not only have farm incomes increased (up to 1978) but the income gap between small and larger farmers has widened. The results of the Farm Management Survey of An Foras Taluntais clearly indicates the widening income gap between farmers in the 1970s. The results of the 1977 survey, for example, indicated that while the proportion of farmers on low incomes remained static as compared with 1976, the proportion with higher incomes increased. In commenting on this situation it was stated in the introduction to the report of the 1977 survey that;

For the most part this report is concerned with the value of production in Irish farming, its associated costs and residual income. Before our entry to the European Economic Community when the prices for farm products were low, the gap in all of these indicators of economic activity between the intensive and unintensive farms are not very great. To that extent it could be said that the reward for intensive production was unduly low. The most striking feature of the most recent Farm Management Surveys is the rapidity with which the entire situation changes when product prices rise. The results for 1977 indicate this quite clearly and showed an acceleration in the rate at which that gap widened. At one end, there is the developing, commercial sector of farming making very rapid progress in financial terms, while at the other end there is the clearest evidence of the existence of a static and low income sector, unaffected by all that is happening in the rest of the agricultural economy.[9]

The low-income sector is mainly concentrated in the western region and average family farm income per farm in Connacht and Ulster falls seriously short of that in Munster or Leinster. By 1979, a year in which farm income declined in all parts of the country, the average family farm income per farm in Ulster was less than a third of that in Munster (Table 2).

The report of the 1979 Farm Management Survey indicates that of 120,000 full-time farmers, almost a third (31 percent) generated an income of less than £2000 as compared with 24 percent in 1978; a further 39 percent had an income of between £2000 and £5000 (36 per cent in 1978) and 30 per cent had an income in excess of £5,000 (40 per cent in 1978).

The widespread decline in farm income experienced during 1979 highlights uncertainty associated with farming as a means of livelihood. Such a drop in income also occurred in 1974. Furthermore, it is usually the least efficient farmers and those engaged in unintensive production who are particularly affected during a slump in the farming sector.

Developments in the farming sector in recent years have been greatly influenced by Ireland's entry into the EEC. It is now

Table 2
Average annual family farm income*
per farm by province 1977-79 (£)

	1977	1978	1979
Connacht	1,716	1,993	1,808
Ulster	1,663	1,766	1,276
Leinster	3,572	4,007	3,401
Munster	4,790	4,806	4,033
Ireland	3,113	3,330	2,816

*Family farm income is gross output less total net expenses. It represents the total return to the family labour, management and capital investment in the farm business.

Source: J.F. Heavey et al, *Farm Management Surveys* 1977, 1978, 1979, An Foras Taluntais.

accepted that price supports alone cannot guarantee an equitable distribution of income in rural areas. In addition emphasis is now placed on policies aimed at structural reform and is embodied in a number of measures such as the Farm Modernisation Scheme and the Farm Retirement Scheme, introduced under the aegis of the Common Agricultural Policy of the EEC.

The underlying philosophy behind the Farm Modernisation Scheme is that aid to farmers for capital and herd expansion should be given in the context of a development plan for the farm rather than for specific projects. Maximum levels of aid are given to farmers (Development Farmers) who can develop their farms over a six-year period to provide an income comparable to average non-agricultural earnings in their region. Lower levels of aid are given to farmers (Commercial Farmers) who already earn at least the average non-agricultural wage and to farmers (Other Farmers) whose resources are not sufficient to allow them to reach a comparable income within the specified time period. The latter group, however, do not require a development plan to qualify for aid towards farm improvements.

During 1979, a total of 4337 applications for aid under the Farm Modernisation Scheme had been classified and the break-down by category was: Commercial (5.4 percent) Development (23.3 percent) and Other (71.3 percent). One of the principal criticisms of the scheme is that it excludes certain farmers from the optimum range of benefits if they are classified as Other. These farmers are excluded because of their limited resources despite the fact that they may have shown both a willingness and ability to maximise their existing resources.

As already indicated, a high proportion of farmers are elderly and single. With their demise a large number of farm holdings will become available for farm restructuring purposes. The Farm Retirement Scheme is designed to contribute to the release of land, thereby accelerating the process of farm consolidation. The Farm Modernisation Scheme provides that farmers whose development plans require additional land should have priority access to land thus released. Since its inception in 1974 the take-up of the scheme has been disappointingly low. Only 421 farmers have participated up to the end of 1979 and about 18,500 acres of land have been released, a figure which is low in relation to the land potentially available for restructuring purposes.

One of the factors which hinders the take-up of the scheme is that in mose cases receipt of an annuity combined with the sale price or rent when the land is leased under the terms of the scheme will lead to the loss of social welfare payments, such as non-contributory old age pension and some ancillary benefits, e.g. medical cards. Other factors which militate against a higher take-up are attachment to land and the status which ownership of land confers in rural areas. In any case, the Farm Retirement Scheme is only one means of facilitating land transfer.

In view of the low income generated by farming in certain parts of the country it is not surprising that some farmers take up non-farm jobs to supplement their income. The system of part-time farming is sometimes viewed by economists as contributing to inefficient use of land which would be more profitably utilised if released for farm restructuring purposes. This view tends to ignore the involuntary nature of part-time farming and that for many small farmers in particular there are valid personal and family incentives to take up a non-farm job. The net result is that the family's income is increased. Furthermore, given the uncertainty associated with farm income itself, the regularity of a non-farm income, particularly for farmers with families, is important.

The creation of off-farm employment opportunities alone, however, is not necessarily the panacea for under-employment and low incomes in rural areas. Much will depend on the type of job opportunities provided and the level of skill required. Inevitably, some sections of the farming population are unlikely to benefit by either agricultural or non-agricultural developments.

In general, existing farm policy measures are focused on that section of the farming population with the greatest potential to respond to the demands of modern agriculture. At the same time low income remains one of the most intractable problems of Irish agriculture and has been reported on extensively over the past few decades.[10] It is important to distinguish between different categories of low-income farmers, particularly in relation to their ability to make the necessary adjustments required to improve their income position.[11] It is now generally accepted that a section of the low-income group cannot be helped to any worthwhile extent by any meaningful policy for agricultural development. Their problems are primarily of a welfare nature though they are in possession of valuable land resources which could be released for farm restructuring. In this context it has been suggested that sufficient cognisance should be taken of the traditional manner by which farmers (even those without direct heirs) transfer land, i.e. land is typically transferred to relatives.[12] The present Farm Retirement Scheme runs counter to this tradition and the emphasis should be on encouraging earlier transfers of land or the use of land through leasing in accordance with the wishes of the landholder.

Other low-income farmers require development schemes more clearly geared towards their special development needs than is the case under the Farm Modernisation Scheme. Kelleher and O'Hara have pointed out than an effective farm development scheme for such farmers should incorporate a development plan, intensive advisory attention, availability of credit and training programmes for farm operators, along with financial rewards based on the achievement of both short and long-term growth targets.[13]

Provision of Services

Here we examine a number of services in order to illustrate the disadvantages experienced by members of rural communities in regard to availability of and access to social services. These services are readily available in most large urban centres.

Transport

To the extent that the public transport system in Ireland is heavily subsidised by the State, it is possible to regard it as a social service. It is also a good example of the problem involved in providing a service in rural areas with low densities of population. Here the major factor is one of cost.

While car ownership in Ireland has increased in recent years, it is inevitable that a sizeable proportion of the population will continue to be dependent on public transport. Elderly persons and those on low incomes, for example, are likely to fall into this category. It is somewhat ironic that in some rural areas there are elderly persons entitled to free travel on public transport but who are unable to avail themselves of the facility. This can arise either because the public transport system does not serve this area or because they live far from the main thoroughfares where the service is provided.

From an economic viewpoint it would be futile to recommend an increase in the provision of bus services in many rural areas, particularly since losses are already being sustained in areas where the service is provided. However, special school buses are provided in rural areas for pupils of primary and post-primary schools. This type of transport, also financed by the State, is used almost exclusively for conveying pupils to and from school. It should be possible to initiate, even on a pilot basis, a scheme whereby these buses could convey elderly persons for shopping or social purposes, especially at weekends.

Health Services

Considerable developments have occurred in the provision of health services during the past decade or so. One such development was the introduction in 1972 of the choice-of-doctor scheme for medical card holders and their dependants. This scheme replaced the dispensary system which originated in 1851 under the Poor Law and which had a stigmatising effect on patients who were segregated from the fee-paying patients at the point of service. In many rural areas, however, there is effectively no choice of doctor. Furthermore, in 1979, approximately two in five persons covered by medical cards in the Western and North-Western Health Board areas lived five miles or more from their doctor as compared with one in twenty in the Eastern Health Board area (Table 3). Distance from doctors is likely to be accentuated by the absence of transport or telephones among this low-income section of the population.

Inadequacies in the dental services have been highlighted on several occasions. The Health Board dental service is available free of charge to medical card holders and their dependants and to children attending national schools. A further service is provided for the majority of social welfare contributors. In a recent report of a joint working party it was acknowledged, in relation to the Health Board service, that;

> . . . availability of treatment is not uniform throughout the country; there are marked differences in the level of service delivered and a comprehensive service is not provided in all cases. Areas which find it relatively easy to recruit dentists, such as Dublin, are better able to meet the needs and provide a more comprehensive range of services. A much less satisfactory situation applies in the areas which traditionally experience difficulty in recruiting and retaining sufficient numbers of staff.[14]

In the child health services a disparity also exists between areas in the provision of developmental clinics. These clinics are confined in the main to towns with populations of 5,000 or over. While some parts of the country are relatively well provided for, others are not, e.g. there are no child developmental clinics in counties Roscommon or Leitrim.

Despite the fact that a greater rationalisation in the distribution of hospitals providing acute care has been recommended,[15] the present situation is that two distinct types of hospitals are emerging, i.e. a limited number of large specialist hospitals in Dublin, Cork, and Galway, and a large number of small general hospitals. Inevitably, certain sections of the rural population will live at a considerable distance from hospitals, whether a hospitals development plan is implemented or not. The aim should be to minimise this disadvantage as much as possible, e.g. by the provision of an efficient ambulance service.

Table 3

Percentage of medical card population living five miles or more from their doctor, December 1979.

Health board	
Eastern	4.5
Midland	28.4
Mid-Western	25.1
North-Eastern	28.2
North-Western	38.3
South-Eastern	25.5
Southern	31.1
Western	40.9
Ireland	25.6

Source: Report of the General Medical Services (Payments) Board for the year ended 31 December, 1979, p. 15.

It is important that the development of an adequate and efficient community care service in rural areas, especially those located at a considerable distance from hospitals, be emphasised. In such areas the demographic structure gives rise to specific problems in relation to health care delivery. The health needs of populations in remote rural areas may be magnified by the incidence of households with aged and incapacitated persons, and the absence of family help in cases of illness is accentuated by geographic isolation. It is not possible to provide all rural areas with the same level of health care services as larger urban centres. The objective should be to minimise the disadvantages associated with remoteness from urban centres to the greatest extent possible. In this context it has been recommended that more public health nurses, social workers and home helps are needed to compensate for deficiencies in the provision of primary medical care and that the provision of adequate back-up services such as an efficient ambulance service, a better telephone service, would offset considerably the problems of the more remote rural areas.[16]

Education

Problems of access also arise in relation to education, although considerable progress has been made in reducing the disadvantages associated with distance from schools. The introduction of free transport as part of the free post-primary education scheme has led to increased participation in second-level education among pupils in rural areas. By 1977 almost one-third of all pupils attending second level schools were being conveyed to these schools under the free transport scheme. Similarly, the introduction of complete State-financed (comprehensive) schools in some rural areas in the 1960s helped to reduce the existing locational imbalance of post-primary schools.

The policy of closing small rural primary schools, which was given an added impetus by the recommendations in the Investment in Education Report of 1965, was reversed in 1977. Between 1967 and 1977 the number of one and two-teacher schools was reduced from 2,920 to 1,262. As a proportion of the total number of primary schools these small schools declined from almost two-thirds in 1967 to less than two-fifths in 1977.

Under the terms of the higher education grant scheme introduced in 1968/69 a differentiation is made between students living within commuting distance of a university and others, and a maintenance grant is payable only in the latter case. Grants are payable subject to a parental means test and, in the case of farmers, land valuation limits are used. The grant system, however, takes no cognisance of parents over the income limit who have to pay for accommodation for their children in university centres. By contrast, parents over the income limit but living within commuting distance of universities do not have to bear this additional cost.

Income Maintenance

With one exception, Smallholders' Assistance, there are no

105

special income maintenance measures catering for the farming population. One of the main gaps in the Irish income maintenance system by comparison with other EEC countries is that the self-employed, including farmers, are not eligible for contributory or insurance-based benefits. Instead they must rely on means-tested payments as the need arises. In 1978 the Department of Social Welfare published a discussion document on social insurance for the self-employed, which outlined the issues/problems involved in introducing a scheme or schemes.[17] The case for including the self-employed in a social insurance scheme is overwhelming. The self-employed, like other members of the community, are vulnerable to invalidity, widowhood and old age. Apart from equity considerations, the extension of social insurance to self-employed persons would lead to the phasing out of means-tested income-maintenance payments.

The one special income-maintenance measure for farmers is the Smallholders' Assistance Scheme introduced in 1966 for farmers in the western region. Since its inception the scheme has come in for much popular criticism. One of the reasons for this is that eligibility for payment was determined not by reference to the farmers actual income but by a notional assessment based on land valuation. Between 1966 and 1976 the basis of assessment remained at £20 per £1 land valuation, despite an increase in farm incomes over the same period. As rates of payments increased each year more farmers became eligible. As a result of changes introduced in the scheme in 1976, 1977 and 1979, the number of claimants was reduced from about 32,000 to 21,500. Farmers on low valuations (up to £10) have continued to benefit under this scheme while others have either lost eligibility or have had their payments reduced.[18]

Housing

Considerable disparities exist in the provision of housing amenities such as piped water supply and sanitary facilities between urban and rural areas. As in the case of public transport, the problem here is also one of cost. It is much more costly to provide these services in rural areas where population density is low than on a scheme basis in urban areas. By 1971 about 154,000 dwellings or two-fifths of all dwellings in rural areas lacked piped water supply and sanitary facilities, as compared with less than 1 per cent of dwellings in urban areas. In the absence of a comprehensive Census since that date it is not possible to estimate the precise progress made in the intervening years. Between 1972 and 1979, however, about 110,000 piped-water installations have been made with grant assistance.[19] On the basis of these figures the situation has improved considerably.

Eligibility for Social Services

At present different agencies use different methods of assessing farm income for purposes of establishing eligibility for certain social services. In relation to Smallholders' Assistance, for example, a notional income per £1 valuation is applied but three notional figures are used, i.e. £30 per £1 valuation for farmers with less than £10 valuation, £50 per £1 valuation for those between £10 and £15 valuation, and £60 per £1 valuation for those between £15 and £20 valuation. In all of the above cases there is the option of factual assessment. For farmers with valuations in excess of £20 a factual assessment is used. Eligibility for all other income-maintenance payments is determined by reference to a factual assessment.

For health services the population is divided into three categories and eligibility for free health services varies according to category. In Category I are medical card holders and their dependants. Qualification for cards is based on a means test. Category II includes those outside Category I but under a specified income limit and Category III contains persons over the specified income limit. Eligibility for medical cards is determined by a factual assessment of farm incomes in six of the Health Board areas and by a notional assessment in the other two.[20] Outside of the medical car category, farmers' eligibility is determined by reference to land valuation limits. Thus farmers with land valuations of less than £60 are in Category II and those with valuations in excess of this figure are in Category III.

Farmers in Categories II and III are liable for a health contribution based on 1 per cent of income which is determined on a notional basis. The notional figure in use in 1979/80 was £117 per £1 land valuation, a figure derived by equating the farmers valuation limit of £60 to the non-farmers' income limit of £7,000 (£7,000 ÷ 60 = 117).[21]

In the case of loans for housing provided by local authorities, a valuation limit (£44) is used. Similarly eligibility for higher education grants are determined by land valuation.

The net result of the system of eligibility described in a necessarily simplified manner above [22] is considerable confusion among claimants and the existence of anomalies. In the case of higher education grants and Categories II and III for health services, assessment is made on the basis of valuation and farmers are not allowed to submit accounts as evidence of income even though this would, in many instances, alter the situation significantly. Furthermore, in the case of health contributions farm income is being assessed by a notional assessment related to non-farm incomes. In a situation where farm incomes decline, as in 1979 and 1980, it seems inequitable that they should have to pay higher contributions simply because non-farm incomes are rising. The use of one standard and equitable method of assessing farm income would considerably reduce much of the confusion and eliminate many of the anomalies which now exist both within and between the agencies concerned with providing social services.

Conclusion

This chapter has examined some of the inequalities which exist both between urban and rural areas and within rural areas. Some of the inequalities such as low income arise from a combination of socio-demographic factors, size of farms and soil quality. Other inequalities arise because of the difficulties involved in providing services to rural areas with a low density of population.

One of the key problems which distinguishes remote rural areas from urban areas, and one of the principal problems to be tackled by policy makers, is access to services. This type of inequality has not been so well publicised as that of low income. Yet access to services is part of the overall problem of rural areas.

It would be facile to suggest that there are easy answers to the problems touched on here. Nor is it likely that some of the disadvantages of living in rural areas can ever be fully eliminated. The objective should be to minimise these to the greatest extent possible. In this context, a necessary precondition for action is the creation of a greater awareness among politicians, policy-makers and the general public of the special problems and needs of rural areas.

REFERENCES

1. Much of the contents of this chapter represents a summary of what the author has written elsewhere, especially in 'Rural Areas: Social Policy Problems', NESC Report No. 19 (Dublin, 1976), and in P. Cummins, P. Cox, and J. Curry, 'Rural Areas; Change and Development NESC Report No. 41 (Dublin, 1978).

2. Jones, J.F., 'Hard Times and the Search for a Frugal Utopia' in *Social Development in Times of Economic Uncertainty*, Proceedings of xxth International Conference on Social Welfare, Hong Kong 1980, Columbia University Press, New York, 1981, p. 36.

3. D. Donnison, 'An Approach to Social Policy', NESC Report No. 8. (Dublin, 1975), pp 39-41.

4. The last comprehensive Census was undertaken in 1971. A more limited Census was carried out in 1979. Some of the data in the following paragraphs refer to 1971, while 1979 data is also used where appropriate.

5. See NESC Report No. 19, pp 10-16.

6. For a more detailed analysis of the demographic features of the farming population see Ibid, pp 16-19.

7. M.J. Gardiner, 'Soils' in D. A. Gillmor (ed.), *Irish Resources and Land Use* (Dublin, 1979), p. 105.

8. Ibid. p. 104.

9. J.F. Heavey et al, *Farm Management Survey 1977*. (Dublin, 1978), p. 1.1

10. Among the reports published are, *Report of Inter-Departmental Committee on the Problems of Small Western Farmers* (Dublin, 1962); J. J. Scully, *Agriculture in the West of Ireland — a Study of the low farm income problem* (Dublin, 1971); *Interim Report of Inter-Departmental Committee on Land Structure Reform* (Dublin, 1977); C. Kelleher and P. O'Hara, *Adjustment Problems of Low Income Farmers* (Dublin, 1978).

11.ʼ See Kelleher and O'Hara, op. cit.

12. NESC Report No. 41, pp 79-81.

13. Kelleher and O'Hara, op. cit. p. 75.

14. Joint Working Party, Department of Health, Irish Dental Association, Health Boards, *Dental Services Report*, (Dublin, 1979), pp 6-7.

15. See *Outline of the Future Hospital System*, Report of the Consultative Council on the General Hospital Services (Dublin, 1968).

16. NESC Report No. 41, p. 127.

17. Department of Social Welfare, *Social Insurance for the Self-Employed A Discussion Paper* (Dublin, 1978).

18. For further discussion on the Smallholders' Assistance Scheme see NESC Report No. 19, pp 57-62, and NESC Report No. 41, pp 83-90.

19. Department of the Environment 'Housing Statistics, December 1979' (Dublin, 1980), p. 6.

20. See *Relate*, Vol. 7 No. 11 (Dublin, 1980).

21. For 1980/81 the non-farm income limit is £8,500 and it was decided to leave the notional figure of £117 per £1 land valuation unaltered thus giving a land valuation limit of £72.65 (£8,500 − 117 = 72.65).

22. For a more detailed analysis of variation in assessment of farm income see J. Curry, 'Variation in the Assessment of Farm Income in Social Administration', *Irish Journal of Agricultural Economics and Rural Sociology*, Vol 7, (Dublin, 1978).

Poverty and Old People

Robbie Gilligan

This chapter examines the extent to which the elderly in the Republic of Ireland are affected by poverty. The evidence used suggests that a substantial majority of the elderly can be judged to be seriously disadvantaged relative to the general population. Possible reasons for the inferior position of the elderly are explored and it is argued that their circumstances have a complex causation which is in part accounted for by the social and economic structure of our modern society.

The profile of the elderly is drawn from statistical and other information relating not only to income but also to possession of consumer durables, housing, health, nutrition, education and mobility. The scope of the profile is considerably hampered by the limitations of Irish social data, but nevertheless it gives a valuable insight into the living standards of most elderly people relative to the general population. The thrust of the profile begs a number of questions which are addressed in the final part of the chapter. The conclusion is a preliminary analysis of some of the factors that may explain the adverse circumstances of these elderly. It is argued that biological or physical decline or individual misfortune are inadequate as explanations for the general trends that have been observed.

It is assumed throughout that the elderly are those aged 65 and over unless otherwise noted. In 1979 there were 361,375 persons aged 65 and over in the State.[1] Contrary to international trends, the proportion of elderly in the population has actually declined in recent years, from 11 percent in 1971 to 10.7 percent in 1979.[2] This proportion compares with 13.7 percent for the EEC as a whole, 15.2 percent in Austria, 15.7 percent in Sweden and 14.4 percent in the UK.[3] In Ireland the elderly are more heavily represented in the rural than in the urban population: the proportions are 13.2 percent of the rural population and 9.1 percent of the urban population.[4] Interestingly, this trend is most marked in some of the poorest counties, as Table 1 based on 1979 data shows.

Table 1

Counties with Highest % Population 65 & over	% Population 65 and over	Ranking of County in National Income per Capita League
Leitrim	17.3	26
Mayo	15.86	24
Roscommon	15.64	21
Sligo	14.31	19
Donegal	10.04	25

Sources: Census of Population 1979;
M. Ross, 'Personal Incomes by County 1975', NESC Report No. 30 (1977)

It is not easy to find substantial discussion of the association between poverty and old age in Irish social policy literature.One important exception is the work of Seamus O'Cinneide on the extent of poverty in Ireland. Writing about low income in 1972 he estimated that 60 percent of the elderly population lived in poverty. However, in the same article O'Cinneide admitted that 'the very idea of a poverty line defined only in terms of current income is outmoded: the limitation and anomalies in the idea have been clearly demonstrated by many writers'.[6]

One of the writers to whom O'Cinneide refers is Townsend.[7] In his most recent and greatest work, Townsend has discussed his approach to a theory of poverty.

Poverty is the lack of resources necessary to permit partic-ipation in the activities, customs and diet commonly app-roved by society. Different kinds of resources have to be examined. The scope, mechanisms and principles of each system controlling the distribution and redistribution of resources have to be studied.[8]

Townsend has identified five sets of resources which he believes are essential to any analysis of poverty and its impact. These are (1) cash income, (2) capital assets, (3) value of employment benefits, (4) value of public social services and (5) private income in kind.[9]

An application of Townsend's model would require a scale and sophistication which is beyond the scope of this chapter. However, the approach to the question of poverty and the elderly here is heavily influenced by Townsend's views. In a modern industrialising society such as Ireland the experience of poverty is as likely to be defined by gross inequality as by the lack of the basic essentials of living such as food or shelter.

The predicament of the deprived elderly cannot be explained by personal misfortune. Their progressive isolation and submergence is derived in part from the dynamic of our urbanising and industrialising society. De Beauvoir has observed, 'Modern technocratic society thinks that knowledge does not accumulate with years but grows out of date. Age brings disqualification with it; age is not an advantage. It is the values associated with youth that are esteemed.'[10] But the increasingly marginalised position of these elderly in relation to the rest of society is also derived, of course, from a further range of factors which have economic, social, political, psychological, demographic and cultural dimensions.

Yet it would be misleading to infer or assume that the elderly are a homogeneous group who share to varying degrees a common deprivation. Titmuss has spoken of there being two nations of elderly.[11] Certainly this seems true in Ireland. There is a minority here, perhaps one-third whose social circumstances are to a greater or lesser extent quite favourable. These people are likely to have belonged to the privileged socio-economic groups throughout their lives. Old age does not rob them of their prestige, status and economic security; it may even enhance it. Of the property-owning elderly, de Beauvoir has said:

> Among the privileged classes, the state of the aged is bound up with the regime of porperty. When property is no longer based upon strength but is institutionalised and firmly guaranteed by law, the character of the owner becomes non-essential and irrelevant — he is identified with his property and it is respected in his person. It is not his individual abilities that matter, but rights; and so age, weakness or even decrepitude are of little consequence. Since wealth usually increases with the years it is therefore no longer the young who start at the top but the older men.[12]

Townsend has observed a similarly favoured status among more prosperous white collar employees, where increasing age will not signal a decline in living standards, 'but a consolidation or maintenance of status and earnings among the best paid, especially non-manual workers'.[13]

The privileged elderly then are those who possess property or other capital assets and have an inflation-proofed income. They will generally include those who have been successful in their career in the professions or in other socially and economically advantaged occupations. They will typically share their household with their spouse and with other family members. They will tend to remain active; their privileged status permits them more easily to retain a meaningful role in everyday life. It goes without saying of course that property and wealth cannot guarantee protection from the problems of loneliness and failing health, but these assets can go a long way towards mitigating their worst effects.

The focus of what follows is very much on the disadvantaged elderly, those for whom each day unfolds further unremitting hardship and the grim routine of poverty. In order to gain a reasonable insight to their deprivation, it is necessary to rely on various indicators direct and indirect, of the circumstances of these elderly.

Income

The traditional measure of poverty has been based on levels of income. It seems appropriate therefore that income should be the first indicator used in this discussion. Marshall has noted important differences in likely income sources between the elderly and the non-elderly and the consequence of these differences in terms of the risk of poverty in old age:

> while the old may still rely to some extent upon market earnings, they are more likely to be dependent upon financial aid from relatives or private charities, upon the produce of accumulated savings, including private pensions schemes, and upon the state retirement pension. Access to income from the alternative sources will determine whether or not an individual of retirement age will fall into poverty.[14]

Irish income data is limited. However, the Household Budget Survey is a valuable source of information about income levels.

The Survey examines domestic expenditure patterns among different categories of households. In 1973 the first national Survey was undertaken based on a sample of all households in the State. Each year since 1973 a sample of all households in urban centres with population of more than 1000 persons has also been undertaken.

For our purposes the HBS can offer information about (1) the proportions of households on low income which are headed by elderly persons, (2) the average weekly income of elderly households compared with the average for all households and (3) the extent of reliance on social welfare and State benefits by elderly compared to all households.

One quarter of all low-income households in the State are headed by an elderly person, yet the elderly make up only 10.7 percent of the population.[15] Households headed by the elderly are 2.7 times more likely to be poor than the average household; the households of the elderly who live alone are three times more likely to be poor.[16]

Estimates based on the HBS (1973) indicate that the average weekly income of an elderly household amounted to 63.65 percent of the average weekly income of all households in the State.[17] This proportion declined for the elderly living alone to 29.14 percent and for the elderly person with one dependent to 48.23 percent.[18] However, those elderly who headed larger households did very much better: these households had an average weekly income that amounted to 98.76 percent of the national average.[19] These figures suggest a marked gap between different categories of elderly households; the 62 percent of elderly in one or two-person households are much more likely to be deprived in terms of income, relative to other households headed by the elderly or to the average national household.[20] These elderly belong to the poorer of Titmuss 'two nations of elderly'.

Poor elderly households rely heavily on the combined value of State transfer payments and benefits in kind to make up their net weekly income. These State benefits make up 68 percent of the net income of those who live alone and 60 percent of the income of households headed by an elderly person with a dependent.[21] These figures compare with 28.7 percent as the proportion made up by State benefits of all kinds in the average household income.[22]

Elderly urban households rely, on average, for 37.4 percent of their income on State transfer payments.[23] This proportion is almost four times greater than the extent to which all urban households rely on State transfer payments.

Social Welfare Pensions

The elderly rely heavily on social welfare payments, partly because of their steady withdrawal from the labour force over the years as illustrated in Table 2.

Table 2

% Males aged 65 & over	1961	1966	1971	1975
gainfully occupied	51.5	48.4	43.9	28.9

Sources: Census of Population 1971; Labour Force Survey 1975

It is only in the agricultural sector that the elderly remain a significant proportion of the work force. But even this group is likely to exist on low incomes: old age in farming is heavily associated with small holdings and therefore generally low incomes (see chapter on rural poverty by John Curry).

The particular dependence of the elderly on social welfare payments makes the statistics about the Department of Social Welfare's payments an important source of information about the income levels of the elderly.

Fitzgerald reckoned that in 1976 85 percent of those over pensionable age (then 67) were receiving weekly payments from the Department of Social Welfare.[24] The proportion is unlikely to have declined markedly in the meantime, as the pension age has since been lowered to 66.

In 1980 36.2 percent of those of pensionable age, 130,860 persons, relied on means-tested, non-contributory Old Age Pensions.[25] Approximately 84.5 percent of these received the maximum rate;[26] for a single person this was £21 or 27.7 percent of net average industrial earnings.[27] In addition, 18 percent of those aged 66 and over, 65,111 persons were in receipt of Contributory Old Age Pension in 1980.[28] This was worth £24.50 to the pensioner under 80.

Fitzgerald reckons that, since a high proportion of contributory pensioners' wives qualify for non-contributory pensions, 'most contributory pensioner households have no substantial income source other than their social welfare pension'.[29] A further 31,734 persons were in receipt of retirement pension; these made up approximately 8 percent of those of pensionable age.[30] Widows' pensions are obviously an important source of income for many elderly women. In 1980 there were almost 70,000 recipients of the contributory widows' pension and 11,242 recipients of the non-contributory pension.[31] Assuming half of those are elderly this means that approximately 40,000 elderly women, or close to 11 percent of the elderly population, rely on these payments. All categories of recipients listed have a total of approximately 10,000 elderly dependents.[32]

Persons with means insufficient to provide the neccessities of subsistance can seek Supplementary Welfare Allowance. This may be payable as sole income or as a supplement to income from another source. In February 1976 the elderly (67 and over) made up 41.1 percent of the recipients of Home Assistance (Supplementary Welfare's previous title).[33] At the same time the elderly made up 52 percent of those receiving Home Assistance as a supplement to their income, perhaps in respect of fuel or rent costs.[34] These figures indicate a heavy over-representation of the elderly in the population of Supplementary Welfare recipients. It suggests that they make up a disproportionate number of those on the very lowest incomes in the State.

Medical Card Eligibility

An indicator of the average income of the elderly can also be found in the numbers eligible for medical cards. Medical cards provide entitlement to free use of health services: eligibility is determined by a means test. Thus the take-up rate can indicate income levels for different sections within the community. In December 1979 36.4 percent of the general population had coverage of this scheme.[35] In Spring 1979 it was estimated that the elderly who make up 10.7 percent of the general population accounted for 23.6 percent of the population covered by medical cards.[36] In July 1978 there were 256,000 elderly persons who were medical card holders (these cards covered in addition 35,000 elderly dependents).[37] Thus approximately 80 percent of the elderly population was deemed officially to have incomes at that time below £26 per week for a single person and £37.50 for a married couple (or the equivalent, by reference to rateable valuation, for farmers). The

117

means test limits for eligibility for medical cards are adjusted regularly in line with the cost of living. It is unlikely that the proportion of elderly beneficiaries will have changed in the interim.

The data on income of medical card holders tend to support, independently, the profile of income of the elderly derived from social welfare data. The latter indicates that approximately 80 percent or so of the elderly population is in receipt of weekly social welfare payments. Perhaps one in five of this group may have an additional source of income (these would be of course, contributory pensioners). From social welfare data, therefore, over 60 percent of the total elderly population can be judged to be on low incomes relative to the general population. The medical card figures certainly appear to corroborate this view. While of necessity, these are relatively crude estimates, they support O'Cinneide's figures and suggest that the position of the elderly may now be even worse.

Expenditure

The elderly households spend an unusually high proportion of their incomes on food, fuel and light. This reflects the relatively small size of their average income and the large part of it taken up by essentials. As incomes rise, these items invariably recede in relative importance in the distribution of expenditure. People on low income are largely deprived of discretionary non-essential spending that is the prerogative of those more fortunate. Table 3 illustrates the relative share of household expenditure taken up by these items in certain categories of elderly households and in all State households.

Table 3

% Weekly Household Expenditure on Selected Items

	Food		Fuel and Light	
	1973	1978	1973	1978
All State households	32.1	28.6	4.8	5.6
Retired households (urban)	–	31.1	–	8.2
Old age pensioner (national) living alone	44.8		13.4	

Source: Household Budget Survey 1973 and 1978 (CSO, Dublin).

In each instance the elderly spend a higher proportion on food, fuel and light than does the average household. This trend is even more marked in the lower income households of pensioners who live alone: in 1973 they devoted a 179 percent greater proportion of their spending to fuel and light than did the average household.

Possession of Consumer Durables

Another possible measure of the relative living standards of the elderly is their possession of modern household appliances. The figures in Table 4 show that elderly households are considerably less well equipped in this regard than the average household.

TABLE 4

	Persons 65 & over Living Alone		Married couple where HOH* 65 & over		All State Households
% Households in possession of	OAP	ALL	HOH with OAP*	All cases	
Washing machine	4.0	5.9	13.0	22.9	44.5
Refrigerator	15.4	19.2	32.4	42.7	53.9

Source: D. Murphy, *Journal of the Social & Statistical Inquiry Society of Ireland*, Vol. 23 (1975-76).
*HOH = Head of Household
*OAP = Old Age Pensioner

The relatively more favourable position of the couples in comparison to those who live alone is of interest, as is the inferior position of those dependent on the Old Age Pension.

Table 5

% Households in Possession of	Retired Urban	All Urban
Vacuum cleaner	53.2	68.40
Spin dryer	5.7	10.82
Washing machine	35.3	64.82
Refrigerator	67.0	85.52
Separate deep freeze	2.4	7.22
Television set	89.4	95.4
Record player	29.5	56.28
Tape cassette recorder	14.81	32.14

Source: Household Budget Survey, Urban Enquiry 1978, special tabulation.

In tables 4 and 5 the relatively low rates of possession of washing machines and fridges are particularly significant since these could reasonably be deemed essential for those elderly who are striving to maintain an independent existence in the community and are, in any event, clearly part of the standard amenities of the average household.

Housing

It is difficult to assemble fully satisfactory data on the housing conditions of the elderly. Nevertheless it is possible to point up certain important trends.

There are a number of differences between the housing circumstances of the elderly when compared with those of the general population. The elderly are more likely to be owner occupiers. They are also likely to live in considerably older housing units which tend also to be somewhat smaller and less well equipped with basic amenities than the housing of the general population.

In 1971 44.7 percent of all housing units in the State were built prior to 1919[38] The only equivalent figures available for the elderly relate to those who live alone, 53 percent of whose housing is built prior to 1919. There were 4.69 rooms per housing unit nationally in 1971.[40] More recent information on urban housing indicates that the average number of rooms per household in urban areas is 5.2 and for elderly urban house-holders, 4.9.[41] A comparison of facilities between elderly and all households again underlines the deprivation of the elderly relative to the general population. Table 6 illustrates this point in respect of urban households.

Table 6

% Households in Possession of	Retired Urban	All Urban
Piped water — hot	81.6	91.2
Bath or shower	73.8	86.15
Toilet (internal)	86.3	91.3
Central heating (all forms)	10.3	29.6
Garage	15.1	21.1

Source: HBS, 1978 Special tabulation.

Table 7 shows again the disadvantage of a more specific category of elderly, those who live alone, in comparison with the general population.

Table 7

% Households in Possession of	Old & Alone Housing	All Housing Units
Electricity	90	96.6*
Piped water	70	78.2**
Use of bath or shower	43	55.4**

Sources: *Household Budget Survey 1973
**Census of Population 1971; B. Power, *Old and Alone in Ireland* (Dublin, 1980)

Table 8 indicates the differences in household tenure between the elderly and the general population. The figures suggest that the elderly fare better in that they are somewhat more likely to be owner-occupiers. However, this can be a liability for the less active and prosperous elderly person. They may lack the skill, financial resources, or the physical capacity to undertake the necessary repairs or home improvements.

Table 8

Household Tenure	Aged 65 & Over Living Alone	Married Couples HOH aged 65 & over	All Households
% Owned outright	52	59.2	47.7
% Owned with Mortgage	8	14.7	23.4
Total	60	73.9	70.7

Source: D. Murphy, '1973 Household Budget Survey: Special Features Results', J.S.S.I.S.I. (1976).

In any discussion of housing of the elderly the achievement by the Department of the Environment and local authorities in observing the Care of the Aged Committee's (1968)[42] recommendation deserve acknowledgement. The Committee's recommended that local authorities would aim to reserve a minimum of 10 percent of their new dwellings for the elderly. Table 9 shows how far this has been done in recent years.

Table 9

Dwellings Provided for Elderly Persons with State Assistance

Year	By Local Authority (including demountable dwellings)	By Voluntary Bodies	Total	Total as % of all Local Authority Dwellings Completed
1975	875	54	930	10.5
1976	763	33	796	10.9
1977	893	51	944	14.9
1978	925	11	936	15.4
1979	681	17	698	11.2

Source: Department of the Environment, personal communication, 1980

Educational Attainment

The elderly tend to have completed their formal education earlier than the general population. The increasing minimum school-leaving age, the increasing social and economic benefit accruing to educational attainment, and 'free' post-primary education are social developments that obviously did not affect their generation. From the 1971 Census of Population it is possible to compute that 75 percent of the elderly completed their full-time education before the age of 15, compared with 55.1 percent of the general population. While no figures are available, it is reasonable to presume from the foregoing that levels of illiteracy would be considerably higher among the elderly than the general population. In the earlier decades of this century, in many urban primary schools pupil-teacher ratios were dramatically less favourable than they are now, even though the present situation still attracts criticism.

Health

The health status of the elderly compares unfavourably with that of the general population. Evidence to support this thesis is drawn from available statistics about morbidity; take-up of health services whether in community, hospital or institutional settings; nutrition and hypothermia.

Morbidity

It is necessary to rely on information relating to the general labour force in order to estimate the general levels of sickness among different age groups, including the elderly. Geary and Dempsey (1979)[43] have done valuable work in this area. Despite deficiencies in the available data, the evidence they have compiled points clearly to a striking preponderance of illness among elderly workers. The figures they use refer to the mid 1960s workforce which at the time contained a considerable number of elderly. (While this data is not entirely satisfactory it is the best available to the author.)

Table 10

Average Duration of Short-Term Disability in Selected Age Groups and Percentage of Time Lost

Average Duration (weeks)

Age Group	16-20	31-35	46-50	51-55	56-60	61-65	66-70	all ages
Men	0.29	1.03	2.16	2.89	4.15	4.93	5.98	1.96
Women	0.56	1.55	2.85	3.20	3.44	3.52	5.36	1.59

Percentage Time Lost

Men	0.6	2.1	4.3	5.8	8.3	9.9	12.0	3.9
Women	1.1	3.1	5.7	6.4	6.9	7.0	10.7	3.2

Source: Geary and Dempsey, 'The Preparation of Statistics of Sickness or Disability in Ireland', *Administration* Vol. 27, No. 2 (Summer 1979).

Table 10 illustrates the fact that the elderly workers are particularly prone to illness. The risk of illness increases gradually with age in adulthood. The risk increases more markedly first among the 51 to 55 age group and then again in the 66 to 70 age group. The males in this latter age group are likely to have a duration of illness almost six times greater than the 31 to 35 age group and three times the average for all ages. It is not surprising therefore to find that the elderly are disproportionately heavy consumers of health care.

Unreported Illness

A further important consideration in relation to the health status of the elderly is the fact that there is substantial international evidence that there is much unreported illness among the elderly.[44] This is commonly illness which can be relatively easily remedied or prevented. As a UK writer has said:

. . . minor, untreated complaints can produce a very sick old person. This would be a typical sequence: an old lady has bad corns and goes to bed. She stays in bed, helped by neighbours, and as a result gets constipated. She has some wax in her ears and doesn't hear too well. In no time at all she is confused, disoriented and quite ill.[45]

Walsh (1980) pleaded for a greater recognition, among all concerned with the elderly, 'of the treatability of much that is labelled old age'.[46] In his study Walsh found among a Dublin population that 'The less symptomatic illness like hypertension, congestive heart failure, sight and mental impairment, deafness, dental disease and food ailments were all grossly under-diagnosed and largely untreated.'[47] Interestingly, Walsh notes a much higher incidence of previously unrecognised sight impairment (32 per cent) than has been found in similar studies in the UK[48]

Nutrition

An important determinant of standards of health is the quality of nutritional intake in any population. In the introduction to an important study of nutrition and the elderly in Ireland published by the National Prices Commission in 1977, the authors summarise the evidence from other studies in Ireland and elsewhere, some of which is detailed here:

*   Sub-clinical malnutrition is probably frequent in the aged and often characterised in particular by Vitamin C deficiency.
*   Overall dietary intake decreases with decreasing income.
*   Those who are housebound or unable to prepare meals are most at risk.
*   The most typical case is likely to be one of the multiple deficiencies.[49]

The investigators expressed serious concern about the quality of diet consumed by the study group of low-income elderly in Dublin. They found that 73 per cent of the elderly studied were living on a nutritionally inadequate diet.[50] The authors admit certain limitations in the study but are confident of its predictive value in estimating the general nutritional status of elderly in similar socio-economic circumstances. Table 11 illustrates some of their more detailed findings.

Table 11

Inadequate intake of	% of Elderly in Study Affected
Energy	31.6
Protein	11.9
Iron	47.8
Vitamin C	56.7
Iron & Vitamin C	31.3
Calcium	17.9
Energy and all nutrients	6

Source: National Prices Commission, 'Some Economic Aspects of the Dietary Intake of Old People' Monthly Report No. 58 (1977) pp. 46-67.

Of the final group in the Table the authors say that while their proportion was relatively small it was of considerable public health significance since the risk of these subjects developing some form of overt malnutrition is high. They note that 'in the largest study ever done of dietary intake of the aged (Palmore, USA, 1971), lack of housing facilities such as running water, cooking, refrigeration and storage facilities were the major determinants of dietary intake'.[51] In this context it is worth recalling Power's (1980) figures that 30 per cent of the old and alone lack all five basic water amenities.[54] In the same survey, 12 per cent expressed varying degrees of dissatisfaction with their food storage arrangements. A similar porportion felt at least somewhat unhappy with their cooking arrangements; typically these were 'single males of farming stock in more remote rural parts'. Another National Prices Commission study of 1978 observed that

> The majority of pensioners seem to exist on a fairly monotonous series of meals . . . there were even instances of pensioners having two meals a day consisting solely of bread butter and tea . . . inevitably this lack of variety is in part due to the fact that limited income restricts the choice of foodstuffs available to the pensioner.[53]

General Practice

General practice remains the focal point for admission to the health care system for individual patients. Gowen, in a study of general practice prior to the introduction of the general medical service under the Health Act 1970, found that the elderly made unusual demands on domiciliary consultations; they accounted 29.91 per cent of all private and 34 per cent of all dispensary (i.e. public) domiciliary consultations.[54]

Gibson, in a later study of a practice in the Skiberreen area of West Cork, found that the elderly made heavy use of the practice's services. The 60 and over age group made up 12 per cent of the local population yet accounted for 55 per cent of all domiciliary and 35 per cent of all surgery consultations.[55]

Hospital and Institutional Care

The elderly make a disproportionate demand on in-patient hospital and institutional care. The elderly account for 36.9 per cent of all bed days in hospital.[56] This is in part due to their considerably longer average duration of stay, as illustrated in Table 12

Table 12

	Total Patients	Average Duration of Stay	% Bed Days
65-74	41,412	16	19.8
75 & over	28,005	20.8	17.1
All ages	324,448	10.3	100

Source: Medico-Social Research Board Hospital In-Patient Enquiry 1979, personal communication, 1981.

The elderly have a similarly heavy take-up of psychiatric in-patient services. They make up 33.2 per cent of the in-patient population of psychiatric units[57] and they are also over-represented among patients admitted on first and subsequent occasions, as illustrated in Table 13.

Table 13

	No. of In-Patients Rate per 100,000	% First Admission	% All Admissions
65-74	1,472	14.8	17.2
75 & over	1,736	14.8	17.2
All ages	578	100	100

Source: O'Hare and Walsh, *The Irish Psychiatric Hospital Census 1971* (Medico-Social Research Board, Dublin); *The Activities of Irish Psychiatric Hospitals and Units* (Medico-Social Research Board, Dublin, 1978, 1980).

These figures underline the substantial over-represenation of the elderly among those receiving psychiatric in-patient care, relative to their proportions in the general population.

The elderly are at greater risk of admission not only to general or psychiatric hospital care but also to institutional care. There are now 17,355 places for the care of the elderly in institutions.[59] Of these 78 per cent are in long-stay nursing settings, 20.05 percent are in welfare homes and the remainder are in rehabilitation/assessment units. In 1975 13.3 percent of these institutional places were filled by the non-elderly.[60] Assuming the same proportion of non-elderly now in 1980, 4.16 percent of the total elderly population is in institutional care. There is evidence that many of these people may be in institutional care inappropriately or prematurely, due to the inadequacy of community supports.

Bourke and Coughlan surveyed fifteen Dublin hospitals in 1966.[61] Fourteen were general type hospitals and in these

17.6 per cent of males and 20.2 per cent of females were 70 years and over. In the remaining hospital, which resembled a 'county welfare home', 56.1 per cent of males and 68.5 per cent of females were aged 75 and over. Bourke and Coughlan reckoned that many of the elderly patients in both the acute general and long-stay chronic hospitals could have been at home or in non-medical residential accommodation.

The Care of the Aged Committee (1968) subsequently observed that

it is better, and probably much cheaper, to help the aged to live in the community than to provide for them in hospitals or other institutions. . . the aim of services provided for the aged should be (inter alia) to enable the aged who can do so to continue to live in their own homes.[62]

McDevitt, Brett and O'Connor (1975) studied the factors determining admission to county homes.[63] They concluded that one significant group among the population of county homes were admitted 'mostly for social and demographic reasons'. They found that 39 per cent of the male patients and 20 percent of the female patients scored high on a measurement scale of self-care capacity and therefore could reasonably be regarded as suitable candidates for care in the community rather than in an institution.

Powell and Powell (1980) found in a study of the population of a long-stay hospital for the elderly in an Irish county, that one quarter of the patients were fully fit and therefore should not have been there.[64] O'Hare and Walsh (1980), commenting on overall psychiatric admission rates (which are disproportionately high for the elderly), say: 'The continuing increase in our admission rates, already very high by international standards must raise questions about our hospitalisation practices and use of alternatives to hospitalisation.'[65]

It is worth noting here that home-help services, which must be the lynch-pin of community-support services for the dependent elderly, received only 0.4 per cent of total non-capital health spending in 1979.[66] The amount, £2.25 million, represented a reduction in real terms over the 1978 figure. The political weakness of the elderly would seem to be relevant here: they cannot command the services they require.

Hypothermia

Hypothermia — the condition of seriously low body temperatures — has become prominent in the public mind as a hazard of old age. This vulnerability is 'due essentially to a life-style which involves a relatively low level of activity and an increased risk in the cold because of poor thermo-regulatory responses and blunted perception of temperature changes.[67] In the UK, Wicks (1978) found that low income, social isolation through living alone, and advancing age were significant but by no means exclusive factors in the incidence of hypothermia.[68] His findings suggest that around 9 per cent of the elderly can be deemed to be 'at risk' of hypothermia. While Wicks emphasises that hypothermia affects the elderly in a fairly random way, he reckons well-heated, insulated and damp-free accommodation, and adequate social security with an income sufficient to meet necessary fuel costs, are important preventive measures. While these are general rather than specific measures and cannot ensure against hypothermia, they require a command over resources which inevitably is beyond the reach of the most deprived elderly. In the SVP survey, Power (1980) found that 25 per cent of the old and alone described themselves as dissatisfied with their heating arrangements; 25 per cent complained they had problems with draughts, 20 per cent with dampness.[69] Households headed by the elderly are far less likely to have central heating than the average household. Power found that only 3 per cent of the old and alone had central heating.[70] In urban areas households headed by retired persons are almost three times less likely to have central heating than is the average household: only 10.3 per cent of those elderly households possess the facility as opposed to 29.5 per cent of all urban households.[71]

In the earlier reference to expenditure it was noted that the elderly devote a particularly high proportion of their weekly spending to fuel and light. Yet despite this there is important indirect evidence to suggest that many elderly, especially the poorest, must live in inadequately heated accommodation either because of the high cost of fuel relative to their income or to the expense and difficulty of achieving satisfactory insulation of their house or flat. The Institute for Industrial Research and Standards reckons that an open fire, probably the most common source of heat for the elderly, would cost £250 for use 16 hours a day over a 200-day heating season.[72] Thus, the typical old person relying on an open coal fire would need to spend upwards of £1 per day for this level of heating during this period. At the moment the State *may* grant a means-tested £3 fuel voucher per week to an elderly person, which is a good deal less than the true cost of sufficient fuel. In this context it is important to note that the rate of increase in the cost of fuel in the twelve months ended mid-November 1980 was approximately double the rate of inflation for the same period.[73]

Mobility

The elderly fare less well than the general population in terms of ease of access and mobility. Getting out and about can often pose great problems. Their independence in this regard can be hampered or restricted by an unfavourable level of physical fitness and health or by the unavailability of suitable means of access, including private and public transport.

Walsh (1980) found that 39 per cent of the elderly he studied were in need of chiropody.[74] In the same study he found 3.8 per cent who were 'in need of walking appliances to maintain independent existence'.[75] Power (1980) found that 36 per cent of the old and alone would find it impossible or very difficult to walk a mile unaided; 29 per cent said they could not leave home for health reasons.[76] McDevitt, Brett and O'Connor (1975) found that 6 per cent of the elderly in the communities they studied were either chair-bound or bed-fast.[77] A study in Athlone (1974) found that 3.3 per cent of the elderly were bed-ridden and a further 12.2 per cent described themselves as severely physically restricted.[78] Personal physical circumstances can therefore seriously confine or preclude opportunities for the elderly to move about outside their own homes.

A UK study found that

The old people who had difficulty walking used the bus less and walked more. Those who did not drive, whether they lived in a household with a car or not, were heavily dependent on pedestrian and bus travel, and travelled less frequently than those who drove.[79]

There is no Irish data about whether the elderly may have markedly different reasons for travelling than the general population. However, it may be useful to look at some British evidence regarding travel patterns of the elderly. The British National Travel Study found that:

Compared with the population as a whole the elderly made 25 per cent fewer journeys for social and recreational purposes and 14 per cent more on shopping journeys, although

130

they made a similar number for personal business.[80]

The British evidence, suggests that the elderly have serious rather than frivolous reasons for travelling. They may rely on getting about to conduct the essential business of their survival: to keep a hospital appointment, to sort out a hitch in pension payments or other welfare problems, to do shopping or to visit a sick relative.

The prevalent assumption of ultimately universal car ownership which, I believe, underpins physical planning, effectively disenfranchises most elderly from adequate access to necessary services, facilities and amenities. The Household Budget Survey (1973) showed that 48 per cent of all households had at least one car.[81] The comparable figure for the elderly living alone was 5 per cent (none of the old age pensioners in this category had a car).[82] A quarter (24.6 per cent) of households made up of a married couple where the head of household was an old age pensioner had a car.[83] Thus the elderly are more likely to be dependent on a public transport system which may all too often be inappropriate infrequent or insensitive to their needs. Table 14 outlines figures for passenger journeys on CIE services. The proportion of journeys undertaken by the elderly is lower than might be expected, even allowing for the kind of physical constraints referred to above. This trend is surprising because firstly they are entitled to free travel on CIE services; secondly they must have recourse to public transport if they are not car owners or cannot arrange a lift from a car owner

Changes in the nature of urban and rural communities may have serious implications for the elderly in terms of their ease of mobility and access. Bosanquet observes that the modern urban environment has become 'a hostile place for the elderly pedestrian . . . (since) . . . distances to be walked have tended to get longer, with less compact development in towns and the replacement of small shops with supermarkets'.[84]

Donnison has noted that, in a context of rural decline and deprivation, the local shop, school, doctor and policeman may be replaced by larger units serving bigger populations from a town easily accessible by car. Bus and rail services may deteriorate or disappear'.[85] This is undoubtedly the experience of many communities in rural Ireland and may go some way towards explaining why in Power (1980) 40 per cent of respondents were not availing themselves of their free travel entitlement.[86] Eligibility may be irrelevant; the appropriate services may not exist. As Curry (1976) comments:

> Ironically, the situation can arise in some rural areas where elderly persons who are entitled to free travel are unable to regularly avail themselves of the facility, either because the public transport is inadequate or because they reside at a considerable distance from the main thoroughfare.[87]

Lifts from neighbours, friends and relatives may play an important part in making travel easier for the elderly, in rural areas particularly. However convenient these may be, to have to rely on them deprives the elderly person of an independence which younger people may take for granted.

TABLE 14

	Total Passenger Journeys (million)	Total Passenger Journeys by Elderly (million)	Total Journeys by Elderly as % of total Passenger Journeys)
Dublin city bus services	167	30	17.9
Other city bus services	28	3.5	12.5
Provincial Bus Services	46.5	2.5	5.3
Railway Services	18	0.5	2.7

Source: CIE, personal communication, 1981.

DEPRIVATION AND DISADVANTAGE

The available evidence points clearly to the conclusion that for the majority, old age entails the experience of a daunting range of deprivation and disadvantage. Jackson has said, 'Growing old is . . . a dynamic process of increasing liabilities and decreasing assets.'[88] About a quarter of a million elderly people living in the State may be trapped in, or close to, poverty. This estimate assumes that 15 per cent of those in receipt of Department of Social Welfare pensions have an additional source of income which permits a comfortable life-style. Thus approximately 25 per cent of the elderly may be materially well off, but for the rest — the other 65 per cent — old age holds the prospect of varying degrees of poverty. This poverty determines their whole lifestyle; it is not just about low income or poor living standards:

> In the last analysis to be poor is not just to be located at the tail end of some distribution of income but to be placed in a particular relationship of inferiority to the wider society. Poverty involves a particular sort of powerlessness, an inability to control the circumstances of one's life in the face of more powerful groups in society.[89]

The political and economic weakness of the elderly has a complex causation: their powerlessness and poverty are not accidental. These result from a sometimes subtle but systematic range of factors which have (inter alia) demographic, economic, psychological, social and geographical dimensions. I now propose to discuss the way which these factors lead to the phenomenon of poverty in old age.

Demographic Factors

The risk of dependence and poverty in old age can often be heavily influenced by the person's demographic characteristics. Writing more than twenty years ago, Townsend described those elderly who seem particularly dependent on institutional and domiciliary services:

> Compared with the population at large many more live alone; more of them are unmarried, more are childless, more have sons but not daughters, and more are separated from daughters when they have them.[90]

Writing more recently in Ireland, Corridan (1975) estimated

that one in eight of the elderly is likely to be dependent and to be 'drawn from the ranks of the childless, the very old and those living alone'.[91]

Approximately 12 per cent of the elderly live alone.[92] They make up 48.3 per cent of all persons living alone.[93] These people are particularly liable to economic and social disadvantage. Power (1980) found that 53 per cent of the old and alone were childless,[94] whereas Corridan (1975) estimates that 37 per cent of all elderly are childless.[95] The correlation of living alone and childlessness, of course, heightens the risk of dependence. The elderly who live alone are at greater risk of admission to institutional care. McDevitt, Brett and O'Connor (1975) found that 41 per cent of the county home populations they studied were living alone prior to admission.[96] Powell and Powell (1980) found in a similar study that approximately 35 per cent had been living alone prior to admission.[97]

Those who live alone are also likely to be poorer. In the earlier discussion on income it was noted that the household of an old person living alone had less than one third of the net average weekly income going into households shared by an elderly person with others. Power (1980) also underlined the serious deficiencies in the housing amenities of the elderly who live alone, as noted earlier.[98] This was particularly a problem in rural areas.

Age and marital status are further important demographic factors. The older elderly, those over 75 years, are more likely to experience a decline in physical function which tends to be associated with a greater risk of dependence and poverty. Marriage seems able to protect the elderly from some of the hazards of old age. The single and widowed are strikingly more vulnerable to admission to long-stay care, for instance.

Economic Factors

In response to economic pressures, Jones notes that social policy usually exhibits the same priorities as primitive people struggling for survival: 'workers first, children and child-bearing women next, and the old last'.[99] Ireland's remarkably high dependency ratio (the ratio between those who are not economically active and those who are) poses this problem of competing priorities very acutely. Ireland has a higher dependency ratio than any of its EEC partners, than any other Western European country, excluding Turkey, and higher than the

USSR, USA, Canada or Japan.[100] A narrow income tax base and the highest unemployment rate of any of the countries mentioned above compound the problems already posed for social policy by the high dependency ratio.[101]

The current prospect of further economic retrenchment suggests a most inclement climate for social reform and the extension in scale and scope of social services. If there are to be cuts in the levels of service or in the rate of growth of services, among the most vulnerable are the elderly who inevitably are quite prolific consumers of health and social services.

The evidence can support Townsend's view that the elderly, in a sense, are trapped in a complex of structural disadvantage and deprivation of society's making. A primary source of this unequal economic status of the elderly is their increasing distance from the market place, both as producer and consumer.

Social and Psychological Factors

Steinman suggests that there are three roles ascribed to the elderly following retirement in modern industrial society: (1) dependant − supplicant; (2) leisure time filler; (3) sick role occupant.[104] The theme of dependency runs clearly through all three. Society expects the elderly to behave as though they are weak and vulnerable. Perhaps because of this it is often assumed that deprivation and decline in old age is due to the biological imperative of senescence rather than to social definitions of the ageing process. Hinton says, 'We must remain aware that a social assumption that elderly people are senescent can contribute to their decline.'[105] Gray draws the important distinction between the disease and ageing processes:

> The probability that one will suffer from strokes, heart disease, bronchitis, and osteo-arthritis in old age, to list but a few common disabling diseases is influenced not only by one's genetic constitution but by external modifiable factors such as working conditions, diet, cigarette smoking and environmental conditions.[106]

He accepts that some dependence in old age is inevitable but reminds us that 'many of the problems of dependence are associated with social deprivation . . . which elderly people share with certain other groups, for example single parent families.'[107]

In our society where the individual's self-esteem and social status rely for their continued validation on his/her economic productivity, the emergence of retirement has deprived the majority of the elderly of this source of status. Participation by the elderly in the labour force has declined steadily over the years (see Table 2). Retirement can deprive the individual of any meaningful role in life. No longer a producer and restricted also in the consumer role because of low income, the individual becomes economically obsolete:

> Thus the old are stigmatised . . . by the myth that they must retire overnight because of some defect in themselves rather than in the economy of the modern Western industrial state with its inability to provide jobs in peacetime equal to the number of citizens able and willing to be employed.[108]

Another source of status in modern society is socio-economic class position. This is clearly a critical factor in determining life chances in old age:

> Living standards in old age are not only a function of class position as signified by present occupation, last occupation prior to retirement or husband's occupation prior to widowhood. They appear also to be a function of life long class position.[109]

Townsend emphasises the link between poverty in old age and unfavourable class position: 'some old people are poor by virtue of their lower life-long class position. Others are poor by virtue of society's imposition upon the elderly of an "underclass" status.'[110]

Political Factors

Kaim-Caudle has hypothesised that the proportion of the elderly in the total population may be a determinant of national pension rates. He notes that these rise where the numbers of elderly increase and that the contrary occurs where the proportion of elderly remains stable. He speculates that this may signify the relative electoral power of the elderly constituency. He concedes, however, that 'political economic and ideological factors quite unconnected with the number and proportion of old people are decisive in determining the level of pension rates'.[111]

The elderly in Ireland are relatively weak numerically and

therefore electorally. They compound this weakness by failing to organise around their common political interests. The National Federation of Pensioners and Pensioners' Associations may be the first sign that this tendency can be reversed. In the US the Grey Panthers, a political pressure group organised by the elderly to promote their interests, has made some impact but its membership remains relatively small. One of the reasons for the absence of any concerted expression of political self-interest by the elderly in Ireland may be their low expectations. Power (1980) found that only 29 per cent of the old and alone, (who tend to be among the most deprived) expressed dissatisfaction with government action on their behalf.[111] However, it is unlikely that succeeding generations will remain so undemanding. Another problem is physical: the elderly tend to be scattered throughout the community and to experience difficulty with mobility and access. This precludes or inhibits the possibility of effective action for many. It is a political fact too that the most deprived are typically less likely to have the energy or organisational skills necessary to influence political decisions or events.

Conclusion

Close to two-thirds of all our elderly have a command over the resources of modern living which is unequal both to their needs and to the norms and expectations of the general population. These elderly have to bear a disproportionately heavy share of the national burden of inequality and deprivation. It may be true that in absolute terms the elderly have had improvements in recent years in pensions and their general living standards. But in relative terms the gap between the elderly and the general population seems actually to have widened.

Poverty obviously is not randomly distributed throughout society. Its incidence is strongly associated with certain social characteristics such as unemployment, illiteracy, chronic illness and economic dependency. The widespread economic dependency of the elderly renders them more vulnerable to poverty than any other age group, except perhaps children. The dice of social prosperity are heavily loaded against the elderly. The triumph of economic priorities in national development threatens them with social redundancy as a consequence of their progressive economic marginalisation. The plight of the elderly therefore is not incidental to the way in which society organises itself. The thrust of economic and social development quite systematically distances the elderly from the mainstream of modern life. Their circumstances are explicable much more in terms of structural and social disadvantage derived from the economic and social system rather than from personal misfortune occurring in the biographies of individual old people. The social isolation of the elderly, their economic obsolescence and their psychological marginalisation are not accidental features of a modern urbanising and industrialising society. Like more 'primitive' societies we too have our rituals for the disposal of the elderly. For some this may mean consignment to long-stay institutional care whether in the guise of a hospital or a welfare home. Illich has criticised this trend as in modern society as 'the contemporary strategy for the disposal of the who have been institutionalised in arguably less hideous forms by most other societies.'[113] Most elderly here still remain in the community. But the majority of these increasingly find themselves excluded from the market place and therefore from the mainstream of a society that is dedicated to economic growth. For them, old age too often entails an insidious decline into poverty and social isolation.

The personal consequences for the elderly of this structurally determined disadvantage and poverty rank low if at all on most political agendas. Policies and priorities are ultimately determined by competing interest groups whose influence derives from some sanction which they can invoke or threaten. The elderly generally lack such sanctions or clout. This is partly because of their relative numerical weakness but also because of their virtual lack of a collective identity of interests.

Note
I would like to thank Mary Whelan for her unceasing encouragement and support in the preparation of this essay and Bob Carroll, Diarmuid McCarthy and Paddy McPhillips for their helpful comments. The final responsibility is, of course, my own. R.G. January, 1981.

REFERENCES

1. *Census of Population 1979* (CSO, Dublin).

2. Ibid.

3. EUROSTAT, *Basic Statistics of the Community*, (Luxembourg, 1979).

4. *Census of Population 1971* (CSO, Dublin).

5. S. O'Cinneide, 'The Extent of Poverty in Ireland', *Social Studies*, Vol 1. No. 4. (August 1972).

6. Ibid.

7. See (i) 'Measures and Explanations of Poverty in High Income and Low Income Counties' in P. Townsend (ed). *The Concept of Poverty* (London, 1970); (ii) B. Abel Smith, *The Poor and the Poorest* (London, 1965).

8. P. Townsend, *Poverty in the United Kingdom* (Harmondsworth, 1979).

9. Ibid, p. 88-89.

10. S. de Beauvoir, *Old Age* (Harmondsworth 1978). p. 237.

11. R. Titmuss.

12. De Beauvoir, op. cit, p 114.

13. P. Townsend, op. cit, p. 676

14. G. P. Marshall, *Social Goals and Economic Perspectives* (Harmondsworth, 1980), p. 162.

15. E. Fitzgerald, 'Alternative Strategies for Family Income Support' Table 2.2 p. 66-67, NESC Report No. 47 (Dublin, 1980).

16. Ibid.

17. Central Statistics Office, *Redistributive Effects of State Taxes and Benefits on Household Incomes in 1973* (Dublin, 1980). The percentage is of final weekly income as defined by the CSO.

18. Ibid.

19. Ibid.

20. Ibid.

21. Ibid.

22. Ibid.

23. Household Budget Survey, 1978, special tabulation (CSO, Dublin).

24. E. Fitzgerald, 'Universality & Selectivity: Social Services in Ireland; NESC Report No. 38 (Dublin, 1978).

25. *Dail Debates,* Vol. 324, No. 1, Cols 53, 54 (11 November 1980).

26. Ibid, Col. 52.

27. Society of St Vincent de Paul, *Submission to Government Concerning the 1981 Budget* (Dublin, 1980).

28. *Dail Debates,* Vol. 324, No. 1, Cols. 53, 54.

29. E. Fitzgerald, op. cit.

30. *Dail Debates,* Vol. 324, No. 1, Cols, 53, 54.

31. Ibid.

32. Ibid.

33. National Committee on Pilot Schemes to Combat Poverty, personal communication 1980.

34. H. Donoghue, *The Supplementary Welfare Allowances Scheme in Practice* (National Committee on Pilot Schemes to Combat Poverty, (Dublin, 1980).

35. *Dail Debates,* Vol. 323 No.4, Col. 621 (22 October, 1980).

36. Department of Health, personal communication, 1980).

37. Ibid.

38. *Census of Population 1979* (CSO, Dublin).

39. B. Power, *Old and Alone in Ireland* (Society of St Vincent de Paul, (Dublin, 1980).

40. *Census of Population 1971* (CSO, Dublin).

41. Household Budget Survey 1978, special tabulation (CSO, Dublin).

42. Ireland, 'The Care of the Aged', Report of Inter-Departmental Committee 1968.

43. R. Geary and M. Dempsey, 'The Preparation of Statistics of Sickness or Disability in Ireland', *Administration*, Vol. 27, No. 2 (Summer 1979).

44. See for instance, works referred to in B. Walsh, 'Previously Unrecognised Treatable Illness in an Irish Elderly Population' *Journal of the Irish Medical Association*, Vol. 73, No. 2 (February 1980).

45. M. Goldring, 'Questions of Age' *The Listener* Vol. 105 No. 2694 (8 January, 1981).

46. B. Walsh, 'Previous Unrecognised Treatable Illness in an Irish Elderly Population' *Journal of the Irish Medical Association*, Vol. 73 No. 2 (February 1980).

47. Ibid.

48. Ibid.

49. National Prices Commission, 'Some Economic Aspects of the Dietary Intake of Old People' Monthly Report No. 58 (Dublin, 1977), pp 46-67.

50. Ibid.

51. Ibid. (The Palmore study is not fully referenced but took place in 1971 and covered more than 50,000 subjects).

52. Power, op. cit.

53. National Prices Commission, 'Old Age Pensioners: Shopping Behaviour and Attitudes Towards Prices', Monthly Report No. 76 (Dublin, 1978).

54. J. Gowen, 'A Report from General Practice in Ireland' *Journal of the Irish Medical Association*, Vol. 65 No. 7 (April 1972).

55. J. Gibson, 'A Study of General Practitioner Consultations and Workload in a Trainee Practice in South-West Ireland' *Journal of the Irish Medical Association*, Vol, 70 No. 5 (April 1977).

56. Medico Social Research Board, Hospital In-Patient Enquiry 1979 (Dublin).

57. A. O'Hare and D. Walsh, *The Irish Psychiatric Hospital Census 1971* (Medico Social Research Board, Dublin).

58. A. O'Hare and D. Walsh, *The Activities of Irish Psychiatric Hospitals and Units 1978* (Medico Social Research Board, Dublin, 1980).

59. Department of Health, personal communication 1980.

60. Department of Health, *Statistical Information Relevant to the Health Services 1980,* Table G 16.

61. G. Bourke and A. Coughlan, *Dublin General Hospital & Geriatric Study* (Dublin, 1966).

62. Ireland, op. cit.

63. D. McDermott, T. Brett and M. O'Connor, *Admission to County Homes: A Study of the Aged in Three Homes and Three Counties in Ireland,* (Medico Social Research Board, Dublin, 1975).

64. A. Powell and F. Powell, 'Too fit for hospitals', *Community Care* 16 October, 1980).

65. O'Hare and Walsh, *Activities of Irish Psychiatric Hospitals and Units 1978.*

66. Department of Health, *Statistical Information Relevant to the Health Services 1980,* Table I 3.

67. K. Collins and E. Hoinville, 'Temperature Requirements in Old Age' *Building Services Engineering Research and Technology,* Vol 1 No. 4 (1980), p. 165-172).

68. M. Wicks, *Old and Cold* (London, 1978).

69. Power, op. cit.

70. Ibid.

71. Household Budget Survey 1978, special tabulation (CSO, Dublin).

72. Institute for Industrial Research and Standards, personal communication 1980.

73. *Consumer Price Index Mid November 1980* (CSO, December 1980). Percentage increase in cost (for twelve months ended mid November 1980) for all items: 18.2; for fuel and light: 36.2.

74. Walsh, op. cit.

75. Ibid.

76. Power, op. cit.

77. McDevitt, Brett and O'Connor, op. cit.

78. Athlone Community Service Council. *A Survey of the Aged* (The Study took place in 1973; date of publication not known).

79. J. Hopkin, P. Robson and S. Town, *Transport and the Elderly: Requirements, Problems and Possible Solutions,* (UK Dept., of the Environment and Dept., of Transport, 1978).

80. National Travel Study 1975/76 referred to in Hopkin, Robson and Town, op. cit.

81. D. Murphy, '1973 Household Budget Survey: Special Features and Results' *Journal of the Statistical and Social Inquiry Society of Ireland* (1975/76).

82. Ibid.

83. Ibid.

84. N. Bosanquet, *A Future for Old Age* (London, 1978) p 56.

85. D. Donnison, 'An Approach to Social Policy', NESC Report No. 8, Dublin (1975).

86. Power, op. cit.

87. J. Curry, 'Rural Areas: Social Planning Problems, NESC Report No. 19, Dublin 1976).

88. D. Jackson, *Poverty,* (London, 1972), p 77.

89. J. Kincaid, *Poverty and Equality in Britain* (Harmondsworth, 1973), p 171.

90. P. Townsend, *The Family Life of Old People* (Harmondsworth, re-printed 1977), p 214.

91. J. Corridan, 'Demography of the Geriatric Problem in Ireland', *Irish Journal of Medical Science,* Vol. 144 No. 4 (1975), pp. 137-42.

92. *Census of Population 1971* (CSO, Dublin).

93. Murphy, op. cit.

94. Power, op. cit.

95. Corridan, op. cit.

96. McDevitt, Brett and O'Connor, op. cit.

97. Powell and Powell, op. cit.

98. Power, op. cit.

99. K. Jones, 'The Social and Cultural Context' in *Easing the Restriction on Ageing* (Age Concern, 1972).

100. EUROSTAT, op. cit.

101. Ibid.

102. P. Townsend, *Poverty in the United Kingdom* (Harmondsworth, 1979).

103. Ibid.

104. R. Steinman, *Serving Elderly People at Risk in Scotland and the United States* (Age Concern n.d.), p.5.

105. J. Hinton, *Dying* (Harmondsworth, 1974) p.64.

106. M. Gray, 'What we can expect at old age', *Community Care* (24 April 1980).

107. Ibid.

108. Steinman, op. cit. p. 4.

109. P. Kaim Caudle *Comparative Social Policy and Social Security* (London, 1973), p. 199.

110. Power, op. cit.

111. I. Illich, *Limits to Medicine* (Harmondsworth, 1977), p 91.

PART II

Poverty, Politics and Policies

Tony Brown

In discussing poverty we are dealing with a major economic and social phenomenon and with a continuing human tragedy which today afflicts many thousands of our fellow-citizens. Poverty is a fact of modern life in this country and the facts of poverty revealed in this volume are, at once, an indictment of our society and a challenge to its political institutions.

Exactly one hundred years ago the great American economic philosopher, Henry George, stated that 'poverty with all its concomitants shows itself in communities just as they develop into the conditions towards which material progress tends. . . (and) this association of poverty with progress is the great enigma of our times'.[1] It is an unhappy fact that these words reamain true now as we enter the last two decades of the twentieth century. Poverty is still significant and widespread in even the most advanced modern countries and continues to pose deep, and largely unanswered, questions for policy-makers and for planners.

The health and progress of a nation and, indeed, of the world may be related directly to its capacity to deal effectively with the needs of all its people, and especially of the disadvantaged. On this will depend the prospects for future political stability and social accord. In the past it has proved possible to ignore those who have fallen behind or who have lost out in the economic or social race. That luxury may not exist for much longer. Injustice and discrimination are no longer tolerable in the opinion of those who can, and will, influence future political development.

Basic Propositions

This chapter will attempt to relate the question of continuing and persistent poverty to the political decision-making system of a democratic society. The elimination of poverty is a task for society as a whole. This theme will be discussed in relation to three broad propositions which may be expressed in the following terms.

Poverty has not become a central political issue in Ireland, nor indeed in other European countries. The poor are seen to be marginal, belonging to many sub-groups within society, and they are unorganised with little political 'muscle'. Some political initiatives on the poverty issue have been made from time to time but so far there has been no real mobilisation of political will.

Policies to deal with the needs of the disadvantaged have evolved largely in a piecemeal fashion and without any firm basis in an analysis of the causes of poverty. Individual social policies are subject to pressure at times of economic difficulty and recession. The essential links between economic and social policy — within a planning framework — have not been made.

Poverty exists because of inherent defects in the economic and social order. Its elimination must, therefore, become a political issue as well as a matter of day-to-day policy. The central political question here relates to the divide between strategies to eliminate poverty and programmes to alleviate distress. Society must be brought to accept the implications of doing away with poverty in all its forms — which must involve deep-seated structural change — and to face up to the costs which must arise.

Poverty — Not a Central Issue

The existence of poverty on a considerable scale is a fact here in Ireland and in all of the countries of Western Europe. A study published early in 1980 pointed to the existence of relative poverty at a level of 20 to 25 per cent of the population in Italy, Belgium and Ireland, 16 per cent in France, up to 10 per cent in the UK and between 3 and 5 per cent in Germany, Norway and Sweden.[2] These percentages add up to a total of many millions of men, women and children. Yet, poverty has not been regarded as a central political issue in any of the countries mentioned. It has largely been left to committed pressure groups together with a few politicians to fight the battle of the poor.

Quite simply, the poor have not become an issue because they do not constitute a recognisable and organised political constituency. People afflicted by poverty are in the minority and they are not a homogenous group within society. Seamus O Cinneide, in his 1971 study, divided the poor in Ireland into five main categories: old people, widows; small farmers; certain groups of the self-employed, and low-paid employees.

To these may be added such groups as single-parent families, prisoners' dependants, isolated individuals and groups, and the long-term unemployed and disabled. Of these, only the unemployed — and even then to a very limited extent — have any real political muscle. One hundred times as many marchers turned out for the 1980 PAYE protest as for the unemployment protest in the same year — and both marches were organised by the same trade union body.

It must also be pointed out that for a significant period since World War II in Europe as a whole the existence of poverty was denied and the view widely advocated and accepted that material deprivation had been effectively dealt with by the growth of the economy and by the steady extension of the whole range of modern social services. Throughout the late 1950s and the 1960s the governments and peoples of the industrialised countries had come to accept as a fact the assertion that poverty had been abolished and that inequality was merely a catch-cry of the malcontent or subversive. This was true in Ireland as elsewhere in Europe.

The 'rediscovery' of poverty, not only in Europe but also in the USA, is a story which had been widely documented. It occurred largely in the 1960s and came about as a result of academic research by such experts as Peter Townsend, Richard Titmuss, Michael Harrington and Seamus O Cinneide. Adrian Sinfield has very succinctly summed up the experience of rediscovery:

> . . .in each country the rediscovery of poverty has had its own form and development, but there also appear to be marked similarities. At each stage of the rediscovery a different stereotype of the poor tends to dominate discussion and to influence the solutions proposed. At first there is a recognition of isolated groups. . . the solution is seen essentially as a small scale one, a tidying up operation. . . in this period inequality is not discussed and the term 'poverty' seldom used. This pattern of finding poverty by categories or groups is important because it tends to confine the policy debate, and to insulate it from wider issues of inequality and from the rest of society generally.[3]

As the facts of poverty became more widely known through the research and writings of the 1960s some political initiatives were taken. In the UK successive governments launched the Urban Aid Programme and the National Community Develop-

ment Project. The USA Administration under Kennedy and Johnson introduced the Manpower Development and Training Act and established the Office of Economic Opportunity which initiated the so-called War Against Poverty. Thus, under the influence largely of academics, the wealthier nations were very slowly, and with little enthusiasm, brought to accept that the poor did still exist and that the progress made had been slow and patchy. Evidence even began to emerge which suggested that inequalities within the richer countries had widened. The various programmes started in this way achieved some success but failed to take root as permanent elements of national policy.

In Ireland, the 1971 Kilkenny Conference on Poverty, at which Seamus O Cinneide presented his celebrated paper, drew some initial verbal support from politicians. One important response was the establishment by the Labour Party of a Working Group on Poverty which produced a detailed report on the subject, followed by a policy statement both of which were adopted by the Annual Party Conferences in 1973 and 1974. The main political thrust of this work was reflected in the Statement of Intent of the National Coalition Parties (Fine Gael and Labour) which won the 1973 General Election.

The Statement of Intent contained the following commitment:

The elimination of poverty and the ending of social injustice will be a major priority in the next Government's programme. The social policy of the new Government will bring immediate assistance to those in need and lay the foundations of longterm policies to root out the causes of low incomes, bad housing and poor educational facilities.

While the main emphasis in government policy in pursuit of these aims lay in the area of increased social welfare benefits and greater provision for local authority house-building, the question of poverty in the hard-core sense was also given attention. In particular, the commitment was taken up and worked on by Frank Cluskey as Parliamentary Secretary to the Minister for Social Welfare and *de facto* Minister for Social Welfare, with a view to its practical implementation.

Frank Cluskey was to a large extent personally responsible for the establishment, in 1974, of the National Committee on Pilot Schemes to Combat Poverty and for the initiation, in 1975, of the European Community Programme to Combat

Poverty. The full history of these initiatives has yet to be told but a major part of the story is related in the Final Report of the National Committee. It can, however, be said that a genuine and positive effort was made to place the issue of poverty clearly on the political agenda, both in Ireland and throughout the European Community.

A great deal of good work was done in the Irish projects and many important lessons have been learned. Action research projects were successfully undertaken in all the member states of the Community. Yet it is true that the problem of poverty remains marginal to economic and social planning at both national and Community level and there is little apparent conviction that this is an issue of the first priority. Apart from the hard-line, right-wing economic and social philosophies which hold sway over many governments today, more fundamental influences must be at play.

The Political Reasons

Why should this be so? Three reasons may be suggested. First, all of the most important anti-poverty initiatives here, as elsewhere, have been directly the result of political decisions made outside the normal channels of decision-making. The Irish programme was the practical implementation of Labour Party thinking rather than the outcome of departmental pondering or the response to public pressure. Much the same can be said of the USA War on Poverty which

> did not arise, as have many great national programmes, from the pressure of overwhelming public demand; the poor had no lobby. Nor was it proposed by the staff thinkers in government agencies who are paid to conceive ideas. . . . it seems clear that the anti-poverty programme was a presidential initiative.[4]

Such beginnings reflect positively on political leadership but do not guarantee success. Governments and ministers, change, and bureaucracies have long time horizons. Only a firm coalition of long-term political commitment, administrative attention and real community involvement (most particularly the participation of the poor themselves) can give a basis for success. In the Irish case the Combat Poverty Programme found itself in 1977 responsible to a minister who made it clear to the Committee that its basic philosophy of social and economic change was unacceptable to him. The programme, in its original form and with its original philosophy, was abruptly — and with minimal consultation — ended in December 1980, though the prospect of continuation now arises from the subsequent change of government.

Second, the poverty issue does not command an effective political constituency. The type of change which must be sought if poverty is to be defeated demands the existence of support capable of sustaining a programme in the face of adversity and sheer hostility. Even the limited Irish programme excited the active opposition of bishops, businessmen and politicians because it sought to stress the powerlessness of the poor and their right to acquire and use power within the community. To deal with such difficulties and pressures it is essential to have built up strong and reliable public backing. Equally it is necessary to enjoy political support at the level of budgetary and administrative decision in order to ensure financial and organisational viability.

Poverty action is always faced with a dilemma in the area of support. Too much backing within the Establishment would tend to reinforce conventional approaches and attitudes. Too much reliance on the support of the poor themselves would involve the danger of marginalisation. Striking the right balance is extremely difficult. Again, the diversity of poverty situations leads to a diversity of sources of support. 'Community action did not lack a constituency: it had too many, whose interests could not be reconciled. So it tended to alienate them all; and, unable to recruit the concerted support for the resources it needs, generated a growing frustration.'[5] Nowhere to date has there emerged a coherent, broad-based movement for change in favour of the poor.

Third, and most fundamental, policies against poverty have not been adequately linked with the mainstream of economic and social development. These policies have tended to be adjuncts to social welfare or labour market policies or to be isolated in the general area of research. The diversity of experiences of poverty already referred to tends to segment anti-poverty programmes and to reduce the prospects of comprehensive approaches. In all of the cases mentioned above — in Britain, America and Ireland — what was started has been no more than an experiement or a pilot project. The break-through to a full-scale (and meaningful) programme has yet to be achieved.

It is sometimes argued that the anti-poverty initiatives which have taken place have been deliberately designed to avoid long-term commitments. There is no real evidence to support this view but there is abundant cause for concern at the lack of planned progression to a further stage of policy development. First steps have been taken with the genuine purpose of creating long-term programmes but without any in-built mechanism for achieving the necessary break-through. It has been strongly argued, for example in the Labour Party policy statement of 1974, that there should be a formal national Plan to Combat Poverty which would lay down the successive steps to be taken and indicate the nature of the resources required.

The history of programmes to deal with poverty demonstrates that there has been no systematic and sustained mobilisation of political will in any country in relation to a continuing and humanly unacceptable situation. This fact constitutes a serious indictment of the democratic political system and of the economic and social values which underpin it.

Poverty and Social Welfare

As has been indicated earlier, one of the arguments used over the years against any special attention to the issue of poverty has been based on the expansion of social provisions in all countries and the rapidly growing commitment of scarce financial resources to income-maintenance and other relevant services. It is an unquestionable fact that such advances have taken place. In Ireland, for example, spending on Social Welfare has grown from £151 million in 1972 to £893 million in 1980 — a factor of almost six to one.

Yet the argument must be made that such growth in social services does not necessarily imply any real change in the relative position of the poor. In a modern society such large outlays are, in fact, necessary in order merely to keep the poor groups in the community at their normal level. No significant improvement in terms of closing the gap in life-styles or life prospects has been achieved.

In this connection, it is important to reflect upon some of the different approaches to Social Welfare which exist in our society.

Political views differ widely. In recent years, ministers responsible for Social Welfare have adopted very contrasting attitudes. Comparison of two such presentations reveal, on the one hand, complacency and lack of comprehension and, on the other, awareness of the real situation.

. . . the Government, despite the economic difficulties, are doing everything they can to ease the lot of the weaker sections of the community.[6]

. . .we must pause, even when considering the very significant progress made. . . to point out for us all the large responsibility which rests on the community to provide for those in need. . . we still have a long way to go.[7]

Irish society contains many selfish and self-interested groups which have seen fit to attack the Social Welfare system. In the mid-1970s there emerged a concerted and powerful campaign by leading businessmen and their organisations seeking cuts in all social services and propounding the theory of 'the survival of the fittest'. The campaign was not without success. Episodes such as this must be taken seriously as a reflection of significant attitudes within our community.

Social Welfare increases are not an adequate response to the poverty issue, and it is vitally important that they should not be considered as such. No foreseeable advance in income-maintenance levels will cope in any real way with the needs of the poor in modern society. A wide range of economic and social changes, involving a real cost of the entire system, is necessary.

Piecemeal Progress

Progress in terms of Irish national policy to deal with the needs of the disadvantaged has come about over the years in a piecemeal fashion. There has been scarcely any coherent planning of social development and the various planning documents of governments have been notably short on social content. Mr Tom Barrington, the former Director of the Institute of Public Administration, has stated very aptly that 'at present the central Departments are very good at preparing what might be called shopping lists in the social area — the Third Programme gives us a good example. But that is not enough.'[8]

Policy discussion on social matters in Ireland has almost totally avoided any consideration of the causes of social problems. Where such analysis has been attempted it has usually been superficial in nature. No sustained effort has yet been made to explore the structural causes of poverty and injustice and, even at the highest levels of the public service, of community organisations and of the Churches, mention of structural factors can still be met with blank incomprehension.

It must be recognised that policy debate in Ireland takes place within a society which is essentially conservative in attitudes and which has never been encouraged to engage in vigorous self-analysis. Simplistic attitudes still predominate. Political debate and the development of policies have been characterised by the same conservatism and lack of commitment to change as is found in the population as a whole. The long history of the continuing politics of the Civil War has been a particularly sad one, trivialising much discussion between the Parties and distracting attention from the main issues in the economic and social spheres. For a variety of reasons, including the impact of the present electoral system and the small size of the population, Irish politics has tended to concentrate on personality issues at the expense of policy considerations. It is only in comparatively recent times that there has been any noticeable movement towards an in-depth or analytical approach to the development of political ideas — or towards debate based on ideological and philosophical concepts.

Inequality

One important concept which has received very little attention in Irish policy discussion is that of inequality. Yet this is the central consideration in any realistic understanding of the notion of social justice and, in particular, in any long-term programme to eliminate poverty. Only when political debate and policy development are directed towards the achievement of the principle of equality can there be real hope of success in combating poverty and deprivation.

The facts of the situation must be fully recognised and understood. A few very simple points will illustrate the nature of our present problems of social injustice. A recent research paper has revealed that extreme discrepancies exist in relation to income distribution. Conclusions based on 1973 data indicate that while the top 9 per cent of the nation's households have 42 per cent of total income, the bottom 19 per cent of households have little more than 4 per cent of income. These figures are paralleled by equally disturbing evidence of an inequitable distribution of capital wealth in Irish society. This is quite extraordinary reflection of a situation of deep-seated inequality — a ratio of ten to one.

The unemployment situation today is only too well known. What must be understood is the essentially long-term nature of this national tragedy. We have never had an unemployment level of less than about fifty or sixty thousand men and women — 5 per cent of the workforce. Today the figure stands at about 11 per cent. The Irish economic system has never fulfilled the very basic responsibility of providing adequate job opportunity for our people and more than a million emigrants in fifty years bear tragic witness to this.

Acceptance of the principle of equality is central to the making of a just society. This principle must be adopted as a practical measuring-rod for all policy, but especially in the area of distribution or resources. The main theme of the early National Economic and Social Council Report on Social Policy was articulated along these lines, proposing that all policies should be assessed by reference to their distributional effects and to the overall goal of greater equality. As might have been expected, the report has been totally ignored in policy-making. Inequalities will be found in all societies at all times. But, in a truly just society they would require to be justified against stringent criteria of general welfare and contribution to the needs of the disadvantaged. 'Inequalities could exist as a result of the application of need, merit and contribution to the common good as criteria for allocating resources. In other words, inequalities could be acceptable only on the grounds of equity.'[9]

The fundamental characteristic of a just society would be that no one or no group should have access to resources surplus to their reasonable needs while any of their fellow citizens remained unable to satisfy their equally reasonable needs. Such a vision of society is very far away from the general thinking of today's Ireland in which concepts such as the 'deserving poor' and the 'idle dole sponger' still command widespread acceptance.

Economic and Social Planning

Policy development in relation to poverty in Ireland requires that there should be integrated economic and social planning and committed political leadership. Social and economic planning must be integrated. There can be no genuine progress towards even the accepted economic goals — such as the attainment of full employment — unless the plans and policies devised to achieve them are properly balanced. Those plans must be of a nature that will provide answers — or the recognisable beginnings of answers — to the major social problems of the day, including those of legal and administrative justice.

In a relevant speech, made when he was Parliamentary Secretary to the Minister for Social Welfare, Frank Cluskey summed up this view in the following terms:

The mere pursuit of goals spelled out in terms of economic advance-growth deficits, balance of payments, even employment or unemployment levels — simply cannot be looked to as the basis for the concerted national effort that is essential. The very process of economic growth can be a self-defeating exercise if it is in itself such as to maintain and reinforce injustice. There must be a clear commitment to the achievement of a balance between what is necessary to meet acceptable economic criteria and what relates specifically to the creation of a more just and equal society.[10]

And Social Planning must be directed towards the real issues as Titmuss has pointed out.

Planning, if it means anything at all in relation to the social and economic needs of the particular groups in society, means the making of decisions about the allocation of resources and claims on resources in the future as well as the present. If we are to plan for the aged to have a larger share of the national income then we are, in effect, planning for others to have less.[11]

Such an approach to planning will require the exercise of real political leadership. People cannot be expected to display wild enthusiasm about policies which call for equality and redistribution. Governments today are constantly made aware of the public attitude to taxation and to costly public services. Yet there cannot be justice, within individual nations or at world level, without redistribution. To fail to accept this fact and to fail to base policy decisions on redistribution will, in the long run, bring about social and policial chaos. While there is much emphasis on the need for economic development it has been correctly pointed out that growth to date has taken place at the cost of justice. All politicians today face the challenge of those words.

In recent times the extraordinary idea has been widely canvassed — not least by finance ministers trying to cope with the aftermath of the recession — that governments cannot legislate or decide on any matter without the sanction of an almost

100 per cent national consensus. That is a view which runs directly counter to the whole democratic tradition within a normal community where the concept of consensus surely implies an acceptance of the rule of the majority within defined rules and limits. The search for full consensus on major policy issues is futile and must increasingly be seen as no more than a mechanism for delaying decision-making or as an alibi for avoiding decisions.

Irish Attitudes

The statement that poverty has its roots in the structures of the present economic and social system is central to any really serious discussion of poverty and of its eventual eradication. That is not to say that there is agreement on the truth or policy implications of the statement — rather, all debate on poverty now revolves around the arguments for and against this view.

For many people, especially in Ireland, poverty is seen only as a result of personal characteristics or circumstances. One recent Irish study found that 'the underlying concept of poverty was one of personal inadequacy or failure rather than possible faults in the social and economic institutions'.[12] Research by the EEC Commission has revealed a remarkable range of attitudes to poverty among the peoples of the Community. The causes of poverty were identified as follows:

TABLE 1

	In the Nine %	In Ireland %
Injustice in society	26	19
Laziness	25	30
Bad luck	16	25
Inevitability	14	16
None of the above	6	4
Don't know	13	6
	100	100

The results for Ireland reveal this country as having basically conservative views on the issues in question. Less than one-fifth of the population believe in the injustice of society as a contributory factor in poverty, compared with 40 per cent in Italy. The extremely high proportion who place the blame on laziness is paralleled in the UK and Luxembourg — and it bears out most accurately the results of previous Irish research and of much general information on the trend of Irish social attitudes. This result is perhaps closely related to another finding of the survey which places excessive drinking at the top of the Irish list of common causes of deprivation — no less than 65 per cent of Irish respondents ranked drink first, compared with a Community average of 28 per cent. These results clearly indicate the range of opinion which exists on the subject. From those who see poverty as little more than a sign of divine disfavour, through the long tradition of welfare response to the more refined theories of the cycle of poverty and the 'culture of poverty', these are views which all tend to see deprivation as an aberration or distortion of the otherwise benign and improving social and economic system. In practical terms these opinions have been reflected in the Poor Law; in the vast expansion of the welfare state with its whole plethora of benefits, services and means tests; in the concentration of attention on educationally deprived areas; and, more recently in the study of the effects of the transmission of deprivation through the family.

The Structural Causes of Poverty

More and more, however, the evidence and the practical experience of all the various studies and programmes points to the fundamentally structural nature of the problem of poverty. The revealing story of the UK Community Development Projects contained in the CDP Inter-Project team report 'Gilding the Ghetto', published just three years ago, is summed up in the following words: '. . .the Poverty Programme, although arising from the problems of poverty and exploitation experienced by those living in the older declining areas, was not developed in order to solve or alleviate *their* problems, but to help the state meet *its* problems in dealing with these people'.[13] The conclusion is that unless policies and actions are geared to meet the underlying causes of need, there cannot be lasting solutions and an end to poverty.

It is surely no longer possible to deny the truth of what Henry George wrote one hundred years ago: 'I assert that the injustice of society, not the niggardliness of nature, is the cause of the want and misery which the current theory attributes to over-population.'[14] He saw very clearly at that stage of the development of the USA economy that somewhere in the innermost working of the system, which was, superficially, opening up a future of great bounty and hope, there were injustices and inequalities which made the persistence of poverty inevitable. Those injustices and inequalities remain within the system to this day. Despite the advances of economic and technological power in modern societies, a process of marginalisation whereby some groups and individuals — and some regions — are by-passed and condemned to relative or absolute misery is to be observed in all modern economies including Ireland. It is to that fact, and to its implications, that attention must be directed in the evolution of our social planning.

In modern Irish society, and in all the so-called advanced societies, there are problems of general and aggravated inequality which affect large numbers of people. The 1975 NESC Report on Social Policy refers to circumstances in which specific inequalities are more extreme and more lasting than could possibly be explained by individual differences; in which specific deprivations are correlated; and in which deprivations and privileges tend to become a pattern within certain groups or families or locations. In other words, inequalities are a continuing part of the overall system and any policies devised to deal with them must be based on a clear understanding of that fact.

Approaches to a Solution

For those who believe that poverty is a function of inequality and that inequality is an inherent part of the socio-economic system inherited by the modern nations of Europe, the battle against poverty must take on a two-fold aspect — with the firm understanding that the two elements are closely linked and that one without the other must be futile. The battle must be fought to alleviate the affects of poverty *and* to bring about the changes in structures essential to the elimination of the scourge of poverty. Only in the context of a commitment to the long-term goal of elimination can even the most enlightened and far-reaching programme of alleviation through the social services and income-maintenance be of any real service. That is the lesson of the welfare state experience of the past thirty years and it is only being learned with the greatest reluctance.

A programme for alleviation of poverty involves the planned application of a whole range of social services (health, income-maintenance, education, housing and personal social services) together with certain economic and financial policies (e.g. the field of taxation) to the particular problems of individuals and groups most in need. Only by a planned approach, with a co-ordinated use of all relevant policy types, can there be any hope of success — and, even then, the danger is that no more than a very limited success rate, with individuals, will ever be achieved.

A programme for elimination, on the other hand, will combine all the positive aspects of alleviation with far-reaching economic, fiscal and legal reforms. Foremost among such reforms must be a real acceptance of the need for, and cost of, substantial redistribution of resources and full employment. A moment's consideration of the implications for the Irish national community of the setting of an early date for the achievement of truly full employment will serve to underline the radical nature of any such policy.

The nub of the whole argument is summed up in the following section from a study of the impact of social security and taxation policies in the UK on the deepseated problems of deprivation in that country.

Any serious attempt to abolish poverty endangers the whole structure of inequality in society — partly because money must be found for the poor at the expense of the rich, but also because such an attempt threatens the values which underwrite social inequality and the whole existing structure of privilege. So long as society is organised on a deeply competitive basis, it appears as indispensable that social failure should exist for individuals as a visible and possible fate. Poverty is such a fate, just as mental illness is another. Poverty cannot be considered as a residual, historically determined defect of an otherwise fair society, but as an integral element that helps support competitive social order. It follows therefore that proposals to reduce poverty often involve very much more than technical and administrative problems. They tend rather to raise issues of principle about the whole structure of society.[15]

There is a long and unhappy history of declarations of political concern for and commitment to the poor. In many countries these declarations have been accompanied by misleading statistical claims about the numbers of those in need, the dimensions of the problem, and so on. What has been singularly absent, in almost every case, has been any deep political analysis of the causes of poverty and any clearly articulated long-term policy to deal with those causes. Unless there is a change in this essential area of political decision there can be no real progress in the fight against poverty.

In the context of the broad subject of social policy against poverty, the only way forward towards any of the long-term goals of our society is through comprehensive and balanced economic and social planning. Especially is this so in respect of poverty, which is a complex problem involving, in every instance, a mixture of economic and social elements and circumstances. Since true planning relates to the definition and statement of objectives and the consequent evolution of policies and actions designed to achieve them, it is basic to any planned approach to poverty that the right objectives should be set, and fully understood.

If political leaders are not prepared to face up to the fact that poverty — as an evil in society which must be removed — can only be tackled by the application of policies which are necessarily radical and costly, then there can be no hope. It would be better to stop the pretence of tackling the problem altogether than to continue with a charade. To argue for generous alleviation is an honest policy approach. To claim that this does anything to remove poverty from society without the addition of appropriate long-term policies is totally dishonest.

In this particular area of social planning there is now a most urgent need for decisions concerning the future direction of policy. Such decisions must be based upon a proper appreciation of the nature of the problem and of the essential components of any solution. They must also be designed to win and maintain the maximum amount of public support and co-operation, not least in terms of willingness to accept the burden of cost involved.

The main thesis of this chapter has been that poverty, arising from inequality can only be effectively dealt with by policies which recognise the fundamental elements of the problem.

The point must be made that equality in the full sense may never be achieveable but that the eradication of structures which remove inequality from the area of random chance and institutionalise it must be a major objective. Tawney put it in the following striking words:

It may well be the case that capricious inequalities are in some measure inevitable, in the sense that, like crime and disease, they are a malady which the most ingenious precautions cannot wholly overcome. But, when crime is known as crime, and disease as disease, the ravages of both are circumscribed by the mere fact that they are recognised for what they are, and described by their proper names,not by flattering euphemisms. And a society which is convinced that inequality is an evil need not be alarmed because evil is one which cannot wholly be subdued. In recognising the poison it will have armed itself with an antidote. It will have deprived inequality of its sting by stripping it of its esteem.[16]

Justice is Indivisible

Ireland, as we have seen, is by European standards, a country afflicted by widespread poverty and need, but it has been correctly pointed out that 'the condition of most of the world is such that even Ireland's poverty may be seen as relative wealth'.[17]

We live in a world in which one billion human beings are illiterate while the means exist to teach them; in which 70 per cent of the children of the Third World are hungry while the means exist to feed them; and in which over eight hundred millions are trapped in deep and degrading mass poverty while the means exist to provide for them. Our world spends twenty times as much each year on the weapons of destruction as it does on development aid. And none of these terrible things happen by accident.

The poverty, illiteracy and misery which are the lot of millions of men, women and children around the world result from injustice and inequality within the economic system. That system gives rise to the powerlessness and exploitation of the poor. Changing the system will require change that is revolutionary in extent and in nature. The consistent call of the peoples of the Third World is for justice and dignity and these will come about only through a remarkable transformation of the world order. Nothing less will do.

But the concept of justice is indivisible. The poverty and injustice of Irish society and the desperate need and exploitation experienced in so many developing countries are linked. They result directly from the same flawed and inhuman system. They will be eradicated only by solutions of the same, far-reaching kind. There is a direct relationship between the willingness of governments in the developed world to commit resources and assist in solving the problems of countries and peoples far away. The refusal of the previous Irish government to accept that widespread poverty here is the result of structural injustices was paralleled by short-sighted and non-analytical approaches to world development needs. It was the same government, in the same year, which first frustrated and then ended the work of Combat Poverty and which cut bilateral aid by 40 per cent.

Finding the lasting solutions to poverty, which are necessary for the social cohesion of Irish society and for the peace of the world, must be seen as a political task. An appropriate mixture of principle, detailed analysis and leadership is what is required. To wait for the emergence of a consensus on the issue will be to wait forever. No great change, no great social or political advance, ever grew out of a consensus. Change must be brought about by courageous political leadership allied to hard and patient political and technical work. Above all it must be brought about by harmonising the skills and insights of people themselves, and especially of poor and deprived people. Policies for people, rather than policies for administrators and institutions, must be developed. For us in Ireland, such policies — and such politics — will demand a break from all that has gone before. But then, what has gone before has made our society what it is.

REFERENCES

1. Henry George, *Progress and Poverty* (reprinted London, 1966).

2. V. George and R. Lawson (eds), *Poverty and Inequality in Common Market Countries* (London, 1980).

3. Adrian Sinfield, 'A comparative View of Poverty Research' *(Social Studies,* Vol. 4, No. 1 (Spring 1975).

4. P. Marris and M. Rein, *Dilemmas of Social Reform* (Harmondsworth, 1974).

5. Marris and Rein, ibid.

6. Dr M. Woods T.D., Minister for Health and Social Welfare. *Dail Debates,* Vol. 325, No. 5, Col. 899.

7. Frank Cluskey T.D., Parliamentary Secretary to the Minister for Social Welfare, speaking in Dail Eireann on the Second Reading of the Social Welfare Bill, 1977.

8. T.J. Barrington, 'Why Don't Things Happen?' Paper delivered to the Action Against Poverty Seminar, Kilkenny, November 1974.

9. V. George and P. Wilding, *Ideology and Social Welfare* (London, 1976).

10. Frank Cluskey T.D., Parliamentary Secretary to the Minister for Social Welfare. Paper delivered to the ICEM Symposium on Social Planning, Dublin, March 1976.

11. Richard Titmuss, *Commitment to Welfare* (London, 1968).

12. Dermot Clifford, 'The Public, the Client, and the Social Services' (Social Studies Occasional Papers in Social Research, 1975).

13. CDP Inter-Project Editorial Team, *Gilding the Ghetto* (London, 1977).

14. George, op. cit.

15. J.C. Kincaid, *Poverty and Equality in Britain* (Harmondsworth, 1973).

16. R.H. Tawney, *Equality* (London, 1964).

17. The Labour Party Programme, 1980.

Poverty and the Church

Writing about the Church and the poor is a thankless task in Ireland today. Few people, I fear, regard Irish poverty as a reality, few, that is, outside the estimated one million of our population who are managing to live below subsistence level. This figure many will reject out of hand. Most of the rest will say that poverty is the State's problem — the Church should not need to meddle.

Certainly we are in a changing society, one that is now more self-centred, more urbanised, more industrialised and competitive than that which the older generation grew up with. The traditional influence of the Church is probably weakening, and, therefore, the alternative of interference by the State in private and social life is becoming more widely acceptable, and, indeed, expected.

The Church, therefore, must use her influence in non-traditional areas. She must accommodate her practice to this social change. She cannot modify her basic teachings, but she can develop the deeper implications of the old truths and express them in language which the new generation, who live in a new milieu, will appreciate. In such a way she can draw the changing scene into her care. The old virtue of almsgiving will thus become voluntary contributions to the underprivileged; widows and orphans, who figured prominently in traditional prayers, will be joined by addicts and social misfits, and homeless and abandoned wives. She will then be doing as St Paul did with the basic teaching of Christ, when, through his urging, and even more so through the impact of his life and the lives of his converts, he made that teaching acceptable to the lives and problems of non-Jews.

One of the frightening aspects of modern life is the extent to which we can all be held responsible for actually creating poverty without being conscious of it. We have accepted competitive success as a norm almost everywhere, in business, in life, and, with even less excuse, in education. Those who reach the top, or near it, succeed; those who do not reach the top fail. The failures are then regarded as inadequate. They are looked on as mainly non-productive. This justifies putting them aside as worthless, or nearly so — and society discusses them as problems, and either hides them away as inmates in large institutions, or herds them as units or hands into depersonalising factories and flats and workers' terraces. Worse still, patronisingly, it gives them, without consultation, what someone decides should be enough to keep body and soul together. They accept this and see no reduction of their basic humanity in doing so.

The fact that the hand-out is uniform for most circumstances, and is seldom sufficient, is bad, but it is by no means the least of the harm done. What has already been done to them is the great wrong; already they are reduced, depersonalised, debased and degraded in their own esteem.

Educating the Poor

The problem has many facets for the Church. In Ireland the Church has had a near monopoly in schools for a long time, in the sense that most schools are and have been religious owned. Not often, however, have we produced anyone able and willing to present a theory of education that would stand out as richly Christian. Neither, indeed, have we produced a richly Christian body of thought on any social topic.

In the sphere of education, we were caught in a trap. We had to be fair to our pupils and their families, and not rock their particular boat. These families were poor for the most part, so we accepted a system that would get them what they wanted, what they came to school for, — a place in the economic system. Many of our pupils did not succeed in spite of our efforts, (and how great these efforts were only someone who had to work the system knows). Some of these chose to emigrate, — we did not have time to prepare them for this either — and they were effectively lost from our sight. We were tragically purblind, for what was done with good intentions can now be used to convict us of neglect.

Indeed it is possible to argue that we had little option. The publication in 1929 of the Encyclical *Divine Illius Magistri* had a specific reason. It was made universal and applied where it should never have been applicable. Such loyalty was no virtue. The theory that the schools were the agents of the parents left them at the mercy of parents, who, because of poverty, needed the shortest road to success for their children. We should have been partners of these parents. Schools did little to inform or educate them, or to meet the needs of those children who could not benefit from the system. Church schools had been set up very often to provide satisfactory alternatives to religiously objectionable ones. They had to compete with these to retain their pupils. At the same time Church schools were kept dependent on State support and were cynically compelled by this dependence to co-operate in many educationally doubtful schemes which the government in power at any particular time required.

It is to the Church's credit that most of her schools were established to teach the poor. They were, however, forced to concentrate on the academically intelligent or bright. The weak got less attention, and little thought was paid to working out a system of education for poor children who would remain poor and who would never 'make it'. How much effort went into discovering talents that were hidden by their poverty; How was the self-defeating attitude of poor children countered?

A more basic fault was the ease with which the Church overlooked the always revolutionary New Testament teaching on the poor and on poverty. Even yet, we do not see the poor as blessed: so we could not teach them this strange truth enunciated in the Sermon on the Mount. Unlike Jesus or the Apostles, we still find it very difficult to identify with the poor, and so to know best how to help them. Probably we do not wish to, or do not feel any great urgency to do so. In many countries the poor were disenchanted with the Church: they were made to feel the Church was not with them because they appeared to have nothing to give. The basic reason was, the Church forgot, and the poor never knew that because they are blessed they have, therefore, most to give — they can give a blessing.

We in Ireland have been fortunate with our poor: literally we have been blessed by them. There has always been a close relationship between the poor, and, indeed, all marginal people, and the Irish Church. What we are as Christian people we own under God to this closeness, for generally speaking our people were the rejects, the ones who had, and still have, no 'contacts', no 'clout', no bargaining power but what the Church provided. They were the ones who feared a rebuff if they asked anything for themselves, and anyway they did not know how to ask.

166

It was they who made our Church, they who blessed us, and they who had a strong influence on the Catholic Church in the English-speaking world. There are signs that many would like to forget our origins in poverty.

Peace and Change

One of the reasons why Jesus chose to be poor and could identify so easily with the poor was that they were not afraid of change. So it was understandable that Jesus had to warn his disciples that when he brought peace, he was not promoting any sort of static peace. Peace must be always striving. Change, movement, is essential to peace, as it is to Christianity — we are a pilgrim Church, a restless one, always on the way to the Father. To get to the Father we have to move to Jesus, letting those lead us who are loaded down with their own heavy burdens of care. 'Those whom the world thinks contemptible are the ones that God has chosen — those who are nothing at all show up those who are everything' (1 Corinthians 1:29).

The rich who came to Jesus, people like Zachaecus or the Roman officer, were prepared to change. They differed from their fellows. The rich have always been afraid of change and this fear colours all their thinking. For the rich, concepts acquire a different meaning, and generally a very static selfish one: peace is a powerful example.

Peace to the rich means that they be left alone, they should not be disturbed. The same can be true of the Church; where she is rich she distrusts change. This is most noticeable whenever the Church emerges from underground. It tends to become institutional and static almost overnight. It aligns itself with the powerful. The changes of Vatican 11 were unwelcome in comfortable Church areas.

The same blindness can affect those who become attached to a valued way of life, to a prestigious ancestor, or even to the founder of a religious community. Such people feel rich in tradition, have riches others do not enjoy: their loyalty can resent and even resist all change. They see no need for growth. or for change to meet changing traditions. Most religious orders were established to meet a particular need and attracted generous people. Some at least became institutions, rich in heritage, but therefore jealous of change, unyielding. They catered for one type of poverty in the name of the Church, but neglected to look at the changing patterns from one generation to the next, or as the inner heart of the poverty grew and showed different more noxious fruits. It is refreshing today to see the superiors of the St Vincent de Paul Society in Ireland exposing new needs to its members, new forms of poverty, reaching out to those whom Pope Paul VI called the new poor of our time.

Our giving, or our teaching for the poor is not all one-sided. The poor have much to give and to teach the Church. We can certainly learn from 'the solidarity of the poor, their sense of sharing and mutual help, their common sense in the presence of theorists and the dreamers, their acuity in the face of love and of death, their patience'. Their life is often 'an act of living an unknown widsom', part of the secret of the poor.

The Bible and The Poor

It was in this spirit of deep insight into real need, of excitement and good news, that Peter and John could preface their reply to the beggarman cripple with the phrase which it would be well if Christians could say more often — they had no money to give him. What we should not forget is that once they helped him, they actually left him financially poor. He could be said to be a self-employed man whose trade disappeared: the Apostles took his livelihood from him when they helped him to walk. But he gave it up joyfully for personal freedom. That exchange, incidentally, is a challenge we are often reluctant, or unable to present, when we call on the young. We are afraid to ask them to renounce prosperity, or we dare not. We are ourselves too attached to things to understand that others may actually be glad to be free of them. The young are not afraid of change: indeed, they have to be conditioned to fear poverty. If the Church fears poverty, as it often seems to, its fear is something that it had to learn, and it certainly was not Jesus or his disciples who taught it.

From incidents like the one with Peter's beggarman, and from many sayings of Jesus, it is understandable that in the proper circumstances the Bible can come as a complete surprise to the reader. It can be an exciting experience for the poor when read not merely in an archaic literary version, but pondered in a modern one. This applies particularly to reading it with a group, with people who are sensitive to one another and sufficiently at ease to be able to ask, can it be true? For this reason the introduction of up-to-date translations rather than established literary translations is so providential. Indeed, the use of vernacular in the scripture and liturgy is more than an important concession to those who are not well educated in the old sense. It is a right. The poor, like others, still need people at times to explain the Bible to them. Not everyone can explain it: ideally there should be people available who have been acquainted with poverty, and people for whom the Bible was and is an experience, a surprise and a consolation.

It is important then that we all return to the Bible to appreciate poverty. There is evil in poverty, but it can be transmuted to good by the poor. It is far too easy to be romantic about poverty, too easy to believe that poverty is approved of by Jesus. We have to sympathise, however, with the 'well-off' people and with many parents when they come to the Bible; they are many passages. even ones that they love as literature, which are anti-wealth and therefore quite disturbing for them and for their aspirations. At least, however, one can offer these, too, some hope; one can say to them with Dag Hammarsk jold, 'Bless your uneasiness: it is a sign that there is still life in you.'

The Irish religious tradition is one where the poor were well cared for. Generosity and hospitality to the poor ranked among the virtues. Even in prayer, perhaps particularly in prayer, the Irish had to be hospitable and think of the needs of others even before their own. Prayer for oneself alone was a *paidir ghann,* a stingy prayer. The giving of merely 'surplus' prayer to others was not enough. In the same tradition we read of a Frenchman visiting the South-West of Ireland in 1790 and wondering at a religion that, he said, 'encouraged politeness and lenience'. (O'Riordain). Fr O'Flynn of the eponymous song was not a false portrait then: he was in the same *sagart a ruin* tradition, pastoral in his life, unselfish, kind. The understanding Christian, generous in his giving to those in any kind of need, was secure and faithful to his own Christianity, to his own faith.

A Practical Faith

While spirit of leniency should be encouraged particularly in relation to the failures and weaknesses of the economically and socially poor, and particularly those weaknesses that stem from environmental or hereditary deficiencies, it should not in any way detract from the personal responsibility of these poor. To ascribe their failings simply to factors beyond their control is to deny them responsibility, and that does nothing either for their dignity or for their freedom. We all have to keep in mind our common responsibility for many of the failings of the poor. This form of brotherhood is essential to the teaching of the Church.

Unemployment

It is difficult, of course, for people like, say, the chronically unemployed father of a family to accept all the talk he may hear about common responsibility, or the excitement or the power of the Gospel and the dynamism of Christianity and the brotherhood of Christians. For him it is rarely anything more than a pipe dream. He is faced every morning with cruel personal, family and social problems arising from his continued unemployment. These destroy his morale and affect his family and life. He cannot be blamed for being cynical and suspicious. The chronically unemployed know hunger. Hunger desensitizes: it is brutalising. It dulls the critical faculties. We accept this for people far away from us. We are slower to accept it for our own. It probably does not occur to us to ask how far continuous undernourishment, falling short of actual hunger, contributes to the same end, even amongst our neighbours.

Such experience as we have would seem to indicate that sub-standard living has many deleterious effects on the critical and even the moral faculties. Along with all the suffering of going without necessities, a chronically unemployed person suffers from the failure of people to appreciate him. He is aware that he is almost certainly regarded as a work-shy malingerer, or one who is unwilling to work because he can draw more from the dole, or from a combination of dole and 'nixers' — dishonest, it other words. Where there was once dynamism there is now total depression, inertia and rejection. This the Church must save him from.

The Church must protect and restore him, and more. Conscious of the Good News she has for him, she must show herself ready to put forward practical suggestions and never cease to make concrete endeavours and involve him in them. She cannot pass this duty and privilege over to others. Accepting her duty and alerting her members to it is part of the Church's responsibility for the poor.

The only real and long-term correction for poverty, unemployment and so on is restraint on the part of those who have plenty, or enough, and have the courage to try to see their restraint is put to good effect. More than that, there must be unselfishness on the part of those who have the power to produce. I do not think the Church emphasises sufficiently this moral duty of intelligent restraint and generosity today, and the duty of making reasonable contributions to the needy. We are not forceful enough in our condemnation of waste. We are too tolerant of consumerism. 'That is how we strike a balance,' as Paul told the Corinthians (2 Corinthians 8:14). The giving of gifts from superfluity is of little religious use (cf. Mark 12:41). We do not assert strongly enough that personal or community growth is not optional for us. Our giving must always hurt. As our selfishness eats into us, superfluity gets smaller and smaller, and soon we cannot afford to give at all. This is a thought not often enough stressed: restraint and genuine generosity are necessary Christian virtues. Here again is a thought we are reluctant to put to the young, and so we fail them.

If those poor referred to were to read the Scriptures in the way suggested, they would become rebels. They would rebel against their own rejection and they would rise up against the waste that is part of modern living. It is out of such rejection that what we call liberation theology has come. Here in Ireland we have need of some new form of liberation theology, one for ourselves. Our poor are not free people. The personal liberty of many of the fringe people of our community is destroyed. The unemployed man is only one example of a person's liberty being so restricted and confined as to be destroyed altogether. He has to stay close to his local unemployment office in order to collect the money to which he is legally entitled. He is expected to take any job that offers, however unsuitable. He has to have a permanent address. When all is said and done, a permanent address is much more than Jesus had.

Community Homes

People forced by age, infirmity or poverty to live in large institutions are expected to sacrifice most of their personal freedom. They cannot, to take a simple humane example, bring in their personal friends to entertain them as they did at home. This restriction is usually in the name of order or efficiency, and appears to continue until the persons involved are virtually isolated. If anyone can speak from experience of Pope Paul VI's 'new loneliness', they can. Such homes derive from an out-

171

moded system of custodial care where little accommodation has been made to new social thinking.

In the same way it would hardly occur to the management of many of the various kinds of institutions to consult the residents already there before accepting a new person to what must be a very tightly packed inter-involved community. The residents cannot be said to be denied freedom of association: they are certainly denied freedom of non-association, a freedom which in this case might be much more necessary. Few object, however. They are poor or old; they do not count and generally have no influential friends to get them accepted: they should, therefore, be duly grateful to all concerned and stay there out of the way!

From the Church's point of view it is unfortunate that religious are often responsible for the day-to-day administration of such homes, and while their intentions are excellent, they have ceased to think about the system and have simply accepted it. Perhaps economic necessity is forcing them. It is definitely another social field where there is need for a bold independent christian policy. People like Jean Vanier do the Church a great service here. It is all the more necessary as we try to serve today's needs of today's poor when we are in such urgent need of their blessing.

Violence and The Poor

Modern living is unfavourable to liberty. Liberty is being dissipated and even killed off. The different acts of violence which we hear of so commonly today contribute to this end. If an old person living alone is molested or attacked at home, every old person in the area lives in fear and is effectively denied freedom. Each attack on women ensures that few women, particularly younger women, feel free to move about, to walk unescorted, to babysit, to look after lonely or ailing people, to do the many things that christian charity might suggest. When a hitch-hiker turns out to be more of a scamp than a traveller, the freedom of hundreds of young people to travel cheaply and adventurously and joyfully is taken from them.

A fact often forgotten is that any sort of violence anywhere destroys many people's freedom. The poor are the first to suffer, and they suffer most. The dreadful state of fear can only be really cured by a total outlawing of violence. We must restore the teaching of the Gospel on care, concern, gentleness and peace to full practice. The poor need this and its protection more than the rich. Because the rich are people of property, society will look after them as its own, and care for them and their property much better. Society indeed cares for property and protects it far more clearly than people. If you have no property, God help you. The Church, as Pope John Paul reminds us, must speak for those who have no one to speak for them.

Conclusion

The excuse is frequently put forward that what one person can do in the Church for the poor is so slight that it has to be negligible. So why try? This is to deny the spectacular increase in output when a few come together to act; to deny the efficacy of specifically christian work and the value of a symbolic act. During the first weeks of the German occupation of Paris Cardinal Suhard said, 'The priest of tomorrow must be prepared to take the initiative, must have a ready ear for souls and situations, must adapt himself so that the Church may be ever young.' What he was thinking of may appear from this illustration: 'A man who lights a candle can give light to a whole procession.'

God uses poor, weak examples, seems to prefer them, indeed, even when they appear useless. St Francis and Brother Charles de Foucauld come to mind. The value of the sign, of the witness, is great: it can be used by God as a true light to the world, and that is why we must let our little light shine. In today's affluent world we need such simple signs more than ever before. We need such witness to bring hope to many people whom affluence will pass by, or whom affluence will disappoint. Hope is a powerful virtue. It is even an extremely powerful instrument in the hands of the poor.

It would be a great mistake, however, to imagine that the poor are always the receivers. In the time of Jesus the educated, the experts, the well-off, took barbaric steps to get rid of the shame of being continuously corrected by the Carpenter's Son. A few days later they found their assembly being addressed by Peter and John. There were 'uneducated lay men' who spoke to them with astonishing assurance. Where they asked, did they get it? We need to learn this assurance, this confidence, from the poor. When we do, many will call us arrogant. They will contest our arguments. Neither Peter nor John, nor, indeed, St Paul, was worried about such a charge of arrogance, or such contempt. They did not care what waters they muddied when they spoke. Quite often today, like Peter or Paul or John, the poor can teach the Church that prudence is a very limited virtue. The world loves prudence. As often as not it is a very convenient hindrance to inconvenient action.

Pope Paul VI was very conscious of all this. He called for a new conscience for our time. He knew what the poor suffer. He recognised the new poor, the product of our time and life-style. He felt that we had forgotten the power, the dynamism to be found in the Gospel, and we ran after other gospels. We must show the chronically unemployed that this is not mere talk. We possess power, we know we do, and we can use and we will. To make it relevant for all we must take careful note of the ever-changing circumstances in which we and they live. Christians live in the world. We must take account of what the Gospel could do today for that poor man if we let it.

In Ireland we have become too fearful of the possible consequences of our actions on our status. We are class conscious. We risk losing some of our newly required comfort. So we do nothing and hope nobody reminds us that the cock is crowing. We concentrate on the mistakes which concerned well-meaning Christians make, categorising them, criticising them, knocking them to the ground in our efforts to do good.

We are the Church, but God help us, all the good it does is that we claim to speak as if we were inerrant, if not quite infallible, and the discordance is not very inspiring.

Note
This chapter is the draft completed by Bishop Peter Birch before his untimely death which prevented him from completing work on reference material.

Poor People and the Law

Walter Walsh

'The law, like the Ritz Hotel, is open to rich and poor alike.'
This remark was almost savage coming from an English judge
at the end of the nineteenth century. His criticism was directed
at the narrow access available to the legal system in his day.
The bitter truth of his comment lingers on in modern Ireland.
In addition to restricted access there is a further link between
poverty and the law, more sinister and more direct: it is the
strong and unrepentant support given by the law to the social
structures which create and maintain poverty in our midst.

The reasons for the traditional failure of the law to confront
such a difficult problem as poverty are not hard to find. For a
start, poor people do not make the rules in our society and laws
are neither made by them nor for them; also, once made, law is
an effective but costly tool and it is not the poor who have
wielded it to their advantage. The sad irony is that one of the
most influential forces in the shaping of society benefits least
of all those who need it most.

The indifference of the law does nothing to hide the grim
realities that 'poor people do exist, in substantial numbers,
in this country; poor people are accorded low status in our
society; poor people have and are accorded few rights in Ireland
today'.[1] Furthermore, future attempts to change this situation
are unlikely to be effective without the aid of the law. This
might not be the case if want of money were their only disadvantage, but unfortunately poverty is a more complex problem. Unmet need and powerlessness on almost every level
combine to achieve their devastating effect. Legal reforms are
necessary to restore to poor people some of the control over
their own lives which is so plainly lacking in their present situation. Such improvements must be made part of a wide-
ranging and determined attack on poverty from every angle.

There are two aspects of the law especially relevant to poor
people, each of which shall be dealt with in turn. Firstly, there
is the effect of legislation and in particular that directed specifi-

cally at areas of social need; the second aspect is the question of legal services and access to justice. The following analysis of both issues rests on the twin assumptions that poverty is remediable and that poverty ought to be remedied. It is also rooted in the belief that radical reform is impossible without the assistance of the law.

Social Medicine

The use of legislation to correct imbalances in our social structures is not new. Already on Ireland's statute books there are numerous examples of government intervention into areas in which the interests of private enterprise have not mingled easily with the common good.[2] This has caused the rise of the welfare state which 'undertakes responsibility for the well-being of those citizens who, because of circumstances beyond their control, cannot provide minimum care, education, housing or subsistence for themselves'.[3]

It is patently clear, however, that poverty has not been frightened away by legislative reforms to date. There has been no planned policy which has set out to identify the problems of the poor and to seek suitable remedies. Instead there has been a series of faltering and disjointed efforts to treat isolated symptoms of structural inequality. Even these timid attempts have failed to incorporate the two ingredients essential in any legislation genuinely intended to help poor people: the creation of clearly defined entitlements to minimum standards in all areas of basic need (e.g. health, education, housing and income) together with the provision of adequate procedures for their enforcement.

Rights without adequate enforcement procedures are equivalent to no rights at all. This point is either pitifully misunderstood or cynically disregarded. Consequently,

'the problem of . . . enforcement of laws designed to protect and benefit the less powerful sections of society is massive. So great is it and so feeble the response by government that it is questionable whether it is useful to go on making such laws if, as at present, they are to go unenforced or largely unenforced. In these circumstances we are led to doubt that such laws are intended to be anything more than elaborate exercises in public relations.'[4]

In other words, to help poor people it is not enough to create merely declaratory rights and obligations. Much of our social legislation does nothing more than this.[5]

These comments are intended not to deny but to confirm the potential importance of progressive legislation in attacking the causes and alleviating the effects of poverty. Perhaps the fatal limitation is that it depends on political courage and public concern for its enactment.

The Myth of Equality Before the Law

Access to legal services is the second aspect of the law immediately important to poor people. In the words of Thomas Ehrlich, a leading American poverty lawyer, 'the thin margins on which poor people live make law a crucial instrument for their survival'.[6] Their bleak situation, however, lends law a darker colour than that seen by those in more comfortable surroundings. For instance, demand for family remedies is often the result of pressures caused by unemployment, overcrowding and shortages of food and money.[7] Equally, the relationship between high crime rates and deprived areas is no coincidence. Expressed in another way, 'poor people are not just like rich people without money'.[8] If and when they see a lawyer, it is normally because they have no choice.

Restricted access to lawyers makes nonsense of the constitutional guarantee that 'all citizens shall, as human persons, be held equal before the law'.[9] The high cost of legal services is the most obvious obstruction to equal access to justice for poor people. But it is not the only factor and its impact has now been lessened by the introduction of limited schemes of legal aid.

The failure of the traditional form of private practice to meet the needs of poor people can be explained by other reasons also. Commercial realities seldom locate solicitors' offices in deprived areas. The geographical divide is widened by the huge cultural gap which sometimes opens up between solicitors and poorer clients and which appears on the surface to separate their interests. Such, indeed, is often the case, solicitors commonly acting as agents or representatives of landlords, employers, trading concerns, moneylenders, police, central and local government bureaucracies, etc. A visit to a solicitor's office comes to be regarded as an intimidating and undesirable experience.

Another obstacle can be doubt or ignorance as to the nature

of the problem. The law has all the complexities and none of the thrills of an Agatha Christie mystery, which is enough to prevent many poor people from enforcing rights which have been unjustly abused. Sometimes even the lawyer does not perceive the legal dimension. 'Job rights, social security, unemployment compensation, public assistance, health insurance, retirement funds, and a host of similar interests tend to be the characteristic forms of economic wealth for the poor.'[10] The legal profession has not yet acquired the skills necessary to protect them.

Legal Aid And Ending The Myth

The narrow boundaries within which the existing legal profession operates leave it far removed from the everyday interests of poor people. Growing awareness of the difficulties faced by deprived sections of the community who are denied legal remedies has prompted the State to shoulder at least some of the burden of providing equal access to justice. It has done this by introducing limited schemes of legal aid in both criminal and civil matters.

The criminal legal aid scheme came into operation in 1965.[11] It covers cases in which the accused is unable to afford a lawyer and the charge is either sufficiently serious or there are exceptional circumstances such as to make legal aid 'essential in the interests of justice'. The scheme provides the free services of a solicitor and, if necessary, counsel to present the case. Its major fault lies in the sweeping discretion open to the judge who decides whether legal aid should be granted or not. This has resulted in uneven application. Also, there is no provision for the giving of advice before the applicant has already been brought to court.

The civil legal aid and advice scheme is a more recent innovation. Its origins are interesting, drawn from three separate sources. The first was the creation of the Free Legal Advice Centres (FLAC) in 1969 by a group of young law students and practitioners. Their intention was to bring about the introduction of a comprehensive scheme of civil legal aid and advice by exposing the extent of unmet legal need and providing advice and assistance free of charge to those unable to afford a lawyer. This organisation dealt with almost 40,000 cases up until the opening of the government scheme in August 1980. It was quick to point out that these figures represented only 'the tip of the iceberg'[12] as the voluntary nature of their work restricted them to part-time centres in urban areas.

Their experience attracted considerable public attention and caused the introduction of the second catalyst, the Pringle Committee on Civil Legal Aid and Advice, which reported in December 1977.[13] It called for the implementation of a scheme based on a combination of the services of law centres and solicitors in private practice. The government failed to act on this and less than two years later were held to be in breach of the European Convention on Human Rights and Fundamental Freedoms by not providing any means for a 47-year-old Cork woman to obtain the legal separation she desired to end her irretrievably broken marriage.[14]

The civil legal aid and advice scheme bears little resemblance to its criminal cousin. It has no basis in statute. Instead, it is run by a Legal Aid Board appointed by the Minister for Justice.[15] In contrast to the criminal scheme it operates from Law Centres established in major towns (ignoring the Pringle Committee's proposals for the use of private practitioners). The scheme is not free, the contribution payable depending on the means of the applicant and whether legal aid, which includes representation in court, or advice only is sought.

Since its introduction the scheme has come under justified attack from concerned groups and individuals.[16] There is no reason for the artificial distinction between civil and criminal cases; the rural community is discriminated against by the decision not to use private practitioners; numerous excluded areas of law severely reduce its potential impact, particularly in matters most vital to poor people such as social welfare and employment tribunals; it does not cover test cases, which can be of substantial benefit to the poor; its highly bureaucratic structures require social welfare recipients and medical card holders to undergo further means tests; there are restrictive income limits; the contribution required is not based on the applicant's actual ability to pay; and there is no room for community development.

The Impartial Lawyer

In the final point lies hidden the most penetrating criticism of the existing legal services, both those provided through private practice and by the State. They depend on a lawyer whose skills are not geared to meet the real needs of poor people.

In the traditional model the lawyer is seen as an objective and impartial dispenser of advice, to all who need it, about law which is a product of tradition and which is also the bedrock of liberal democracy. His job is to apply rules in a mechanical fashion, not to enquire too closely into their effect. Obedience to the traditional model is encouraged by a system of legal education which bows to the demands of commerical practice. But the independence and impartiality promised by this approach is, like the Scarlet Pimpernel, elusive. A lawyer who unquestioningly serves the status quo maintains it. The elimination of poverty demands that the status quo be changed.

The traditional model is defective because it is incapable of treating anything but the symptoms of poverty. One of the most discouraging impressions for those working in the FLAC centres, with their unrivalled experience in providing legal services for the poor, was the depressing regularity with which their clients returned. Most legal difficulties were the inevitable and tragic products of the hopeless situation in which poor people find themselves. The individual casework approach taken by existing legal services leaves untouched the structural imbalances which cause the problems. Such work has been compared with that of doctors who regularly put splints on patients who have fallen through an open manhole. Surely it is better to cover the manhole than to continue patching up the broken bones? In the words of one community worker:

'Casework can be said to have served the present system admirably, since its basic assumption is that there is nothing wrong with society, and that problems are the problems of individuals who cannot adjust in some way. This individual emphasis on clients' problems obscures the situation of a human condition viewed collectively and the simple recognition of poverty as a structural phenomenon rather than as an individual misfortune'.[17]

The New Wave in Legal Services for the Poor

This analysis suggests that existing legal services are constitutionally incapable of tackling the underlying causes of poverty. Alternatives have been sought. As Nick Warren, solicitor of the Child Poverty Action Group, says: 'The poor do not think that solicitors have anything to offer. At present, they are probably right but this need not and should not be the case.'[18] The exception in Ireland to the standard pattern of legal neglect of the poor is the Coolock Community Law Centre.

The movement to establish community or neighbourhood law centres began during the 'War on Poverty' introduced in the USA by the Johnson administration in the early sixties. As it is described by one writer: 'The New Wave in legal services is a recognition that the overriding interest of the poor is the elimination of poverty, an interest which lawyers for the poor must represent as advocates.'[19] It demands that the lawyer abandon his traditional role of so-called impartiality and instead campaign energetically for the cause of the poor. The idea spread to the United Kingdom where there are now over thirty community law centres in operation.

In practice their approaches vary between aggressive and wide-ranging strategies to upset rules of law and administration which maintain the 'structural imbalance' of the system against the poor, and less ambitious attempts to simply provide access to the law within the community.[20] In an Irish context, the work of the Coolock Community Law Centre in Dublin has been affected by two particular disadvantages since its foundation by FLAC in 1975. Firstly, it has never had secure funding for more than a year in advance; and, secondly, it has been forced to spend much time on individual casework due to the lack of civil legal aid during the first five years of its existence.

These obstacles have not prevented the Coolock Community Law Centre from making a significant impact in an area marked by high unemployment and its attendant problems. Its aims are threefold: to provide a full-time free legal service to individuals and groups within the community; to tackle with the local people problems arising from the casework where an individual solution would be either legally impossible or only satisfactory in the short term; and to promote a knowledge and awareness of legal rights within the community.[21]

In achieving these objectives, two steps are seen as essential. One is the employment of a Community Law Officer to develop the centre as a neighbourhood resource and to enable it to deal with underlying grievances revealed by individual casework. The other is local involvement and participation, principally through the appointment of a Management Committee representing community and tenants' associations, trade unions, youth clubs and so on. Dave Ellis, the Community Law Officer, points out that these organisations 'are the real strength of working class people and any community law centre worth its salt places itself firmly in a position of supporting such groups'.[22] The centre is now fully independent of FLAC and under complete control of the local Management Committee.

The most graphic way of describing the work done by the Coolock Community Law Centre is to give examples. These may be broken down into the following categories:

(a) *The Test Case* is one of any kind which is likely to set a beneficial precedent for people in the area. For instance the centre mounted a successful legal challenge in the Supreme Court to the ESB practice of cutting off the electricity supply to people who had fallen into arrears, without giving them a fair chance to pay.

(b) *The Group Case,* in which the centre acts on behalf of a number of people, whether they have formed an organisation or not. The Coolock Community Law Centre recently represented the next-of-kin of the victims in the public enquiry into the Stardust Disaster, which took place in its own area.

(c) *Community Development* requires helping local organisations to get off the ground, advising them on possible courses of action and representing them where necessary. The Coolock Women's Group is a case in point. The solicitor, Maire Bates, felt that the women she was helping with regard to family problems were still isolated despite successful legal action. The group was formed and now provides welcome support to local mothers bringing up children alone or in difficult circumstances.

(d) *Community Education* involves informing people of their rights and how to obtain them. The Community Law Officer has made several once-off talks to various bodies, run a series of citizens' rights courses and given classes to senior school students on a comprehensive range of legal rights and obligations. Publications include guides on employment, social welfare and disabled persons' rights, a leaflet on legal aid and a regular newsletter circulated in the area.

(e) *Community Research* is carried out into social grievances exposed by the casework. A major survey on the effectiveness of barring orders was instrumental in bringing about changes in the relevant legislation.[23] More recently the centre published a critical study of the social welfare appeals system.[24]

(f) *The Individual Case* is a necessary remedy to personal problems, though it should not be allowed to swallow up the other work of the centre.

These illustrations of the work done by a community law centre indicate its potential value in striking at the economic, social and psychological paralysis which is the most crippling feature of poverty. It is one way of giving poor people the extra leverage necessary to compensate for their weaker position in society.

Conclusion

It would be naive to expect that the law can provide perfect solutions to all of the difficulties of poor people. Indeed, traditional emphasis on a purely legal answer to problems often arising from bad environmental conditions has proved particularly inappropriate. What the law can do is act as a double-edged weapon in fighting poverty through legislation and adequate legal services. One point that is clear from this brief examination is that both edges of the blade are in need of sharpening.

Whose job is this? Neither central government nor private practice have been eager to take on the responsibility of ensuring equal access to justice. At present the dilemma is manifested in the schizoid personality of the Incorporated Law Society of Ireland, which combines the mutually incompatible roles of custodian of the public interest and representative body of the solicitors' profession.

A more promising future lies in the creation of an independent public body responsible for the provision of adequate and suitable legal services for the whole community and with special reference to the needs of poor people.[25] Such a body could be called the Legal Services Commission and represent legal and social interests on both professional and voluntary levels. It would operate a comprehensive scheme of civil and criminal legal aid, combining private practitioners with community law centres. In its relationship with the centres it would provide financial support and demand certain requirements without infringing the principle of local control. It would publish information on legal rights and services. The Legal Services Commission would also conduct research into the extent of unmet legal needs, for example in rural areas, and seek possible remedies.

Poverty will not go away just because we ignore it. It will stay with us until we are prepared to make an unqualified commitment to the concepts of justice and equality in Irish society. It will afflict large numbers of people unlucky enough to be born into the wrong environment or to be thrown unwillingly into hardship. The law should be used to challenge this situation, not to support it.

So long as we do nothing, we richly deserve the poet's angry reproach: 'Unequal laws unto a savage race.'[26]

REFERENCES

1. Final Report of the National Committee on Pilot Schemes to Combat Poverty (1980).

2. Social legislation includes numerous statutes governing social welfare, health, housing, education, tenants' rights, employment, consumer protection and other areas.

3. Charles Reich, 'The New Property', Yale Law Journal 73 (1964) 733.

4. Brent Community Law Centre, First Report (1975) at p. 30.

5. An outstanding example is the appeals system established under the Social Welfare (Consolidation) Act, 1981.

6. Thomas Ehrlich, 'Legal Services for Poor People', Catholic University Law Review 30 (1981) 483.

7. According to the FLAC Report 1978, family law accounted for over 40 per cent of the caseload of the Free Legal Advice Centres.

8. Stephen Wexler, 'Practising Law for Poor People', Yale Law Journal 79(1970) 1049.

9. Bunreacht na hEireann, Article 40. 1.

10. Carlin and Howard, 'Legal Representation and Class Justice', UCLA Law Review 12 (1965) 381.

11. Criminal Justice (Legal Aid) Act, 1962.

12. FLAC Report 1978.

13. 'Report of the Committee on Civil Legal Aid and Advice', Prl. 6862, 1977 (The Pringle Report).

14. Johanna Airey v. Republic of Ireland (European Court of Human Rights, 9 October 1979, 6289).

15. 'Scheme of Civil Legal Aid and Advice', Prl. 8543, 1979.

16. For a very thorough critique see 'It's Rough Justice with Legal Aid' published by the Free Legal Advice Centres (2nd Ed. February 1981).

17. Alex Dunn, 'The Role of the Lawyer in the Community', unpublished, an address to the Conference on the Provision of Alternative Legal Services, Walsall, 10 January 1975.

18. 'Poverty', December 1977 no. 38 (Child Poverty Action Group).

19. Lowenstein and Waggoner, 'Neighbourhood Law Offices: the New Wave in Legal Services for the Poor', Harvard Law Review 80(1967) 805.

20. Useful descriptions of the movement in the UK are contained in 'Report and Analysis of a Community Law Centre' (Newham Rights Centre, 1975) and 'Community Need and Law Centre Practice' (Adamstown Community Trust, 1978).

21. FLAC Report 1978.

22. Dave Ellis, 'Legal Aid and the Community Centres', addressing the FLAC Seminar on 'Access to Justice and Law Centres in Ireland', Mansion House, 28 May 1977. Reprinted in the Solicitors' Gazette (July 1977) 115.

23. The survey into s.22 of the Family Law (Maintenance of Spouses and Children) Act 1976, was entitled 'Barred' (Coolock Community Law Centre, 1978) Its proposals were implemented by the Family Law (Maintenance of Spouses and Children) Act, 1981.

24. 'Social Welfare Appeals' (Coolock Community Law Centre, 1980).

25. In the USA an independent, non-profit body along these lines was set up by the Legal Services Corporation Act (1974).

26. Lord Alfred Tennyson, 'Ulysses.'

Poverty and Social Work

Noreen Kearney

In a critique of Townsend's recent monumental study of poverty in the United Kingdom[1] the reviewer makes the following statement:

> There can be few subjects which have caused more confusion, conflict, and uncertainty in social work than today's poverty and what the professional response to encountering it, thinking about it and working with human beings experiencing it, ought to be. Explanations for its existence in individuals, families and groups may range from the baldly structuralist to the unadorned personal pathologists, but COSW courses have done remarkably little to shift the mythology equating poverty with sin or to merge the deserving and the undeserving.[2]

This devastating criticism may at first glance evoke a defensive and angry reaction from social workers, more especially as the author of the statement, herself a social worker who for many years was involved in the training of social workers, could be seen as 'letting the side down'. However, on more careful consideration the validity of the view expressed becomes evident, not only in relation to the profession in the UK but also in relation to current practice in Ireland.

Yesterday's poverty did not pose the moral dilemma for charitable workers which modern, carefully screened and university trained professional social workers grapple with. Late nineteenth-century philanthropists clearly distinguished between the deserving or 'helpable' poor and those beggars and paupers whose thriftlessness and importunity determined that they be shunned like poison[3] and dealt with under the Poor Law legislation. Nowadays, with the principle of non-judgemental attitudes enshrined as one of the most sacredly observed precepts of social work, this moralistic approach of the pioneers in the Charity Organisation Society is spoken of with mild amusement, and a rather patronising acceptance. The religious and lay workers of that era are excused for not knowing any better, the assumption being that in these days of enlightenment, social workers equipped with psychological and sociological theory know exactly what should be done for and with their clients who are experiencing poverty.

It is quite clear where the early social workers stood when it came to helping the poor and the COS were in no way apologetic when describing their *modus operandi:*

> We have for convenience sake considered those in distress either as the indigent who are habitually in want, or as those who can be saved or rescued from indigence. The former, making allowance, of course, for special circumstances in each individual instance, we call, for want of a better word, ineligible for charity — the latter eligible.[4]

Eligibility was established by a system of investigation which included the gathering of detailed information on the applicant for help, the reason for his distress, the best method of helping and how future self-support could be organised, all of which was the responsibility of a worker for the COS with the title of almoner.[5]

In the UK, the forerunner of today's social worker was concerned only with the poor, her *raison d'etre* was the relief of poverty and her preoccupation with investigation into the poor person's circumstances was an attempt to ensure that any help given would not serve merely to undermine the recipient's independence. 'Ostentatious mendicancy', as one writer described it,[6] was the result of indiscriminate alms-giving and Octavia Hill, when a member of the first local committee of the COS in 1889, expressed her disapproval of the way charity was being dispensed at that time:

> I am quite awed when I think what our impatient charity is doing to the poor of London. Men who should hold up their heads as self-respecting fathers of families, learning to sing like beggars in the streets — all because we give pennies.[7]

It is not quite so clear where social workers now stand when faced with a poor client or, more specifically, when asked for assistance with a financial problem. Recent research in the UK has revealed marked ambivalence on the part of staffs of social service departments when it comes to giving material help in cash or kind which they are empowered to do under the Children and Young Persons Act (1963) in England and Wales, and more recent legislation in Scotland and Northern Ireland.[8] The research showed widespread discrepancies in the amounts paid and the situations deemed as constituting an emergency from region to region and from one officer to another.

Many social workers were unhappy about the extent to which they were faced by demands, or needs, for money payments. What is interesting about the view of those who were unhappy about this problem is that their arguments against widespread payments ranged from the 'tough' stand-point that clients should 'stand on their own feet', to radical arguments against social services discretion on grounds of equity.[9]

The views of one senior social worker in this report would make one wonder if things have changed that much since the COS's day:

So if any family with children claims not to have any food in the house I would expect the social worker to inspect the pantry and I will need satisfying that this has been done. I do not allow money to be handed over. If it's food the family is short of then the social worker must buy the food. I realise it makes more work for them but this is what social work is all about. I'm sorry if I sound extremely hard but not one penny of Section One money must be spent on cigarettes and beer, and it can so easily do so if you hand over four or five quid.[10]

It might be worth looking briefly at what happened to social work in the eighty years between the two statements above in an effort to understand some of the attitudes and approaches to poverty manifested by social workers.

Social Work as a Profession

In their search for professional status since the early part of this century, social workers have seemed desperately to want to distance themselves from the image of 'do-gooder' and the charitable worker. One way of doing this was to provide train-ing for those interested or already involved in such work, and as early as 1896 the COS instituted a scheme of lectures and practical work for its visitors and social workers: 'Many have no aptitude for almoner's work, none can do it to good purpose without study and training.'[11] By 1912 the course had been taken over by the London School of Economics and Schools of Social Education had been established in several other centres in England. By now also social work had moved into hospitals (the first hospital almoner was appointed to the Royal Free Hospital in London's Hampstead in 1895) and in 1907 a Hospital Almoners Council came into being and was given responsibility for the selection, training and appointment of almoners. Again, the hospital almoner's work was strictly concerned with the poor, her function being to ascertain who was entitled to free treatment and to ensure in so far as it was possible to do so that the benefits of medical treatment were not wasted because of the patient's poverty and consequent inability to feed, clothe and care for himself adequately.

There were two features of this development in the training and employment of social workers in England which are worth noting: the workers were exclusively female, and they tended to be drawn from the middle and upper classes.[12]

> Almoning operated entirely as an elite, paid occupation exclusively recruited from among middle-class women . . . they were deeply committed to systematic professional training and in their attempts to achieve some degree of self-government and occupational control they modelled themselves on the values of professionalism which they shared with the men of their own social class.[13]

These characteristics were to be replicated in Ireland when almoners were introduced in the 1920s, and to this day the profession in Ireland is largely middle class and female,[14] which undoubtedly has affected the manner in which it is perceived by others, not only by administrators and other professionals, but perhaps more importantly, by its clientele.

In the twenties, this need to be seen as professionals led to what Woodroofe has described as the 'psychiatric deluge',[15] when case-workers in the United States of America adopted psychoanalytic theory as the main basis for training and practice. The popularity of Freudian theory in the USA gave a great boost to the newly emerging specialism of psychiatric social work and to case workers generally, and was responsible for the emergence of the diagnostic school of social work which concerned itself more with those factors in the client's personality, background and even subconscious which had led to the presenting problem, and less with the actual problem and its speedy resolution. As Woodroofe puts it:

189

Instead of the older type of social history which furnished relentlessly utilitarian details about parents, children, wages, delinquencies, sicknesses, operations, schooling and jobs there now appeared a case history recording the client's introspection and the attempt of the worker, often in alliance with the psychiatrist, to edit and interpret the client's subconscious.[16]

This approach lives on to this day and although in Ireland it may never have been carried to the extreme limits observable in American practice, at times there has been undue emphasis on diagnosis or assessment both in training and in practice, with very lengthy reports being compiled on the background histories of clients and with much time being spent in formulating the reasons for the client's predicament. The part all this investigation played in helping to tackle the presenting problem or in planning for future action is doubtful, and certainly the expectations of many families were falsely raised, when after a battery of interviews and visits in the early stages following referral to an agency they found themselves still left to cope on their own with the situation which originally had led them to seek help.

The Irish Experience

Professional social work was introduced into Ireland in 1920 when the Adelaide Hospital appointed the first almoner to its staff. During the next thirty years almoners were employed by almost all the other Dublin hospitals, and also by a variety of other organisations. As there was no professional training within the State at that time, all of these women were trained abroad, the majority in the Institute of Almoners in London, and brought with them the philosophy which had evolved from the professionalising of the COS. From the early 1950s psychiatric social workers began to appear on the scene, again trained outside the country, in the UK or the United States, and heavily influenced by Freudian theory. The first appointees were to private hospitals and clinics (and some to the teaching staff of universities), and the Health Act of 1953 relieved hospital almoners (who shortly afterwards were to change their title to medical social worker) of the duties they had formerly discharged in investigating patients' financial eligibility for treatment. Thus professional social workers in

Ireland had succeeded in severing the connection between their work and poverty.

Did this mean that poor people ceased to be clients of social workers? Most definitely not, and figures in recent years show that poverty is a significant factor in the lives of people referred to social work agencies. Social workers, however, have striven hard to prove that their function is much wider than simply giving practical help, and ever since the hospital almoners' battle to shed their clerical means-testing role by refusing to process the forms used to establish a patient's entitlement to free hospital treatment after 1953, the profession has been keen to demonstrate the importance of its therapeutic role, as successive annual reports of the professional bodies show.

> It lay with medical and lay Boards of the Hospital to see that almoners did the work for which they were trained, and to relieve them of the numberless tasks which served to absorb too great a part of their working day.[17] . . . (The speaker) pointed out that much more was required of almoners than to solve material needs, for great were the emotional, personal and family difficulties retarding or hindering certain patients' recoveries, or preventing them accepting treatment.[18]

More than twenty years later, when the Irish Association of Social Workers had been reconstituted, social workers indicated that they still believed that their true function was not understood and the professional association was seen as a means of correcting this situation. The first 'Object of the Association' was

> To provide a professional organisation for and of those engaged in social work and to promote and advance such work, its standards and ideals, the education and training of social workers and *to foster public knowledge and appreciation of their work.*[19]

A newspaper article at the time quoted a social worker as saying, 'No, we're not doing any effective work . . . partly because the attitude towards social workers here is all wrong — it's as if we were sort of plain clothes nuns.'[20]

This confusion of roles for social workers was compounded by the reliance on voluntary bodies in Ireland to provide social services. Whereas Beveridge[21] had cleared the way for social workers in the UK to come into their own, as it were, after

1948 and concentrate on matters other than problems arising from poverty, believing (falsely as it turned out) that the new legislation would sweep away all the remaining vestiges of material deprivation and its concomitant misery, there was no such hope held out to Irish social workers. Their genuine and justified need to establish the importance of professional training, and perhaps more importantly, their professional autonomy, created real difficulties for workers who, while keenly aware of the plight of the poor, were determined not to be confined to filling out claim forms for financial assistance or to paying out a few pounds from a Samaritan fund.

Changes in training for social workers were introduced in the late 1950s and 1960s, with the diploma courses being gradually replaced by three or four-year degree courses offering students in Ireland the possibility for the first time of obtaining an honours degree in social science or social studies. These expanded courses saw the introduction to the curriculum of sociology as a core subject given equal weight with social policy and psychology, and with a consequent weakening of the emphasis on psychological theory. The previous imbalance was further redressed by a move away from casework as the exclusive method of practice, as the more novel methods (to Ireland) of group work and community work were included in training. This shift in emphasis was accelerated by the establishment of the first professional training course in the country, the Diploma in Applied Social Studies offered by University College Dublin from 1968, whose proposed syllabus proclaimed that the social work theory taught would include service to individuals, groups and communities. This course also followed the by now accepted trend in the UK in that it offered generic training, equipping its students to work in any field or specialism they should choose.

All of this paved the way for a renewed interest in social reform, which Woodroofe maintains had been sadly neglected by social workers in the preceding decades.

From the 1920s to the early 1950s, except for the dramatic years of the depression, social work displayed little of its previous concern with reform and social policy . . . Perhaps social work, pursuing the professional hare, wisely preferred to leave this broader public purpose to specialised agencies and professional groups better adapted than itself for reform.[21]

She was writing of the situation in the USA and the UK, and although practice in Ireland tended to follow trends in those much more highly developed societies, there were distinct differences too. Social workers in Ireland had bravely tried to influence social policy in the period Woodroofe refers to, and the records of the Irish Region of the Institute of Almoners provide ample proof of this — lengthy correspondence with government departments, the Hospitals Commission, County Medical Officers of Health, the universities, on matters as diverse as the difficulty in transferring epileptic patients from a voluntary hospital to an institution catering for their needs, the exclusion of women from jury service and the value of appointing almoners to work in the tuberculosis service. However, social workers were so few in numbers that no matter how vocal they were, there would have been no question of their bringing about major policy changes in the areas which were causing most hardship during that era — emigration, unemployment, and inevitably in the wake of these two, poverty. It was a disheartening time for social workers and many left Ireland to seek posts in other countries where their contribution was in urgent demand.

Social Service Councils

In the more mellow climate of the 1960s it became easier for social workers to look beyond their individual clients and begin to move away from their institutional bases. Social Service Councils, a new arrival on the scene, brought social workers out into the community where they would work side by side with volunteers and other professionals in identifying local needs, and, in a more co-ordinated way than previously, address themselves to the problems of a given geographical area or parish. This spontaneous growth of councils which were founded to bring together the many organisations which were engaged in providing personnel social services, gave social workers employed by such voluntary councils the opportunity to engage in other methods of social work as well as casework, notably in advocacy and social action. Many of the Social Service Councils had as one of their aims the improvement of services through lobbying the statutory authorities, and in some instances where this was not written into the formal constitution of the council, it nevertheless was one of the important activities of the organisation and its staff.

The rediscovery of poverty in the UK and the War on Poverty programmes in the USA were also having their impact on social work in Ireland at this time, and community organisation was given a guarded welcome as a form of intervention which might be applicable to the peculiar situation in Ireland, where personal social services were largely the responsibility of the voluntary sector and had been allowed to develop in an *ad hoc* fashion, and were therefore somewhat disorganised. After decades of neglect and uninterest, the government of the day saw this co-ordinated service approach as a possible way of harnessing voluntary effort and saving the State as much money as possible. Through modest funding, first through care-of-the-aged grants and subsequently, through grants for services which the statutory authorities would otherwise have had to provide, Social Service Councils were given official recognition and the impression was created that needs were being met by a happy combination of statutory and voluntary services throughout the land. This was not the case, of course, and it was not until the Health Board Community Care teams were appointed after the 1970 Health Act that it could be said that a minimum of personal social service provision was available in all parts of the country. However, one of the effects of delegating such service provision as there was to Social Service Councils was to ensure that they had little time left to engage in social action, or even in co-ordination in some cases. A study of one council found that it had failed to forge links at a policy level with other relevant authorities:

> Staff effort is concentrated principally on providing services rather than co-ordination or assessment . . . although the social workers themselves have a clear idea of what they are doing in their own work there is a failure to pursue the general issues. These issues are the inadequacy of certain state benefits, housing problems of certain groups and other problems which are common to a large number of clients.[23]

Working in relative isolation, usually single-handed, these social workers were quickly inundated with cases and so, once again, casework became the predominant activity of community-based social workers, as it was to remain even with the rapid growth of the profession in the 1970s.

Casework and its Limitations

On the social action front, corporate activity has been undertaken by the Irish Association of Social Workers, and by individual social workers who were closely associated with such movements as CARE, Children First, The Association for the Welfare of Children in Hospital and many others, but in day-to-day practice in their employing agencies, social workers in the main keep to the tried and tested method — casework with individuals. That the individuals are suffering from problems that may not be of their making and over which they have no control, while recognised by the workers, does not deter them from helping the client to tolerate his intolerable situation. In a study undertaken in a new housing estate in North Dublin in 1975, the researcher found that although the social workers in the area identified the principal problems as being of a structural nature, they did not see themselves as being in a position to do anything about changing those structures. Having cited unemployment, material poverty and lack of amenities as posing the main difficulties for their clients, they yet failed to offer anything other than a casework service to the people of the area.[24]

This impression that social workers rely heavily on casework as their chosen method of intervention is borne out by the experience of those teaching on social work courses. To arrange field-work placements for students who want to acquire skills in group work or community work is extraordinarily difficult, so much so that frequently community workers who are not formally trained and who do not consider themselves as social workers, have been asked to supervise students on professional courses, and have done so most willingly. The result of this paucity of field experience is that the newly qualified social worker emerges from training bursting with the theory of community development, advocacy, welfare rights and group dynamics, but with practical experience of casework only. It is not surprising, therefore, that this is the method the neophyte continues to practise on finding employment.

But is casework an appropriate response to poverty? Whether social workers like it or not, a significant proportion of their clientele is poor, as a glance at their case-loads will reveal. A study in Tallaght in 1974 showed that 20 per cent of the cases referred to social workers in the area were referred because of financial problems, and a third of all clients were either unemployed or suffering some financial hardship.[25] A survey carried out in a county in the mid-west in 1976/77 produced much the same picture — 20 out of 83 families in financial

195

need, with unemployment featuring in 23 of the families.[26] In one of the Eastern Health Board community care areas, the social work team of eleven between them had 748 cases on their books during the first six months of 1980; over a third of the clients were described as having financial problems, and 113 were unemployed. During the period in question a total of 61 people had approached this team looking for assistance with an electricity bill![27]

What can social workers do in the face of such demand? They can decline to become involved in financial problems, on the basis that it is not the social worker's function to deal with such matters; other problems must be given priority. In one Eastern Health Board area, this seems to be the case and for very valid reasons. The referrals to this team were so numerous that only very critical or serious problems could be accepted as cases, with approximately three-quarters of new referrals being relegated to a 'no further action' category. A student on placement in the agency was asked to look at these rejected cases, to ascertain the characteristics of the referrals. Over a period of three months in 1980, of 190 cases judged to require no action on the part of the social work staff, 24 per cent had come seeking financial help and another 24 per cent sought assistance with housing. The priority in this area is child neglect or non-accidental injury to children and although low income may be a contributory factor in cases of that kind, no social worker could justify taking on every debt and financial crisis which turned up on her duty day.

Where no further action is taken on behalf of clients, they can be, and very often are, referred to another service, and in the case of financial hardship this is usually the Community Welfare Officer or the Society of St Vincent de Paul (SVP). Under the supplementary welfare allowance scheme, officers have a responsibility to give information regarding benefits and entitlements to people who are not clear as to what may be available to them. In reality, even when it has been established than an applicant has no means of paying an outstanding rent or electricity bill and is in danger of being evicted or having supply disconnected, the statutory services frequently fail to make any adequate response and the family or individual must resort to some charitable organisation. The SVP are relied on in what might be described as a cavalier fashion by social workers in Ireland, South and North. In a recent survey carried out by the Society it emerged that whereas 6 per cent of elderly people living alone in the Republic are visited regularly by the SVP, only 4 per cent have the services of a social worker, despite the extent of deprivation of these old people as described in the study,[28] even where the workers have access to money for families in exceptional need as is the case in Northern Ireland. In Stevenson and Parsloe's research a social worker in the North is quoted as saying of the Society: 'We use it so often I'm inclined to think of them as another statutory agency!'[29]

Conclusion

Is there any other action open to social workers if something is to be done to tackle the grinding, constant poverty of so many of their clients? Social action through welfare rights programmes, energetic advocacy and wider involvement with the poor in an effort to politicise them, as well as agency reform, are strategies suggested by Holman when he argues that 'social workers should accept involvement in combating poverty',[30] (the implication being that frequently they do not). The recent report of the Combat Poverty Committee pointed to how success can be achieved by social workers in working with very deprived families if they are prepared to utilise these methods, and as in the case of the Newpark Close project, actually move in and live with the deprived community.[31] This kind of approach requires careful research, and there is evidence that social workers in Ireland are improving their recording systems[32] and will soon be in a better position to provide the necessary data to bolster whatever case they are making with or on behalf of their clients to administrators and policy-makers. The publication in 1981 of *Youth and Justice* by staff and students of the Social Science Department of University College Dublin has helped to convince social workers that appealing for change and improvement in social services on the basis of generalised, emotional demands, has little effect other than to discredit the profession. Hard data must be gathered systematically and used constructively if we are to influence social policy.

With over 700 social workers now employed in Ireland, professional social work is on a firm enough footing to be able to decide what it wants to do, without any apologies or self-deprecatory explanations of the kind which have bedevilled it in the past. It is a young profession with half of its members under 30 years of age, many of them eager to try out new ways to meeting social need. There is no evidence that the problem of poverty is decreasing and some evidence to indicate that it may be on the increase. One of the most active workers for social reform in this country posed a daunting challenge to her colleagues when speaking at an International Seminar in Dublin in 1979.

The social work profession played a major role in the search for more rational ways of organising welfare services and we now recognise that the delivery of these services should be focussed primarily on communities rather than on specific client groups. Nevertheless, we have not succeeded in ridding the services of the old approach which is still dominant although it no longer accords with social work attitudes and knowledge . . . The objectives of social work would be better served if we ensured that policy-makers and the public were made aware of the facts of social deprivation as we experience them and that social work services are not provided as an *alternative* to radical reforms which are needed.[33]

It would be unfortunate if knowledge of the extent of social and material deprivation were to remain hidden in the case records of social workers because of an inherited fear that to be too closely associated with the poor in some way detracts from their professionalism.

REFERENCES

1. P. Townsend, *Poverty in the United Kingdom*, (London, 1979).

2. K. Carmichael in *The British Journal of Social Work* Vol. 10, No. 4., (Winter 1980). 542

3. G.D. Williams, *Dublin Charities* (Dublin, 1902), p.2.

4. C.S. Loch, *The Charities Register and Digest* (1895), p. ix.

5. Ibid, p. x xi.

6. H. Bosanquet, *Social Work in London 1869-1912* (1914), p. 26.

7. C.O.S. Occasional Paper, first series, No. 15, p. 25, quoted by K. Woodroofe in *From Charity to Social Work* (1961), p. 25.

8. O. Stevenson, and P. Parsloe, *Social Service Teams: The Practitioners' View* (1978).

9. Stevenson and Parsloe, ibid, p. 234.

10. Ibid. p. 228.

11. Loch, op. cit. p.x.

12. R.G. Walton, *Women in Social Work* (London, 1975) pp. 43-7.

13. N. Parry and J. Parry, in *Social Work, Welfare and the State* (London, 1979) p. 30.

14. Unpublished figures from the Department of Health, 1980.

15. Woodroofe, *From Charity to Social Work*, pp. 118-47.

16. Ibid, p. 131.

17. Institute of Almoners (Irish Regional Committee(16th Annual Report, 1953.

18. Ibid, 21st Annual Report, 1958/59.

19. Irish Assosiation of Social Workers *Constitution*.

20. *The Irish Times*, 8 March, 1969.

21. Sir William Beveridge whose report *Social Insurance and Allied Services*, published in 1942 was the basis for the sweeping changes in social service provision legislated for by the Labour government in 1948.

22. Woodroofe, op. cit., p. 220.

23. Study of a Social Service Council. Unpublished report of Combat Poverty Committee.

24. S. Duncan, 'The Politics of Welfare in a Dublin Working Class Area', M. Litt, thesis, Trinity College, Dublin, 1975).

25. A. Lavan, *Social Work Services in Tallaght*, A Working Party Report, p. 19.

26. Unpublished report of Combat Poverty Committee.

27. Figures provided by social work team.

28. B. Power, *Old and Alone in Ireland* (Dublin, 1980).

29. Stevenson and Parsloe, op. cit, p. 269.

30. R. Holman, *Poverty*, p. 279.

31. National Committee on Pilot Schemes to Combat Poverty, *Final Report*, pp. 137-9.

32. A. Lavan, and L. Lunny, 'Putting it on Record' in *Community Care*, 19 June, 1980.

33. N. O'Daly, Programme of International Federation of Social Workers European Seminar, August 1979, Opening Address.

Equity and the Financing of Education

A Dale Tussing

The system of finance for education in Ireland runs against the interests of the poor, the working class and the large majority of Irish people. It is essentially a regressive system, in which the many support the few. And there are demands that the few who benefit must be given more.

In these respects, Ireland does not differ from most other countries. Education, which has a reputation for being an equalising force in society, tends instead to perpetuate and aggravate income and class differentials. But the regressive contribution of education in Ireland is perhaps more extreme than in most other countries. Let me try to summarise that situation briefly:

(1)Participation rates in Irish education taper off sharply in the years of age immediately after the compulsory attendance age of 15. In 1979 only 68 per cent of 16 year olds were in full-time education, only 48 per cent of 17 year olds, 27 percent of 18 year olds and 16 per cent of 19 year olds. This high drop-out rate is one of the major problems facing Irish education, and one of Ireland's major social problems.

(2) There is a remarkable imbalance in the distribution of public money among the three levels of the Irish educational system. In 1979 only £303 in public funds was spent for each pupil in national schools, £542 for each second-level pupil and £1343 for each third-level pupil, exclusive of the grant scheme. In addition, £716 per grantee was spent in the third-level grant scheme. Fees cover only about 15 per cent of third-level costs. As a result of the low per-pupil expenditure in national school, classes of forty pupils and above are still common, many schools are in intolerable condition, and few special provisions are made for centre-city and other disadvantaged pupils.

(3) In the secondary sector, expenditures appear to be higher per-pupil for the schooling of better-off pupils. My own research (Tussing, 1978) indicates that fee-charging schools,

those which elected not to participate in the free scheme (but which, anomalously, get most of their funds from the tax payer), spend substantially more per pupil than schools in the free scheme. Even within the free scheme, my research shows that per pupil expenditures are significantly higher in the high-income areas of Dublin and its suburbs that they are in the low-income areas.

(4) Studies of the social class backgrounds of Irish university students show them to come disproportionately from the upper social class groups, but more importantly show virtually no change between 1964/65 and 1978/79 (Barlow, 1981). This is particularly significant because between these dates, the free scheme for second-level education, the free transport scheme and the higher education grants scheme were all developed. All three of these were justified in terms of equality of educational opportunity, and if successful should have made a dent in the social class make-up of university students.

(5) The Irish educational system is more effective than those of most other countries in perpetuating or reproducing the existing highly stratified social class make-up of Ireland (Rottman, Hannan, Hardiman and Wiley, forthcoming).

Putting all of this together, what is required for social justice is a substantial redistribution of the public resources going to the various levels of the Irish educational system. More money per pupil is needed in first level. At the same time, there is no reason to continue the very high level of subsidisation of third level.

This position appears to be quite controversial, not only among the well-off, who would admittedly be made worse off by adoption of a progressive redistribution of educational resources, not only in the Union of Students in Ireland, which represents third-level students as an interest group, but among some well-meaning and progressive people who see it as an attack on an important objective — free education for all. Let us examine the proposition, from the perspective of the principle of *equity*.

The Question

The question is this: Who should pay for education — employers, students (and their families), or society at large? Specifically, who should pay the post-compulsory education? Should third-level education, for example, be free, or nearly so, to all comers?

202

One reason for all confusion surrounding these questions is that the subject of education and its role in society is clouded by an immense amount of mythology, due in large part to the fact that education is a central part of the legitimising ideology of Western capitalism.

One of the most persistent, and at the same time pernicious, myths concerning schooling is that it contributes to social and economic equality. The truth is the opposite of this. In fact, in almost every country in the world, schooling reinforces and heightens existing inequalities. In the USA, studies have shown that poor children begin school with a significant disadvantage, as measured in IQ, and that schooling *widens* rather than narrows the IQ gap. Low-income, lower-class children do more poorly in school than do other children; they spend fewer years in school. Less is spent, per pupil per year, on their account, and such evidence as we have suggests that they are dealt with prejudiciously by and in the schools, in ways which contribute further to their poor performances.

These differences in schooling lead in adult years to increased lifelong differences in incomes. Thus schooling is part of a vicious circle, in which existing inequalities are repeatedly passed on, from generation to generation. Schooling is not, of course, the ultimate and sole source of these inequalities. It merely accepts, reinforces and heightens them. But this is far from the usual image of schools as a major motor of equalisation.

Educational differences not only account for lifelong earnings differences, but they legitimate them as well. Most people appear to accept as fair and proper that those with less schooling *should* earn less, even though the distribution of schooling may be itself inequitable. Schooling thus has a major role in perhaps the most widely accepted ideology of *inequality* in the Western Word.

It was stated above that educational differences *account for* earnings differences. We do not really understand the nature of the relationship between education and earned income. One should not leap to the conclusion that the relationship is *casual*, at least in the usual sense. The orthodox view, that schooling increases one's productivity, and that as people are paid in accordance with productivity, those with more schooling are paid more, seems to be losing favour, at least amongst educational economists. First, it does not accord with the apparent nature of much of education, whose connection to

203

productivity must be subtle indeed, if it exists. Moreover, studies appear to indicate that the skills and knowledge required on almost every job are acquired *on the job*, in either formal or informal training, from other employees (Thurow, 1975), Third, it has been found that recent increases in the equality of the distribution of education have done nothing, or virtually nothing, to alter the distribution of earned incomes, in those countries with adequate statistics on these.

An improvement over the orthodox theory is the 'job competition theory' offered by Professor Lester Thurow of the Economics Department in the Massachusetts Institute of Technology (Thurow, 1975). According to Professor Thurow, the set of jobs available to be filled in any society — what he calls the 'jobs distribution' — is determined by underlying economic forces which are more or less independent of the educational attainments of members of the labour force. That jobs distribution, by itself and without reference to education or educational differences, determines such things as the earned income distribution, the amount of unemployment, the amount of wage poverty, etc. If schooling plays little or no part in these things, what is its role? The answer is that one's education determines his or her position in the 'labour queue' which orders one's access to favoured positions in the jobs distribution. Those with more or better education are ahead of others in the queue for jobs, and hence get the best positions, receive on-the-job training and earn high incomes.

The distinction between the two theories can be put in another way.In what was referred to above as the orthodox theory, the distribution of education determines the distribution of earned incomes. If one wants to understand the distribution of earned income, one needs to look only at one distribution, namely that of persons, with their educational levels and their productivities. In Thurow's job competition theory, however, one must look at *two* distributions. First, there is the jobs distribution, which gives the shape of the earned income distribution. Then there is the labour queue — the distribution of persons and their education, which gives the identity of the actual person who will fill each job, and which, then, puts names on the earned income distribution provided by the jobs distribution.

In the orthodox productivity theory, in order to change the distribution of earned income, we must change the distribution of education. But in the job competition theory, changing the distribution or amount of education may change who gets each income, but it will not change the shape of the earned income distribution. Educational enrichment programmes for the poor, if they are successful, may move some people out of poverty, but only by moving them ahead of others in the queue for a fixed set of jobs. The amount of poverty will not decline. If everyone is given an additional year of schooling, neither the amount nor the distribution of earned income will change (abstracting from the marvellous effects an extra year of schooling for all would have on the incomes of those who work in the education system).[1]

These two are not the only theories seeking to explain the links between educational differences and earned income differences. There is, for example, the theory that the causation runs largely from income (or social class) to schooling. There is another theory, which has a large number of adherents, that the education system operates, among other things, as a giant screening system, which serves to locate, identify and certify those young people with the most potential for each of a number of skilled positions in the economy. According to this so-called screening hypothesis, the schools do not so much create abilities as find them.

Whatever the casual link, two things seem clear: children whose families have higher incomes and social positions tend on the average to get significantly more and better educations than those with lower incomes and social positions. And those children with more and better educations tend, in turn, to get higher incomes and social positions than those children with lesser educations.

Of course, students are not the only beneficiaries of education. Employers often benefit as well.

According to orthodox economic theory, employers benefit from 'specific education' and students benefit from 'general education'. Specific education (or training) imparts skills, abilities, attitudes, etc., that are uniquely appropriate to employment with a single employer. The student who has such skills cannot sell them to the highest bidder in the market, and hence will be unable to raise his or her wage as a consequence of the education. Therefore if they want students to undertake specific education, employers will have to provide it or pay for it. General education imparts skills, abilities, attitudes, etc., that are appropriate to a number of employers. Students can sell their augmented labour power on the market for more money than can be earned by those who have not studied because the competition of employers for their skills will drive up their wages. Employers, then, will not pay for general education, because they cannot appropriate the benefits for themselves.

This theory is framed in competitive markets and cannot be accepted without considerable qualification. For example, employees who have been given specific training at their employers' expense can nonetheless sometimes reap some of its benefits by effective trade union action. On the other hand, concerted action by employers can hold down wages and provide employers with a share even of the gains from general education. More basically, it seems incontrovertible that employers as a class benefit from the existence of a national education system, and that, lacking it, they would have to provide a certain amount of education and training, of a 'general' sort, at their own expense.

Ireland has a long educational tradition, but until relatively recently the major function of schooling was seen to be religious, moral and intellectual training, and the transmission of culture, language and ideology. As consequences, the following were true to a degree greater in Ireland than elsewhere: (1) the education of girls was given equal emphasis to that of boys; (2) the curriculum was weighted in the direction of such highly verbal subjects as literature, religion, Irish and Latin; and (3) schooling was simple and cheap (Tussing, 1978).

The orientation was changed in the late 1950s and early 1960s as part of the industrialisation strategy associated with the T.K. Whitaker White Paper of 1958, *A Programme for Economic Expansion.* The central event in the re-orientation was the publication in 1962 of *Investment in Education,* but institutional changes in the system in the late 1960s, and since, are associated with the new approach. Today it is fully accepted that the principal purpose of the education system is to prepare Irish children and young people for employment.

Studies everywhere show a relationship between years of education and income. Though there are, needless to say, fewer studies in Ireland than in such places as the USA and UK, the existing Irish literature is consistent with that of other countries in that it shows a strong correlation between education and earnings. The data are in accord with everyone's casual observation: pay and schooling are positively associated.

The studies show, specifically, that *differences* in schooling

206

are associated with differences in income. To the extent that there is, in a society, a standard level of education attained by everyone, or nearly everyone, that level will not, of course, account for income differentials. In the USA that common level is the completion of high school. In Ireland, it is today the age 15, beyond which attendance is no longer compulsory. By definition, differences in amounts of schooling through age 15 will not explain income differences in Ireland (though qualitative differences might); differences in amounts of schooling beyond those years — in effect, senior cycle of second level and third level — are the contributors to social inequality.

This is not, of course, to say that everyone who receives a senior or third-level education will have a higher income as a consequence. The relationship is an average one, not a mechanically deterministic one. If members of upper classes were all provided with cash grants for financial or productive investment at the age of 21, instead of an education, they would as a consequence have higher average lifelong incomes than those not receiving such grants, even though it seems certain that some individuals receiving grants would find their way to bankruptcy anyway, and some not receiving grants might nonetheless achieve success.

To the extent that average incomes are higher for the more educated than the less educated, the benefits of education are appropriated by the student, rather than, on the one hand, employers, or on the other, society at large.

Standards of Equity

Let us turn now to a discussion of competing standards of equity. We will review three quite different principles: the principle of reciprocal justice, equality of opportunity and egalitarianism.

Reciprocal Justice

'Reciprocal justice' is the justice of equal exhange. One gets what one pays for, and vice versa. In income distribution, this principle justifies inequality, if and to the extent that members of society *produce* unequally. Adherents to this point of view tend to oppose government interventions in the distribution of income, by taxes and transfer payments, legal minimum wages or similar devices, on the assumption that the distribution of income that results from market forces properly tends to reflect differences in economic productivity. That is, obviously, an enormous assumption.

In the context of this doctrine of reciprocal justice, let me discuss the distinction between education as a private good and education as a public good.[2] In economics, a distinction exists between 'private' goods, which benefit only the buyer (together with his or her family and others whom the buyer seeks to benefit), and 'public' goods, whose benefits flow to all or to a significant portion of society. Food is a private good. The doctrine of reciprocal justice says that food ought to be paid for by its consumer. The national defence is a public good, however, which is consumed equally by all, irrespective of the amounts they pay for it; the doctrine of reciprocal justice says that it ought to be paid for collectively.

How does this public-private distinction apply within education? Schooling often provides benefits that flow not only to the learner but to society as a whole. It is in large part through schooling that language, culture, history and national identity are perpetuated. Modern social, political, and economic systems demand of their participants a certain minimal level of education, a level which seems continually to be on the rise. The fact that there is a large social interest in education is indicated not only by public schemes for its provision, but also by the almost universal tendency of societies to make a certain amount of education compulsory. But education is a *quasi*-public good. It stands midway between public and private goods, and has characteristics of each. Its *principal* beneficiaries typically are the pupils, who receive benefits in both current or consumption form (the enjoyment of learning, of socialising with peers, of recreation, etc.) and in investment form (yielding lifelong enhanced potential earnings, as well as enchanced enjoyment of literature, music, etc.). But society in general benefits as well.

Moreover — and this is an important point — in providing society with persons having needed skills, in educating doctors, scientists, managers, teachers and economists, the schools provide a *private* benefit, so long as those skills are sold in labour markets in appropriate quantities. The fact that a product or service is essential does not, obviously, make it a public good. It is a commonplace that essential products — food, clothing, shelter — are provided through the market every day, i.e. that they are private goods. It is only when the market fails to provide the good, or provides it in the wrong amounts, that the good loses its private character. So it is with skills, provided by the education system.

To the extent that the education system provides people with skills they *don't sell,* which they use in their roles as parents, citizens, neighbours and vehicles for the preservation and continuation of culture and nationality, to that extent the education system provides a public good. Reciprocal justice tells us that society, as a whole, should pay for these benefits, even to the extent of compensating the student for income foregone, where the student could have taken gainful employment instead of learning. But the corollary of this is that to the extent that the education system provides people with skills they subsequently sell, or otherwise provides them with higher earning potential, to that extent the education system provides a private good. Reciprocal justice tells us that the learner, and not society, should pay for these benefits.

Not all levels of education have the same mix of public and private aspects. The early years of primary schooling fit better the definition of public goods. It is then that primary socialisation, literacy and numeracy education, and cultural indoctrination occur. Moreover, as schooling is for practical purposes universal at this level, even where it does provide skills which are subsequently sold, it does not contribute thereby to earnings *differentials,* except through quality differences. At higher levels, however, schooling moves closer to being a private good. It ceases to be universal, and it makes a major contribution to lifelong earnings differentials, as well as to other socio-economic differentiation. One possible rule of thumb is that schooling in the years of compulsory attendance (ages 6 to 15) be considered to be essentially public in character. Beyond the age of compulsory schooling, i.e. in senior cycle and third level, education is more nearly private in the distribution of its benefits. At these levels, subsequent employment and earnings opportunities vary with schooling.

Obviously, the Irish system of finance of education does not accord with the principle of reciprocal justice, at least as here interpreted. Senior cycle, second-level schooling is free, except that foregone income is not compensated for. And third-level education is heavily subsidised. The effect is not dissimilar to a grant of stocks, bonds or savings accounts by the government to the upper strata of the income distribution. Society makes the investment, in most cases, but the individual appropriates the return.

Equality of Opportunity

The second principle of justice I want to examine is that of equality of opportunity. If any theory of equity is espoused officially by the Irish State, by politicians, students, teachers and institutions, it is this one. Indeed, the free scheme for second-level education, and the Higher Education Grants Scheme, are offered in the name of equality of opportunity.

This theory is closely related to the principle of reciprocal justice. Indeed, it may be viewed as a qualified or modified version of the latter. Like the principle of reciprocal justice, and in spite of the word 'equality' in its name, the principle of equality of opportunity justifies *inequality* in incomes and social positions.

Society, this doctrine holds, ought to permit each of its members to become whatever he or she is capable of becoming. It should not treat them differentially on account of their race, religion, sex or place of origin, or incomes or social classes of their parents. Education has a major place in this philosophy. Schooling is to be equally available to all persons, regardless of their backgrounds of their financial resources. No one is to be denied the opportunity of schooling by virtue of inadequate means. This principle does not require that poor pupils, or indeed anyone, be permitted to go as far in school as they desire. Instead, it means that admission to each level will be on the grounds of merit and merit alone.

If substantial equality of opportunity is provided, then the principle of reciprocal justice is hard to attain, or even define. Can one argue that people should be paid in accordance with their productivities, as measured by the market, when the ability to develop one's skills and abilities is not afforded equally to all? This is why and how the principle of equality of opportunity stands as a qualification of the principle of reciprocal justice: market-based income distribution is patently *unfair* when opportunities are unequal. It is also how and why equality of opportunity can be called a philosophy of inegalitarianism. It sees as acceptable and legitimate such income differences as exist so long as all members of society are provided with equality of opportunity. It envisions in a completely just society a substantial degree of inequality.

Free public education is often justified on the grounds

of equality of opportunity. But free public education is neither necessary nor sufficient in order to attain equality of opportunity. It is not *necessary*, in the sense that equality of opportunity would not seem to require taxpayer subsidies for the education of the wealthy, but only for those meritorious students whose limited means would keep them back. And it would not be sufficient, for equality of opportunity, even in education, is impaired by much more than school fees. Reasonable equality of opportunity requires that all children, even in their pre-natal months, be assured a healthy, nutritious, poison-free environment. There is now substantial evidence concerning the enormous and often irreversible consequences of undernourishment, environmental poison such as lead, and physical injury — all of which have disproportionate impacts on poor children. Reasonable equality of opportunity may require some enhanced early-childhood learning experiences for many children of poor backgrounds, so that they may enter school on a more nearly equal footing with other pupils. Reasonable equality of opportunity, in so far as it involves school expenditures, probably requires concentration on first level. The consequences of inadequate schooling at that level probably cannot be rectified, and certainly cannot be rectified at any reasonable cost, at later stages. And it is undoubtedly true that inadequate primary schooling, even if equally inadequate for all, has a more deleterious effect on the disadvantaged child than on others, since she or he must put more reliance on schooling, relative to other influences.

To ignore the infantile environment and pre-school learning, and to beggar first level, and then to claim to offer equality of opportunity on the basis of free second-level education and a Higher Education Grants Scheme is ludicrous. It is all the more so when it is recalled that many pupils still cannot continue through senior cycle for economic reasons, that the Higher Education Grants Scheme is so structured as to fail even to permit all those with poorer backgrounds who somehow make it through to third level to pursue a higher education without help from family,[3] and that a more stringent requirement — four leaving certificate honours instead of two — is imposed on grants recipients than on university entrants, a patent and prima facie violation of equality of opportunity.

What does this all have to do with fees for third-level education? First, it means that free or heavily subsidised third-level education, as at present, cannot be justified on the grounds of equality of opportunity, and indeed may even detract from equality of educational opportunity if it takes educational resources from such things as a more adequate higher education grants system, maintenance grants for needy senior cycle students, improved primary schooling, pre-school enrichment programmes, and a safe and healthy pre-natal and infantile environment.

Egalitarianism

The third equity principle I want to examine is my own view, egalitarianism. As I use the term here, egalitarianism refers to the position that the distribution of income and/or wealth ought to be made more equal. Some egalitarians seek absolute equality in incomes; others seek only a smaller spread between highest and lowest; still others concentrate on eliminating poverty. None of these is the same as the principle of reciprocal justice which, as noted, tends to accept the inequality that arises from the market. And it is not the same as the doctrine of equality of opportunity, which also envisions, even in perfection, substantial inequality in society.

Not only do egalitarians differ on how far they would go in redistributing income and wealth, but they also differ in the philosophic underpinnings of their egalitarianism. Some are utilitarians who, like A.C. Pigou, see social welfare as being maximised if money is taken from the rich, for whom each extra penny or pound has little utility, and given to the poor, for whom it has so much. Some are socialists, like Oskar Lange, who not only view inequality as a violation of natural justice, but who also want each consumer to have an equal weight in the market, in determining what gets produced. Some, like philosopher John Rawls, argue from unique ethical positions, Rawls holds that if we were somehow able, as a group, to determine the shape of society's income distribution in advance, before we knew where each of us would be placed in that distribution, we would concentrate on minimising the worst that could happen to us, which means that we would concentrate on raising the level of the lowest as much as we could.

Schooling is often linked to an egalitarian point of view. But, as I argued earlier, school systems are not egalitarian institutions. Far from contributing to a reduction in the social and economic distinctions in society, they enhance them. How would schooling be arranged and financed, in capitalist societies,

212

if the designers of an education system sought truly egalitarian goals? It must be assumed that free education would be means-tested. Low-income pupils would not only be given schooling, books and materials free of charge, but to the extent necessary they would be paid stipends as well, to replace lost income. Medium-income pupils would receive lesser subsidies. High-income pupils would be charged in full. Indeed, these would be the approaches of a rather moderate set of egalitarians. A more purely egalitarian approach would be to allocate *places in school* in such a way as to make the school system a positive agent for the redistribution of advantage. Even educationally meritorious pupils with money in hand to pay for their educations would not be assured entry to any level of the system.

Against such a standard, no school system, not even that of the socialist countries of Eastern Europe, can be called egalitarian.[4] Perhaps the closest in the world to an egalitarian system is that of Cuba. The standard may be defective in that it is so far from practice as not to provide a useful guide for evaluating school finance. Nonetheless, it is instructive to contemplate truly how far we are from school systems which would contribute to greater equality in society.

If one were to look systematically at the educational systems of Western democracies, searching for the most egregious examples of inegalitarianism, where the system and its institutions promoted, fostered and enhanced inequality in society, free or subsidised third-level education would surely be high on the list. To justify an arrangement such as the present one in Ireland on the basis of egalitarianism, when its effect is so inegalitarian, is extraordinary.

As this writer stated in a paper read recently to the 'Phil' (Trinity College, Dublin, Philosophical Society):

Let me put my own philosophical position as plainly and succinctly as possible. I seek a world in which education on all levels is free to all. But I cannot argue for free or heavily subsidised third-level education in a world in which (a) access to it is limited by a variety of other social influences to a small and privileged sector of the community; and in which (b) lifelong incomes are significantly influenced by access to third-level education. In short, I see as inequitable in the extreme a system in which the mass of the people pay the very high costs of third-level education so that the minority who benefit from it can demand that the mass of people pay

213

them again, in doctors' and lawyers' fees, salaries of senior civil servants and researchers in institutes such as the ESRI, and incomes of bankers and business persons.

As Karl Marx wrote, 'If in some states . . . higher education institutions are . . . 'free', that only means in fact defraying the cost of the education of the upper classes from the general tax receipts.' For those more comfortable with Milton Friedman than with Marx, let me quote him to similar effect: 'One of the greatest scandals is government subsidisation of higher schooling. There is no policy which so clearly and at so large a scale imposes costs on low-income people to provide subsidies to high-income people'. And for those whose allegiance is firmly middle-of-the-road, I quote from Christopher Jencks: 'In a society where individuals are free to retain most of the economic benefits of their education for themselves it seems reasonable to ask them to pay most of the costs.'[5]

I have stated that I seek a world in which education at all levels is free to all. That would, however, be one in which *all* goods would be distributed according to need, and the market as we know it would be absent. We do not live in such a world. Instead, we live under capitalism, in an environment of scarcity. I reject the idea that socialism, or for that matter equality of educational opportunity, can be built by starting with third-level education. The day when it will be appropriate to provide free third-level education to all who seek it will also be a day on which access to third-level education will not be affected by social class, and on which incomes will not be affected by one's educational attainment.

Conclusion

In spite of its reputation, free education is not necessarily progressive. Experience in Ireland has shown that where access to the higher levels of education is restricted in other ways, free or subsidised schooling serves mainly to provide for an upward fiscal redistribution. In the case of education, not only tax money, but life chances, are involved.

That being the case, why do so many apparently well-meaning people hold the contrary view? Why the confusion about priorities in the financing of education? There seems to be three main reasons for the confusion.

First, people often react to familiar slogans, and do not bother with the necessary analysis. When the newspapers headline, 'end to free education', people react instinctively. The case is similar to that of 'free health care for all', a slogan now being used to support a similarly regressive policy proposal (see my essay, 'Poverty and the Development of the Health Services', in this volume).

Second, there seems to be no tradition in Ireland, among the trade unions, those concerned with poverty or among the political left, of critical analysis of public expenditure programmes. Spending is good, and 'cuts' are bad. There is no concept that some public expenditures may be regressive or reactionary in their impact. Even the PAYE revolts did not focus on individual expenditure programmes.

And third, discussions of social policy, whether among politicians, intellectuals or even political left-wingers, are dominated by those with higher-than-average schooling, often by those with university degrees. There is an unconscious self-bias amongst this group that leads them to identify their own needs with the needs of the nation.

All three of these reasons relate to ignorance or prejudice. A dispassionate analysis of the financing of education in Ireland shows that the first priority lies in the primary level. That is the level whose needs are most crucial at the moment, in order to improve equity, whatever the standard or principle of equity favoured. It is also the level most seriously under-financed at the moment.

REFERENCES

1. This is not an argument against educational enrichment programmes, especially in Ireland or any other small open economy. If the effect of such programmes is essentially redistributive, pushing some towards the front of the labour queue and others necessarily towards the back, the redistribution may be international in scope. If Ireland pursues aggressive educational policies, Irish students may be pushed ahead of those from other countries in the competition.

2. I first drew this distinction in my ESRI paper (Tussing, 1978), and the discussion proved controversial. I take this opportunity to explain the point more fully.

3. This was written before the July 1981 changes in the Grants Scheme, which I have not had an opportunity to analyse.

4. However, since the ratio of the highest income to the lowest is lower in socialist countries than in capitalist countries (though it varies quite considerably among socialist societies), unequal access to schooling does not have the effect on lifelong incomes that it has in the West.

5. I am indebted for these quotations to a paper by Tony Barlow (A.C. Barlow, 1979).

Poverty and the Development of Health Services

A Dale Tussing

The purpose of this essay is to discuss priorities in the development of the public health services from the standpoint of the
needs of the poor. As will be seen, the needs of the poor in this
area are frequently best served by strengthening services
available to the whole population.

It is not really clear how priorities in the development of
the health services are established at present. Ministers for
Health often make dramatic announcements of changes — usually
the availability free of charge of services previously available
only at a fee. Sometimes, as in 1981, these announcements
come on the eve of an election. Other changes are worked out
in annual negotiations on National Understandings. These are
often in furtherance of positions taken by the Irish Congress of
Trade Unions. Such processes as these are not adapted to the
development of a coherent, rational health care financing
scheme. At the same time they often do not cater to the needs
of the most disadvantaged members of society.

Here, we will first review the present position regarding
health, entitlement to medical care and utilisation among the
poor. Then we will examine the dangers posed by further
developments along the line of changes of the recent past.
Finally, we will lay out an alternative set of policy developments
which will achieve more urgent objectives.

The Present Position

It is a well-established proposition that low-income persons face
more health hazards than the rest of the population. While there
are no income — or class-based morbidity data in the Republic
of Ireland, what evidence exists points strongly in the same
direction here:

Evidence . . . [points] to higher prevalence of a number of
illnesses in Ireland among the poor than in the population
at large: coronary heart disease and hypertension in

217

particular and diseases of the circulatory system in general; diseases of the blood and blood-forming organs; lung cancer in particular, and neoplasms in general; cirrhosis of the liver in particular, and diseases of the digestive system in general; respiratory tuberculosis; bronchitis, emphysema, and asthma; alcoholism and schizophrenia and all other reported reasons for admission to psychiatric hospitals and units; and accidents, poisonings, and violence (Tussing, 1981).

In other countries, the relatively poorer health of the low-income population arises out of their less adequate housing, nutrition and other living conditions; their higher consumption of tobacco and alcohol products; their relatively greater present-orientedness and correspondingly lower prevention consciousness; the inferiority of the medical care available to them; and their lower utilisation of medical care.

In Ireland, it is hard to sustain the last two points. With some qualifications,[1] the poor have available to them the same medical services as are available to the rest of the population. And, on average, low-income persons appear to have higher medical care utilisation than the rest of the population.[2]

Roughly the lowest third of the income distribution, the persons with so-called Category 1 eligibility under the Health Services, once called 'full eligibility' and still called the Medical Card population, have the full range of medical and para-medical services available to them without charge. They can be treated by a general practitioner (GP) of their choice without charge. They can avail of free dental, ophthalmic and aural services. They are eligible for free medical, surgical and midwifery maternity care. Consultant specialist services, both in- and out-patient, are free to them. Prescribed medicines, for which there is a charge in many wholly socialised schemes, are also free to them. Hospitalisation, including room accommodation, x-ray and other diagnostic services, ambulance transport and ancillary services are free. A range of para-medical services, such as public health nursing, chiropody, social worker consultation etc., are available without charge.

Utilisation statistics indicate that the medical care population have more GP consultations per year, have more visits to out-patient hospital departments per year, use more prescription items per year, and have more nights in hospital per year than the rest of the population.[3] In short, the evidence is that low-income people need more medical care services, have more medical care services made available to them, and use more medical care services than others in the Irish population.

There are some important qualifications to these statements. High GP utilisation among the medical card population reflects in part physician-generated demand, which may not necessarily be in response to actual medical needs.[4] High utilisation does not necessarily mean good care, and high consumption of pharmaceutical medicines by the medical card population is increasingly accepted as a problem. There are allegations that doctors spend less time with low-income patients and are more likely to favour pharmaceutical medicines over more time-consuming and careful diagnostic procedures.[5] Most important, while average utilisation may be high, some low-income persons who need medical care do not receive it at all, as we will see below.

Even with these qualifications, it must be stated that medical care available to the poor is of a high standard, and no one finds poverty a barrier to generally adequate medical care.[6]

Progress of the Health Services

Apart from administrative reorganisations, there are two general ways in which the health services can expand. Some developments provide or extend needed services and facilities beyond the levels at which they are now provided, or improve the quality of existing services. Others provide public money in place of private money for existing services. Both of these are important and useful. The first way extends the level and range of medical care. The second advances Ireland further toward a system of medical care free to all at the point of use.

In recent years, there has been an excessive emphasis on the second type of development. As an example, we will focus in this essay on the policy of the Irish Congress of Trade Unions. Congress has recently established as its 'first priority' a 'free hospital service for the entire population', which, it states, 'could be achieved by the abolition of the income limit for limited (Category 11) eligibility for the health services' (Cassells, 1980). This is a change of the second type: it substitutes public money for private money, for a service for the top 15 per cent of the income distribution. Its establishment as a 'first priority' implies that this change is more important than *any* possible change of the first type — any increase in level or quality of medical care. It is argued here that it is not, and that the proposed change would use resources not really needed by the top 15 per cent which might otherwise go to improving the system and extending its outreach to disadvantaged groups. It is also argued that there are dangers involved in adding to the free services unless other reforms are also adopted at the same time to keep the system efficient and rational.

For a number of years Congress has been on record as advocating a national comprehensive health service which is free for all at the point of use. Congress's approach has been to press for incremental changes which, bit by bit, move the Irish health services towards that long-run goal. This piecemeal strategy is realistic, as there appears to be little possibility that political conditions will soon permit a sweeping reform of the health care system.

Within the strategy of incremental change, Congress has chosen to concentrate on the income limit for Category 11 (or 'limited') eligibility. Since the mid 1970s, the approach has been to seek increases in the upper-income limit for eligibility. In 1980 Congress adopted the position that there should be no upper-income limit, i.e. that Category 111 should be abolished, and Category 11 eligibility should be extended to all, other than the Medical Card population. At present, the major difference between Categories 11 and 111 concerns consultant specialist services, which are available free to those covered under the former but not to those under the latter. Hence the main effect of the ICTU proposal would be to extend free consultant services to the 15 per cent of the population not entitled to these at the present.

As the strategy of piecemeal development is pursued, and as, one by one, beneficiaries and services are transferred from the 'fee' category to the 'free' category, it is important that other, structural reforms and changes be introduced. Indeed, the structural changes should usually precede the abolition of fees and charges. The reason is that if one were to take the existing Irish health care system and simply make it free at the point of use, the result would not be an Irish version of the UK National Health Service, which (whatever its faults) is a planned and coherent scheme for the delivery and finance of health services, but instead something of a monstrosity.

There are four reasons for opposing the selection of Category Category 11 eligibility for all as the next step in the development of the health services. (1) Without structural reforms elsewhere in the health care system, the change could be explosively expensive and wasteful of resources, with much of the rise in expenditures going as added income to doctors, rather than to pay for new health care resources. (2) The change would further encourage hospital as opposed to community care. (3) The change implies an upwards redistribution of income, and would amount to a windfall gain to the wealthiest groups in society. And (4), most important, there are more important priorities for health care expenditures, as steps towards a universal health service. Each of these points will be developed in detail.

Explosively Expensive.

When the 'choice-of-doctor' scheme was introduced in place of the old dispensary system, its cost far exceeded even the highest predictions and there were those who thought that general practitioners were raiding the Exchequer. A very real danger exists that a similar pattern could repeat under the proposed change.

Simply to take the existing health care system, with the present methods of remuneration of doctors, and in the absence of review procedures which exist in many countries, and to make it free for all users, would be to create a system with no checks or inhibitions on costs whatever. In general, three sorts of checks are possible in health care systems:

(i) Requiring patients to bear some part of the costs of medical care, through fees, prices and other charges;

(ii) requiring providers — doctors, hospitals, chemists, etc. — to bear part of the costs of providing health care; and

(iii) employing administrative review procedures to oversee the resource-using decisions made by providers.

There is ample evidence that all of these are actually effective, if well thought-out and designed systems are introduced and applied. Where patients pay fees, utilisation is lower than where services are free. How doctors and hospitals are paid clearly influences consultation rates, admitting rates, average stays in hospital, etc. Administrative review procedures are capable of not only controlling utilisation but of making resource use more rational.

If less reliance is to be placed on patient fees, then more reliance must necessarily be placed on the other two devices.

Of the three types of checks, the first, patient charges, is in general less desirable than the others available. One reason is that fees and charges may deter necessary as well as excessive utilisation of health care. This is more likely to be the case, however for low- than high-income persons, so it has less force in the present case. Another reason is that most utilisation decisions are made by providers of health care, not by patients.

The second form of check is found where an uncompensated cost is borne by the *providers* of health care, thereby leading them to resist excessive resource use. Two examples will make clear what is meant: the remuneration of general practitioners and the financing of public hospitals. There are three main ways GPs are paid: on a fee-for-service (i.e. fee per consultation) basis, as in Ireland; on a capitation system, as in the British NHS; and by salary, as in Eastern European socialist countries. In the capitation system, GPs are paid according to the number of public patients registered with them and they are not further compensated for consultations. Thus the capitation system is an example of the second type of check. If the GP must see patients without being paid for each home or office visit, then he or she bears the cost of those visits — not, to be sure, out of pocket in money form, but in the form of time and effort expended. Consultation rates are higher in a fee-for-service system than in a capitation system. For example, the consultation rate for the medical card population in Ireland is higher than that for comparable groups in the UK. It is reasonable to believe that a major reason for the higher consultation rate in Ireland is that GPs are paid on a fee-for-service basis, whereas in the UK they are paid on a capitation basis, since the cost to the patient is nil in both cases. Irish doctors are in a position materially to influence their own incomes, by stimulating or failing to discourage extra or unnecessary consultations. It is noteworthy that British consultation rates, unlike those in Ireland, are not rising, and indeed are actually lower today than in the 1950s. In Italy, where the entire system of health care financing has recently been changed, in order to control costs and make the system more rational, GPs formerly paid on a fee-for-service basis are now paid on a capitation basis, and specialists practising in public health centres who had been paid on a fee-for-service basis are to be paid on a salaried basis. The changed method of compensating GPs has led to lower consultation rates (Abel-Smith and Maynard, 1978).

In general, two techniques have been used to finance public hospitals. The State either pays them on the basis of patient-days, or provides them with an annual budget arrived at through an administrative procedure which does not take into account patient-days. It is widely believed that paying hospitals by patient-days often encourages hospitals to prolong patient days. Where an annual budget is provided, hospitals are encouraged to hold down hospital stays, because the hospital, in effect, bears the cost of extended stays. This technique is, then, an example of the second type of check. The Italian reform referred to above also involves shifting the technique by which public hospitals are financed from patient-days to annual budgets. Public hospitals in Ireland are financed by annual budgets. However, many consultant specialists, who in this country make the basic decisions regarding patient stays, *are* paid on a patient-day basis, a technique which is said to encourage excessive hospital stays (Kelly, 1976).

A system in which services are free to the patient, and under which the provider is paid on a fee-for-service or patient-day basis, open-ended as to total amount, would appear to encourage the highest utilisation rates. To some doctors, such a combination would be the equivalent of a blank cheque. This is the basis for saying that the change proposed by the ICTU might be explosively expensive unless other changes are made in the system.

The third type of check involves administrative review procedures to oversee the resource-using decisions made by providers. (The same procedures also oversee medical decisions as well.) The review procedures found in other countries bear such names as medical audit, peer review, bed utilisation review and professional standards review. Most of the monitoring is effectively self-policing by the profession. Medical societies have peer review committees; hospital doctors comprise bed utilisation committees; and government agencies call upon doctors in the various specialities to organise professional standards review procedures. In some cases, private insurance companies review claims, not only to detect fraud, but to assure that the procedures chosen by providers are medically efficacious and the most cost-effective available. And in some cases State health departments engage in similar medical audit procedures. These devices are almost unknown in Ireland. They need to be considered and developed in an Irish context, and their results evaluated, well ahead of further changes that would weaken or abolish other checks.

Ireland spends an unusually large fraction of Gross Domestic Product on health care, for the income levels in this country — as much as 6.6 percent, as compared with 5.2 percent in the UK and an (unweighted) average of 5.9 per cent in the EEC, apart from Ireland (1975 figures).[7]

Percentage of GDP spent on health care is an ambiguous statistic. Such figures are often taken to indicate the adequacy of health care programmes, and, so interpreted, would reflect favourably on Ireland. But they can also be interpreted as reflecting the costliness of health care, and such an interpretation would apply with some force in this country. Culyer and Maynard comment on an estimate that public plus VHI health expenditure was 5.7 percent of GNP in 1975: The paradox of these figures is that public expenditure in Ireland (including VHI) at 5.7 percent of GNP provides very limited health care coverage whilst a smaller proportion of UK Gross National Product provides 100 percent coverage' (Culyer and Maynard, 1976).

One reason health care appears to be costly here is that the medical card system is what has been described as a 'hospital-oriented' one. Over half of current public expenditure on health goes for general hospitals, while less than one-fifth goes for community services, including general practitioners. What is more, in the last three years the former proportion has been rising, and the latter falling. The hospitalisation rate, measured by annual admissions per 1000 population, is high — about 23 percent higher than in the UK in 1975. The hospital orientation is also shown by the fact that Ireland has an unusually low ratio of GPs to population) fewer than 75 percent of the number, per 100,000 population, found in Germany, France, Italy, the Netherlands, Belgium or Denmark — but a higher ratio of nurses to population that any other EEC nation.

What are the reasons for this hospital orientation? One may be that many GPs, working in isolation from other medical practitioners, and unsure of their diagnoses and procedures, use referral to specialists and hospitalisation as a safety net. In the 'Gowan Report' (Gowan, 1972), which reports on a study of general practice, initiated and planned by the South of Ireland Faculty of the Royle College of General Practitioners, and executed by general practitioners in the early 1970s, the following appears:

With few exceptions, general practice in Ireland is a free enterprise type of medical care. It has been described as having cottage industry qualities, and because single-handed practices predominate, consulting hours, quality and variety of services vary enormously . . . Advances in technical medical care, surgery premises (and) doctor grouping are, of course, developing in the cities, but, by and large, general practitioners outside these areas continue to practice from their homes, using little or no ancillary help, relying heavily on wives for quasi-secretarial and other administrative services.

There are some indications, especially from referral rates, that the level of acute medical care is more haphazard than in the United Kingdom, and Irish doctors still having a too-ready recourse to direct hospital admission to solve their patients' problems.

A Dublin GP, in a survey of his own practice, found himself referring 22 percent of patients seen to hospital out-patient departments, and commented, surprisingly candidly,

Some of my general practitioner colleagues will consider that sending one in every five patients for investigations would seem to be overdoing it. It is possible that this reflects my lack of confidence in my clinical acumen (Berber, 1974).

In medical systems around the world, the emphasis is increasingly on community care services, i.e. primary care by general practitioners, nurses, midwives and para-medical personnel, and on prevention — as contrasted with hospitalisation. The emphasis is for sound medical reasons and is a reaction to over-institutionalisation in the recent past; but it can result in economies as well. Perhaps one reason for the hospital orientation of Irish medical care is that the Irish system has, with some notable exceptions, been slower than many others to shift to the new community emphasis.

Another reason may be that for a majority of the population, hospitalisation is free, while primary care in the community is not. To medical card holders and their dependents, all services are free. To others, the pricing of medical care provides incentives to hospitalisation. Those with Category 11 eligibility can avail of free hospital maintenance, and free treatment by consultant specialists. Those with VHI insurance are in a similar situation. But both must pay for GP consultations.

It may be fairly argued that the incentive structure — free

hospitalisation and charges for the GP visits — has only a minor influence on the choice between hospital and community care, which is typically more strongly influenced by other factors. But it may also be argued that whatever is brought to bear on health care, decisions ought to encourage rational and economical behaviour, rather than the opposite.

The proposed extension of Category 11 eligibility status to the top 15 per cent of the income distribution would use resources which might otherwise go toward strengthening primary care and improving outreach to disadvantaged groups; and at the same time it would tilt the incentive structure facing the public still further in the direction of hospital care. What is really needed is a shift in the opposite direction.

An Upward Redistribution of Income

To provide free, at Exchequer expense, services which hitherto had borne a price, and which are received solely by the highest income groups in society, would be to redistribute income in a regressive, i.e. upwards fashion. At the same time such a move would be likely to leave Ireland with no change at all in the total resources going to health care, by substituting public money for private money. Those with incomes of £10,000, £15,000, £20,000 and more would receive free what they formerly paid for, and consequently would be able to use their increased disposable incomes for other uses — food, drink, automobiles, foreign holidays, etc. All of this is obvious and need not be belaboured.

Such windfall gains and regressive redistribution appears inevitable at some point if one follows the step-by-step, piecemeal approach to the attainment of a universal heath care system. But such a step should be pushed further into the future — after PAYE reforms, perhaps.

Furthermore, perhaps consideration should be given to limiting the regressively redistributive impact of moving to free hospitalisation for all, or other such changes. In Ireland, private hospital care — care in private beds of public hospitals as well as private hospitals, and as private, fee-paying patients of consultant specialists — is affected by very considerably subsidies, both direct and indirect, including tax relief. In the end, the private patient pays but a fraction of the social cost of his or her hospital care. Perhaps an extension of the public system to all should be coupled with and to an extent paid for from a curtailment of subsidies to the private system.

Other Priorities

There are a number of potential uses of medical care resources which have higher priority than extension of Category 11 eligibility to those currently in Category 111. Two are chosen for discussion here: strengthening of primary and community care; and improved outreach to elderly and other disadvantaged populations. As might be clear. these are overlapping if not identical objectives. They will be discussed separately, however, though briefly.

As is clear from some earlier comments, there are weaknesses in the organisation of general practice in Ireland today. One recent survey of general practice (Shannon, 1976) concluded, 'The isolation of the Irish general practitioner, both geographically and intellectually, needs urgent attention . . .' The required strengthening involves group practice and utilisation of non-doctor personnel, including social workers as well as nurses, midwives, para-medical personnel and even clerical staff. At the moment no financial incentives exist for such organisational reform. At the same time GPs are in need of continuing education, more frequent communication among themselves, and some system of peer review and evaluation. Both the State and the profession surely owe the public an assurance that doctors are competent. There is no doubt that such assurance is lacking at present.

The health services make available to low-income persons, without charge, and to all but the wealthiest, with minimal charges, a full range of health care services of a generally high quality. There is little known, however, about the effective outreach of the system. Do those who need care actually receive it? Such limited information as exists is extremely discouraging. In what appears to be the first and only study of unrecognised treatable illness in any Irish population, Walsh (1980) surveyed an elderly, and evidently poor, population in North Dublin. These persons were actually called upon, in person, by doctors and, with their permission, given medical examinations. The results are important and shocking. In 105 persons, there were 174 undiagnosed treatable illnesses, including 33 cases of uncorrected and uninvestigated visual impairment, 22 cases of previously unrecognised mental impairment, 10 cases of hypertension and five cases of congestive heart failure.[8] In addition to these, there were a large number of cases of previously diagnosed conditions not currently being treated or controlled, in some cases the person did not have a medical card to which he or she was entitled, and in other cases because the person was not entitled to a medical card. Commenting on the latter, Dr Walsh states,

> One feels that a more lenient attitude should be taken, especially as regards savings and pensions that exceed the stated limits, when assessing eligibility for Medical Cards of retired people because of the high prevalence of illness in this age group and of the obvious suffering endured by those who lose out on essential services.

The 105 persons examined by Walsh were not, in general, 'lost' to the health care system, or persons who failed to see general practitioners or who were unknown to public health nurses. The findings indicate, in the words of Professor Sir Ferguson Anderson (quoted, with obvious understatement, by Walsh), that 'the self-reporting of illness is not a satisfactory method of detecting disease at an early stage' in the elderly, a comment perhaps applicable to other poor and disadvantaged persons as well. That such a large fraction of the surveyed group should suffer the inconvenience, and even suffering, of untreated ill health and needless risk of death, as is revealed in this study, in a medical care system which uses 6.6 percent of Gross Domestic Product, is indeed a reflection on that system, and especially on its primary and community care. It is difficult to read this article and still believe that free consultant services for the top 15 percent of the income distribution is the highest priority for the development of the Irish health services.

Some Urgent Objectives

A programme for the development of the health services should depend on insights from other perspectives than an economist's, needless to say. But it is with some confidence that all of the following are put ahead, in a chronological sense, of extension of free consultant specialist care to those who currently have Category lll eligibility.

(1) Re-organisation of primary care. General practice needs re-organisation and strengthening. The objectives should be (a) better care by doctors; (b) better outreach and community orientation; and (c) economy. Group practice should be encouraged, with group-practice-based nurses, social workers, para-medics, etc. GPs need more contact among themselves, more

in-service education, and more peer review. Obviously, better outreach is required for the elderly, and perhaps for other disadvantaged groups. One possibility is annual physical examinations for all Old Age Pensioners, in the pattern of national school physical examinations.

(2) *Eligibility.* Dr Walsh's suggestion, that medical cards be available more liberally to the aged, should be taken up. At least the aged require more ready access to GP and other primary care — eyeglasses, hearing aids, dentures, orthopaedic aids, and the like, which does sound very much like medical cards. The cost of medical cards for *all* persons aged 65 and over would probably not be great, as relatively few persons in this age group lack Medical Cards at present. And while this group does undoubtedly include a few wealthy persons, such a move would be less regressive with respect to income than abolishing the Category ll ceiling. With respect to Category ll eligibility, two problems ought to be addressed. One concerns automatic index-linking of the cut-off. It is absurd that anyone should have services to which they are entitled taken away, on account of a nominal income increase which may leave them with lower real (i.e. inflation-adjusted) incomes. The other concerns basing eligibility on family status. At present, a spouse who has no independent income is regarded as a dependent of the other spouse and is therefore in the same eligibility category, while a spouse with independent income is in a category of his or her own, based on his or her income. The number of children is not taken into account. This structure creates two anomalies. One is that some families will have Category ll eligibility with higher family incomes than some families with Category lll eligibility. The other is that need, as indicated by number of children, is not taken into account, so that families with less need have Category ll eligibility and those with more need only Category lll eligibility, in many cases.

(3) *Free general practitioner care.* Free primary care, mainly from GPs, has a decided priority over further extension of free hospitalisation. One purpose is to strengthen health care in the community. Another is to redress the undesirable (price) incentive structure that now faces much of the public. Free GP service should be linked, however, with checks on GP utilisation or costs.

(4) *Checks on GP costs.* Checks are needed on GP costs. Ideally, whether the General Medical Service (which pays for general practitioner care and prescription medicines for the medical card population) is expanded as suggested above or not,

doctors should be paid on a capitation basis, a technique which has proved itself around the world to be the one with the fewest faults. If such a change is not politically on at the moment, one might consider a device recently introduced in the Federal Republic of Germany, where GPs are paid on a fee-for-service basis. Since 1976 any increase in the volumn of doctors' services above an agreed limit has led to proportionate reduction in the level of fees, to keep the annual growth in cost to 8 percent. This is applied on a national basis, so individual doctors still have an incentive to maximise the number of consultations; but for doctors, it can mean running in order to stand (nearly) still, so that utilisation rises faster than expenditure. In addition, meaningful peer review, or lacking that some State monitoring, is long past due in Irish general practice. Prescribing and referral rates should be reviewed, along with consulting rates.

(5) *Consultant specialist remuneration.* Consultant specialists should not be paid by patient day. The best technique is based on salary. Consultant specialists also require some peer review machinery, including bed utilisation committees in hospitals. The system under which specialists have absolute control on a given number of beds ought to be examined critically. Peer review should be nationally based, and a very close look should be given at doctors whose resort to surgery, or other procedures, and average patient stays in hospital, exceeds norms established by committee.

(6) *Review procedures.* As has already been noted in (4) and (5) above, medical care in Ireland should be strengthened by the development of a set of review procedures, where reliance in the main would be on peer review rather than State monitoring, unless the former is not forthcoming.

(7) *Limit subsidies to the private system.* Those in Ireland advocating a national comprehensive health service for all free at the point of use should give serious attention to precisely the kind of health service they seek. In particular, a question arises as to the relationship between public and private sectors of the medical care system, and the extent of public subsidies to the private sector. Low-income people are concerned with the large subsidies given in Ireland to the private sector, both because these divert medical care resources which properly belong to the public sector, and because they strengthen a dual system of medical care in which the public system necessarily becomes second choice.

A full separation of public from private systems may be too radical a shift for Ireland at the moment. Such a policy would undoubedly be resisted still more stoutly by consultant specialists among others than the current ICTU proposal of free consultant services for all. That latter proposal would not only leave the private system intact, but continue the generous subsidies which it now receives. But a policy of separation would seriously threaten the very existence of many lucrative private consultant practices.

Therefore, realism requires that we accept that such a change is not feasible at the moment. But further increases in explicit and implicit subsidies to the private system should be limited, and some existing subsidies should be carefully scrutinised. More to the point, further increases in public health services available to high-income persons, such as the proposed abolition of an income limit for Category 11 eligibility, should be paid for by reductions in the subsidy to private care. Such a policy would mean that Ireland could move towards a comprehensive public system without the necessity of regressive shifts in financing.

Conclusion

It was stated at the beginning of this essay that there are two general ways in which the health services can expand. In the first way, the level or quality of the services is increased and more resources go to providing medical care to the Irish population. In the second way, services already provided for a fee become free; no more resources go to medical care, but public money replaces private money. This essay has argued that it is in the interest of the low-income population to emphasise the first of these types of changes rather than the second. It has argued that the system needs to develop and strengthen internal checks on excessive utilisation before further services are provided free. And it has argued that when and if further services are shifted from the fee category to the free category, there are higher priorities than free consultant services for the wealthy, priorities such as medical cards for the elderly, or a free GP service, both of which might strengthen community care relative to hospitalisation.

It has been stated that the changes proposed here would serve the needs of the poor. But it will be clear that in fact they serve the needs of the working class and the whole population. They constitute an agenda for progress in the health services.

REFERENCES

1. The qualifications are these: low-income people and others see, in general, the same general practitioners, but the GPs may devote more time and care to the treatment of the non-poor (see note 5). When they use the services of a specialist, whether on an out-patient or an in-patient basis, private patients are likely to be treated by the consultant personally, while public patients may be treated by less-experienced junior doctors. Moreover, public patients may have to wait longer to get into hospital (Tussing, 1981).

2. It is common in other countries, including the UK, to find relatively lower utilisation rates among low-income people, in spite of their greater demonstrated need for medical care. In Ireland, according to the results of a household survey this author conducted for the Economic and Social Research Institute, the results of which will be published shortly in an ESRI paper, utilisation is generally higher among low-income persons.

3. The source of this statement is the survey referred to in note 2.

4. There is a substantial literature in health economics on physician behaviour, which includes a number of tests of the hypothesis that doctors stimulate demand for their own services in patterns which are unrelated to patients' medical needs and which are related to doctors' income needs. Studies from the USA, Canada and the Netherlands, and other countries where doctors are paid on a fee basis, confirm such physician behaviour. Similar econometric tests have been performed in Ireland and show similar results. The evidence for these statements will be published in the paper referred to in note 2.

5. These allegations come from doctors themselves, among others. One doctor is quoted in the *Irish Times* (9 March 1981) as saying, "Look, if I prescribe a drug for a GMS (public) patient, I will prescribe the best available, which may or may not be the most expensive. But if it is a private patient, who I know has a large mortgage and other liabilities, then I will think harder before I prescribe a drug at all. This is partly because I have time to think about it, whereas the GMS scheme does not pay me enough to give the same time and thought to the GMS patient.'

232

6. One possible exception concerns very large families with Category III eligibility. Medical card or Category I eligibility depends on income, family size, other expenses, etc., while Category II eligibility depends solely on income, with number of dependents or other circumstances wholly ignored. This means that a very large family with just too much income to qualify for Category II may have difficulty if hospitalisation meant substantial consultants' bills.

7. In 1980 medical care used close to 8 per cent of GDP, a figure which is not used in the text because of the absence of comparative data from other countries for that year.

8. In addition to these, the following were discovered: two cases of previously unrecognised anaemia and two of macrocytosis, as well as one previously known but currently untreated case of anaemia; six cases of prieviously treated but uncontrolled hypertension; six cases of previously treated but uncontrolled congestive heart failure; three cases of newly discovered and one case of previously treated but uncontrolled chronic bronchitis; one new case and two known but uncontrolled cases of angina; one uncontrolled case of peptic ulcer; three new and four known but uncontrolled cases of osteoarthritis; four new cases of deafness which were cleared by cleaning the ears of wax; two new cases and two known but uncontrolled cases of severe deafness from other causes; one new case of skin carcinoma; two new cases of diabetes; two cases each of urinary and faecal incontinence; one case of osteomalacia; one case of hyperthyroidism; two cases of severe lice infestation; one case of moderate hypokalaemia; one case of pneumonia; sixteen cases of severe dental disease; forty-one cases in need of chiropody; three cases of depression; three cases of severe anxiety; four cases in need of walking appliances; one case of multiple sclerosis; four cases of ankle oedema; and one case of abdominal carcinoma.

Poverty and Community Work

Michael Mernagh

The concepts of 'poverty' and 'community work' in themselves cover a multitute of complex experiences and practices and this poses a challenge that is compounded by the task of attempting to uncover these realities within an Irish context.

The harsh reality of poverty and various methods undertaken to combat it are not new to Ireland. The majority of our senior citizens will have experienced poverty at some stage of their lives, and the bitter legacy of the struggle for survival by the population as a whole since the mid-nineteenth century has left its social and psychological mark on the nation.

The many 'self-help' responses of the people as exemplified in the Land League and the co-operative movements and in the rural and urban Community Development and Action projects stand as evidence of the quest for economic, social, cultural and political viability and identity of deprived people in Ireland. If Ireland has had long experience of both poverty and community work approaches, what therefore is the difficulty in learning some lessons from the past and charting a more precise direction for future action? As a concerned people we seem to be too close to these experiences to be able to analyse, conceptualise and sythesise them in an objective and unified manner. It is hardly an accident of history that other Western nations with lesser experience in this area have produced economists and political and social scientists who have undertaken such studies.

This has resulted in a multiplicity of questionable and confusing practices in social planning and action, practices which are not always underpinned by any clear precise theory or philosophy.

The general assumption that people understand what poverty is and where it exists is not borne out in practice. The nature, causes and extent of poverty have long been the subject of debate and are likely to continue to need further investigation and clarification if this age-old evil is to be adequately tackled.

The concept of community work is likewise open to many interpretations and we lack a universally agreed definition in this area.

The purpose of this chapter is to contribute to the debate on these issues, drawing on recent experiences arising out of the work of Combat Poverty.

The Poverty in Question

How we perceive a problem determines how we respond to it. Poverty can be seen as a condition of disadvantage relative to the standards and life style of other people in that particular society. This is in contrast to the notion of absolute poverty where the poor are seen to be existing in conditions below a minimum acceptable level, regardless of the gap between them and the rest of society. Many millions of 'third-world' people who are forced to exist in apalling conditions are afflicted by absolute poverty. If, however, we accept the description of the poor as those individuals and families whose financial and other resources, fall seriously below those commanded by the average person in society, then we must admit to the fact that there are many people — perhaps a million — presently suffering varying degrees of poverty in Ireland. The most obvious manifestations are lack of money, bad housing, unemployment, poor educational attainment, bad environment, lack of adequate food and clothing, and above all a sense of exclusion and helplessness.

The Causes of Poverty

If there are conflicting views as to the existence and extent of poverty there are even more divergent views as to its causes. The following is a brief resume of these perceived major causes.

Pathological/Psychological/Cultural Causes

This view holds that if people are poor it is largely their own fault and is due to their personal inability to cope with the challenges facing them. This inability is believed to derive from personality factors originating in childhood. The underlying assumption here is that economic growth is good, natural and inevitable, that the general standard of living is rising and that it is a question of "accelerating' this growth in order to eliminate

235

persistent pockets of poverty. The poor should be taught to 'manage' better. The model of social change inherent in this argument is a cyclical/organic/authoritarian one, viewing society as an organism analogus to the human body. According to this model social change follows a 'biological' pattern of birth, maturity, death. It is organic in that society has no unrelated parts, no autonomous social classes or groups with conflicting self-interests, no sharp separation between functional entities, between Church and State. There is one, single, organic, social fabric, organised around the 'common good' to which all parts are subordinated. The governing principle underlying this model is authoritarian and hierarchical. Society is considered to be an ascending social pyramid, controlled at the top with little participation from the bottom. The few direct the many, and those who control see themselves as the guardians and interpreters of the social process: how the society should function, how order should be kept, how the 'common good' should be served, and what represents threats internally and externally to the life of this society. According to this model, significant or novel change is viewed as deviant or pathological and it must be absorbed into the system or rejected outright, as the human body either absorbs or rejects a transplant.

Historically, this model can be seen to have guided the traditional European societies and influenced the development of the Western Catholic Church. A landed aristocracy and a hierarchically structured clergy constituted the ruling elite, and their reaction to any challenge to the status quo was the same — absorption or suppression. Such control was justified on ideological grounds by appeals to the 'divine right of kings', the demands of 'right order', the preservation of 'sacred tradition' and 'social doctrine' and the assertion that this is the way things have been always done. In Ireland this model has been strongly mirrored in the *modus vivendi* of both Church and State, particularly in this century.

Inadequate Communications

This view holds that a basic adequate framework of services and benefits exists already to deal with the problem of poverty if only these benefits and services were proberly availed of by the poor. It is assumed that while acknowledging its complexity the administrative system of the country is generally sound with minor adjustments required to ensure a better delivery of services to the poor.

Lack of Adequate Income.

This view holds that poverty is essentially an economic problem and that if basic levels of income were substantially increased the problem would be largely solved.

Those who argue that poverty is largely a 'communications' and 'economic' problem adopt a *liberal* model of change which is evolutionary/pluralistic/managerial. According to this model, change in history is not cyclic but progressive and the best approach to change is to embrace it, stepping forward into the future rather that retreating to the past. Change in this instant is viewed as progress as society gradually moves onward and upward. A healthy society is marked by individualism and innovation thriving in an expanding economic 'free market' system. The governing principle is *managerial* through balancing the system and ensuring greater communication between the various sub-systems. As Ireland moves from a traditional to a more pluralistic and affluent society one can examine the growth of bureaucracy and its efforts to provide services and achieve balance between various vested interests.

Inequalities Inherent in the Structures of Society

This structural view of poverty which was emphasised in Ireland by the National Committee on Pilot Schemes to Combat Poverty, and which underpinned its programme of 1974-80, holds that poverty is largely a result of the inequalities inherent in the social economic and political systems which have built up over the years. Any long-term solution to poverty requires a redistribution of resources and power in society which implies basic changes in the social, economic and political systems of the country.

The most obvious manifestations of poverty were, according to the Committee, lack of money, bad housing, bad environment, lack of adequate food and clothing. However, equally important, and in some cases more important, was the sense of exclusion felt by poor people. Lack of resources, of self-confidence, discrimination and the stigma associated with poverty made it difficult for poor people to play a full part in the life of the community. They tended to feel that they were 'passengers', that their situation was hopeless, and that they had little control over their lives or of decisions that affected them. This sense of powerlessness could extend to whole communities in what might be described as deprived or disadvantaged areas.

The Committee saw poverty as both relative (to the life-style of the more affluent members of the particular society) and structural (rooted in the inequalities within this society.

Those who argue that poverty is primarily 'structural' and rooted in the unequal distribution of power and resources whereby certain people have access to the wealth, power and privilege at the expense of others, call for radical changes to ensure a redistribution of this power and resources as an answer to poverty. While the traditional model sees society as unchanging, and the liberal model sees it as constantly progressing without changing its basic structures, this *radical model* requires that basic transformations occur as the events of history bring about fundamentally new stages. According to the radical interpretation of change, all parts of society are related to other parts. Consequently, decisions regarding any one area have implications for the whole. Thus the increased energy costs have effected costs in all other areas of living resulting in a general recession, and the whims of consumers in America or Europe can determine the employment patterns in this country. In an attempt to find a solution to this dilemma the radical model proposes the concept of participation as its governing principle. The traditional model leaves little room for participation since it accepts that society be governed by an authoritarian elite. The liberal model, while allowing for participation of a sort, ensures that basic decisions are left in the hands of a managerial elite. The radical model, however, requires direct input from local people into political, economic, social, cultural and educational domains.

The 'common good' is seen as the consequences of co-operative participation by people in decisions and developments effecting their lives. The stress on participation, creativity and community implies a different attitude to change from that of the traditional and liberal of reformist perspectives. The traditional perspective sees change as a deviance which should be suppressed. The liberal perspective sees change as something superficial which requires management; the radical perspective, however, sees change as a potentially creative factor which should be allowed to follow its natural course. The tensions produced by change are accepted as the result of participation and the source of transformation within society or communities. When faced with conflct within society the radical response is to seek creative ways that lead to more innovative forms of society through fundamental change.

Poverty in Ireland

How is the issue of poverty perceived in Ireland?

In a survey on poverty carried out by the EEC[1] only 19 per cent of those interviewed in Ireland felt that poverty was due to injustice within the society, whereas 30 per cent felt that it was due to laziness while a further 25 per cent believed that it was due to misfortune. Although these views were expressed by a small random sample of the population (1000 persons) they do represent the current views of Irish people. They pose a serious challenge for anyone attempting to find long-term solutions to the problem of poverty.

Community Work

'Community Work' like 'poverty' does not easily lend itself to clear and precise definition. This generic term is nowadays used to include community development, community organisation, community action, and community or cultural animation. While these concepts have their origins in British, American or French experiences, embodying different strategies and tactics, and are underpinned by different philosophies, there has been practically no discussion in Ireland with regard to their precise meaning and usage. They are frequently, and in my view, wrongly, interchanged to described different realities, with the term 'community development' tending to enjoy more currency. While there is some overlap it is nevertheless important to separate these concepts in terms of their origins, strategies, tactics, and philosophies.

Community Development

This had its origins in the British colonial experience, particularly in West Africa. While this movement with its dualistic approach — government and people — was applied in a colonial situation, it may well seem to be applicable to our situation in Ireland. We have now reached a stage where some local government authorities seem to recognise a problem with regard to disadvantaged groups and communities and are taking steps to solve it. Resources are made available and development personnel are appointed with career structures. The Health

Board Community Care teams and their community workers, the County Development teams and officers and the Dublin Corporation Community Development officers, are examples of this. However, given the grass-roots and people-centred nature of Community Development this trend would seem to be fraught with contradictions. Any Community Development approach which attempts to respond to local 'felt needs' by way of 'self-help' action is in the words of Roland Warren, 'not a system maintenance but a system disturbing approach. In this sense it is revolutionary.[2] If therefore we are to adhere to the traditional meaning and definition of Community Development, it would appear that certain statutory bodies in Ireland are attempting to use this radical arm of community work to promote their response to change. A closer examination of current community work activities undertaken by these agencies will reveal that such is hardly the case and perhaps their activities might better be submuned under the arm of community work called 'Community Organisation'.

Community Organisation

Many social scientists see this as restricted to the creation, employment and co-ordination of social institutions and services. It had its origin in the United States. The Gulbenkian Report 'Community Work and Social Change' links Community Organisation directly to social work and, in the United States at least, sees it as having evolved from charity organisations and social welfare councils and agencies. Its major function is the co-ordination and linkage of existing agencies and institutions for the more effective use and delivery of services. It would seem to differ from Community Development both in its philosophy, its context, its aims, its relation to the decision-making structures and in its strategies and tactics. Community Organisation assumes that the 'system' is basically sound and just, with little need for radical change.

It attempts to adjust the activities of existing systems and agencies to cope with any strain or dislocation that occurs. In this context, people in communities who are the clients of the process find that initiative and action does on the whole flow downwards to them rather than originating with them or from them. The operative word is co-ordination, and much of the Community Organisation process is concerned with this. In this form of Community Organisation there seems to be little room for the concepts of self-help and self-direction which are at the heart of Community Development. This necessarily leads to the question of where independent initiative and action really lie. As social change accelerates and the problems of our consumer-oriented, industralising society grow in number and complexity, the more powerless and disadvantaged sections begin to rapidly lose out in the competitive battle which ensues.

In the past decade, therefore, there has been a rapid increase in the number of non-official bodies that have come to be concerned with social processes and issues. This had been particularly true of deprived communities and neighbourhoods that have been caught up in urban redevelopment and planning. Such large-scale disturbances have resulted in the growth of action groups, protest and pressure groups, all of whom have the common characteristics of being outside the existing power and decision-making structures and are demanding that decision-making be placed at the lowest possible level consonant with local control over local affairs. These often spontaneous movements can be subsumed under the concept of Community Action.

Community Action

This can justly described as the radical wing of Community Development and is concerned to ensure a more equitable 'dialogue' between the government and the governed, and a more equitable sharing of the power and resources in society. This 'root' of all community action is recognised in the second Gulbenkian Report as − 'A consciousness of the remoteness of the structure of power, the growing complexity of the bureaucratic apparatus and the control which that apparatus has over peoples' lives . . . the growing dissatisfaction which these bring". This report arrives at the following definition of community action. 'Community action, then, involves the poor and others who identify with them, in developing an awareness of a common situation which is to be countered by collective action.'

The growth in the number and types of these activities is a phenomenon of our time. Some have sprung up in response to the exercise of power by some external authority, such as central or local government planning or 'big business' organisations. The intention is to stop decisions being implemented or to amend them in ways congenial to the 'action groups'. The

241

housing action group of Dublin North Centre City is an example of this kind of action.

Community Action frequently takes on a political emphasis in that it is concerned with bringing about a more equitable distribution of power and resources in society.

Cultural Animation

This has community development orientation is perhaps, conceptually the most vague in Ireland. The main 'raison d'etre' of this form of community work to 'to provide a stimulus to the mental, physical and emotional life of people in a particular area which will move them to undertake a wider range of experience through which they will find a greater degree of self-realisation, self-expression and awareness of belonging to a community over which they can exercise some control and to which they have a contribution to make'.[3]

The conceptual development of 'animation', which has its roots in the French approach to Community Development, has taken place mainly in continental Europe, especially under the aegis of the Council of Europe, but to say the terms 'socio-cultural animation' and 'animateur' are freely used in the English language. The term centres upon the notion of cultural democracy. This implies giving disadvantaged people access to their culture and to the promotion of peoples' art and culture at all levels, and for all groups in society. The Waterford Arts for All and the Dublin North Centre City training projects of Combat Poverty are examples of the usage of this approach.

The Combat Poverty Community Work Experience

The Combat Poverty programme carried out under the aegis of the National Committee on Pilot Schemes to Combat Poverty and which was terminated in December 1980 merits special attention as the most recent attempt to use community work models in Ireland. Its brief was (1) to bring about practical intervention in areas of deprivation or amongst groups in need; (2) to increase public awareness of the problem of poverty; (3) to contribute to the evolution of effective long-term policies against poverty.

The Committee was responsible for the operation of some twenty-four schemes, thirteen of which were local Community-based projects. Since the projects were 'pilot' ones, both innovation and participation were stressed as key concepts to be used in any approaches adopted. The Committee understood that such an operation would involve risk-taking and were prepared to accept the consequences. In terms of approaches and the models of community work used it is not possible to treat this subject in depth since not all projects used the same model. A range of factors, such as the specific context of each project in terms of its environment, local people and issues and the composition, temperament and experiences of the full-time terms differed greatly. Generally it can be said that all four models as outlined above were used to varying degrees by different projects. Some projects attempted to incorporate all four models in their approaches and a more intensive evaluation might indicate the tensions and indeed failures which resulted from such attempts. Many projects, however, in accepting the Committee's structural analysis of poverty as rooted in inequality attempted to provide deprived groups with more power and 'say' on issues of importance to them. The innovativeness of the methods and approaches used to achieve this could be summarised as follows:

The Use of the Action-Research Approach

Action research can be described as an approach to social change and development which consists in putting research at the service of people in such a manner that they are enabled to use it to analyse the problems facing them, take informed action on such problems and evaluate its effectiveness. In attempting to use this approach teams of combined social action and research personnel worked together with people in local projects. Many difficulties were encountered within the projects.

In some cases the role of research was subordinated to the action and the co-operative efforts needed to ensure integration of Action-Research-Reflection within team structures created difficulties for individual team members. While one could point to its successful usage in some projects, the overall experience of the programme would indicate that while this appraoch is in the long term the most authentic one in working with local groups, it is also the most difficult in practice. It still requires further refinement and high degrees of maturity and skill are demanded of those who attempt to use it. In this context the experiences of the Combat Poverty teams need to be reflected upon and shared with a wider audience. I believe that case studies of the use of action-research by various projects would greatly contribute to refinement and development of this approach which is quite new in Ireland.

The Use of the Community Action-Education Model in the Programme.

While certain use was made of the Community Organisation and development models as outlined above, the most innovative method used was what could be termed the community Action-Education method.[4] This is variously described in the Committee's final report as one which 'involves the development of techniques to help people to see the connections between experiences, events and structures, to help people analyse their situation . . . To enable people to work together to develop and market their limited resources in a co-operative manner . . . to heighten peoples' awareness of the economic, social, educational and other structures impinging on their lives and to provide them with the necessary means and skills to bring about change in their situation'.[5] The report outlines the following broad phases which certain projects experiences:

The Pre-Development Phase: This phase, which was seen as very important in terms of building up trust with disadvantaged groups while resisting dependency and changing their expectations of themselves and the role of the professional community worker, required twelve to eighteen months to carry through. During this period teams tried to determine the needs of people, to build up community profiles of the project locations in terms of problems and resources available, and to plan projects with people based on an analysis of these community profiles. This educational phase was not without its tension and conflicts, both within teams and among people, as projects attempted to prepare the ground for a more creative and co-operative approach by disadvantaged groups to the problem of their powerlessness. This vital 'entry into areas' or 'pre-development' phase holds many lessons for community workers and may well determine the kinds of change which can, with their assistance, be brought about in areas of deprivation or amongst groups in need. It is this particular phase which, on the ground, separates the Community Development and Action from Community Organisation in terms of different community work approaches. The normal tendency of professional workers during this phase is to go in and 'get things done for people' often

244

without due regard to the issue of whether these 'things' correspond to the real needs of people or indeed whether people want to get involved in doing them for themselves.

The Planning/Implementation Phase As the title suggests, this phase was concerned with enabling groups to plan and implement action to deal with problems facing them. Emphasis was placed on the process of developing peoples' consciousness and cohesiveness in analysing, planning and working together, providing a forum for group action reflection. This involved facilitating groups in handling conflict, in dealing with power-sharing and decision-making, and developing intra-group communication. While the community work literature deals at length with the importance of 'process', it is a reality that is often either forgotten or deliberately pushed aside in community work practice, as many agencies and community workers in Ireland are not able to handle the tension and confrontation which such a process may throw up. Yet many will agree that creative change cannot come about without attention to this process. This of course begs the question as to whether those who plan community work programmes and employ community workers are really anxious to bring about change. The problem with community work methods and techniques is that they can also be used to prevent change. The process of facilitating disadvantaged people in acquiring information on their rights, in creating awareness, and in promoting the ideas of co-operation and participation was carried out in many of the Combat Poverty projects.

The Evaluation Phase This involved the teams and local people in constant monitoring and reflection on the action proposed or undertaken, and is necessary for groups who intend to plan further projects or activities. The phase helped groups to externalise and analyse the effectiveness of their action and the dynamic of power-sharing and participation, both between themselves and with other structures and organisations with which they came in contact. Here again community work practice often falls far short of the ideal as this important stage is often neglected even by those whose task it is to be concerned with this aspect of the work. In terms of education, the most effective work undertaken in the Combat Poverty Programme was carried out in these projects which were committed to and ensured that this evaluation phase was not neglected.

The Linkage Phase The view had been expressed from an early stage within the programme that the problems of inequality and powerlessness which might be peculiar to local areas are often created by social and economic forces operating on a far wider scale. It is therefore important to create forums, regional and national, for groups suffering from the same problem to come together to share their experiences and to plan for common action on a wide basis. During the short life-span of the programme such forums were organised by both workers and 'interest' groups. The expertise of consultants was used in an effort to enable people to discuss and plan common strategies. The final report outlines examples of such linkages. This particular phase highlights at once both the potential and limitations of community work in combatting powerlessness and deprivation.

In the Action-Education method used in the programme, stress was laid on the problem of definition, analysis and planning and the participation of local people in this process. Attention to this process often resulted in deprived people gaining confidence to take strong and direct action on issues of importance to them. Whenever these issues were of a controversial nature or posed a challenge to certain authorities, tensions resulted at local levels. An opposition to change led to alliances between those who desired to preserve the 'status quo'. That these alliances often consisted of representatives of Church, State and private business, indicates the serious difficulties facing disadvantaged groups and those community workers who attempt to use this model in enabling groups to bring about change. Both are labelled 'subversives' and the central issue is often lost sight of. While there is always a need for delicacy and sensitivity on the part of community workers who use this model, it is only to be expected that its usage in challenging for change will often lead to the kind of confrontation experienced in some of the Combat Poverty projects. The fact that such individual incidents of confrontation resulted in a labelling of the entire programme as 'dangerous' 'subversive' or a 'waste of money', should not be allowed to negate the validity and importance of this particular community work model in the struggle against poverty. As a model and a strategy it requires further development and refinement, but it is misleading to categorise it as 'conflict oriented'.

The strategy of seeking after justice with and for the poor can often lead to conflicts with those who are in a privileged, wealthy or powerful position. As already stated, the different models have certain tactics in common and the important thing for community workers and their agencies is to understand what model that are promoting and to what purpose. In addition it is of the utmost importance to understand the overall framework within which one is operating because such a framework often exposes the limitations of all community work models.

The Potential and Limitations of Community Work in Combating Poverty

A number of the Combat Poverty project reports highlight the limitations of community work as a way of attempting to get poor people to participate in the betterment of their 'communities'. They argue that people are so taken up with the business of day-to-day survival — as a result of bad housing, lack of an adequate income, lack of access to reasonable facilities of any kind and lack of information regarding their rights and entitlements — that they either have no time to 'participate' or do not see the relevance of such 'participation'. They further argue that some forms of community work show it to be a form of 'poverty management' or more specifically the management of discontent, and a way of providing bits and pieces of services 'on the cheap' instead of developing proper services. True, major issues in the fields of employment, health, education, income maintenance and so on require resources which are not readily available below the national level. Furthermore many of the problems facing deprived areas and disadvantaged groups in Ireland (as elsewhere) are complex, interrelated ones which cannot be solved by marginal local arrangements or 'self-help' efforts alone.

They require major responses from central and local government which entail radical changes in policy and a redistribution of resources. All that localised community action can do is to register local opinion and mobilise local effort and resources to apply a little leverage in key areas. When such local efrort and action begins to bring pressure for change to bear on institutions, the latter is often either to attempt to suppress, discredit and diffuse such efforts, or to absorb them into the system. The poverty programme in Ireland as elsewhere has experienced these responses. Attempts by certain institutions and individuals to block change at local levels, thus preserving the status quo, cannot entirely succeed if the conceptual basis of community work is stressed as an educational one, not in any formal educational sense but in the acquisition of new skills, and development of innate abilities, confidence and attitudes to change among deprived people. It does, however, seem that isolated community-based attempts to effect major socio-economic changes are rarely successful, but underlying the argument of those who say that effective community work requires close liaison with both central and local government is a specific set of value assumptions about the nature of society and the roles and relationship of institutions, agencies and people in fostering such a society. While the particular community work model already referred to as Community Organisation can promote such a liaison, it is doubtful if either Community Development or Community Action/Education can for long support such a thesis.

Towards a Future

Despite the many economic, social and educational advances over the past two decades, poverty and the gap between the rich and the poor, the powerful and the powerless, is still very much in evidence. Any scheme to combat poverty which is genuine and serious must try to help people to bridge this gap and approaches which have not been effective must not be duplicated. Integrity and, in the case of poverty, moral imperative require this. If community work is to be used as a key strategy in the fight against poverty and injustice, its usage must be based on a more explicit analysis of the problem and its causes in Irish society. Too many agencies both statutory and voluntary have been engaged in the fight against poverty and in the promotion of what they term 'community work' without a clear and explicit analysis of the problem and a precise understanding of the particular community work model which they are attempting to use. The Poverty Committee was at least quite explicit in its understanding of poverty and how it wished to tackle it. While many agencies and individuals might disagree with Combat Poverty's philosophy, their own particular philosophy has never been clarified. Those who steered the poverty programme would, I am sure, do it somewhat differently could they do it again. Nevertheless, steering a new course is far too easy.

Considerable advice can be quarried out of the experiences of the past six years. Much of this is of the nature of signposts and orientations, the community work as a strategy for change in Ireland requires further development, reflection and discussion. More openness and honesty is also needed by those who are attempting to promote community work in Ireland. These include the many agencies, both statutory and voluntary, academic institutions and practitioners in the field. As we enter into a more intense, urbanised and industralising society, new problems begin to arise. These may not be associated so much with the standard of living or material poverty but rather with the very organisations that are attempting to solve them. While the need to enhance the economic position of disadvantaged groups is still paramount, the further need to improve and clarify the relationships of deprived people with authorities and institutions who 'manage' their lives is becoming more important. The exigences of large-scale, long-term planning, of efficiency, production and increasing rationalisation is producing an 'alienation' characterised in Ireland as elsewhere, by loss of identify, a sense of powerlessness of 'someone else making all the decisions'. If community work is seen as a means of eliminating this alienation by attempting to place individuals and groups firmly in the decision-making process, then it may well move into a new phase in Ireland where the new problem area is not merely economic but social, psychological and political, where community work in terms of 'prophetic action' will be properly validated. As we move towards this phase the various community work models and disciplines will become clearly separated and organisations attempting to confine them will be seen to be entering into a contradiction. No one who is concerned with the promotion of justice should fear such an eventuaity and pershaps community work as a strategy to combat poverty will have come into its own.

REFERENCES

1. 'The Perception of Poverty in Europe' (Commission of the European Communities, March 1977).

2. R. Warren (ed), 'Community Development and Social Work Practice'.

3. J. A. Simpson, 'General Aspects of Animation' in Information Bulletin 4/1975 (Council of Europe).

4. This method closely resembles the psycho-social method of conscientization developed by the Brazilian educationalist Paolo Freire.

5. Final Report — Pilot Schemes to Combat Poverty 1974-1980. National Committee on Pilot Schemes to Combat Poverty (Dublin, December 1980), pp. 190-200.

Pilot and Demonstration Projects as Political Events.

S.M. Miller with Barbara Tomaskovic — Devey, and Donald Tomaskovic — Devey

Since the late 1950s, and growingly in the '60s and '70s, pilot or demonstration projects have become fairly common in a number of countries, particularly the USA, as a way of 'testing out' concepts and models in small-scale programmes with the presumed objective of seeing whether they are worthy of being adopted on a broader scale or institutionalised on a permanent basis in the institution where they have been tried out. They are regarded as 'social microscopes', permitting the detailed magnification of social processes and thereby providing governments with the data on which to formulate policies.

Under the rubric of pilot or demonstration projects, a wide variety of studies have been made. The range of the technique in terms of subject matter is extraordinarily wide: from studies of the positive and negative impact of drugs, the effects of housing allowances on the housing market and the poor, the significance of new pedagogic methods on the achievements of school children, to the labour market responses of poor families guaranteed a basic income. Obviously, it is a flexible technique, and its apparent flexibility may have led to its inappropriate use in many circumstances.

Characteristically, the key feature of the pilot or demonstration project is that it has a research component. Where research clearly drives the project, it is often regarded as a 'social experiment'. In this form, researchers control who receive or are are excluded from the impact of the pilot, so that 'control groups' can be set up to isolate the effects of the carefully specified interventions from general social and economic processes that may be influencing results. The researchers determine in detail (and with minimal later modification) what is to be provided as a benefit or service to those involved as recipients, clients, subjects or beneficiaries; usually, different variants of benefits or services are offered in order to study their impact. In the income-maintenance experiment in the USA, for example, the subject families were divided into different groups; these could vary by the level of the basic income guarantee that was provided and by the tax rate on the income from working that a family earned beyond the guaranteed income floor.

At the other extreme from this narrowed, research-oriented, tightly controlled intervention is the broad-based pilot or demonstration which is the focus of this chapter. Here, a broad range of services and interventions are offered a sizable community or neighbourhood; control groups are very difficult. if not impossible, to segregate or identify as having appropriate characteristics. The administrators of the programme, the service-providers, are in command, determining what they provide and how, modifying and changing their activities and services in order to improve them during the course of the pilot. The broad-based demonstration, such as Combat Poverty, is not likely to be research driven, but programme focused. The needs of an effective programme rather than those of rigorous research come first.

Despite the dissimilarities of social experiments and broad-based pilots, they emerge from a common perspective. They are formed by the pursuit of 'technocratic rationality' in the development of social policy. The hope is that 'science', careful study, can provide leads, if not answers, for the solution of pressing social problems As a consequence, 'evaluation' or 'evaluation research' are prized terms for they seem to offer confident, reliable information on 'what works' and 'what doesn't work', which politicians and high administrators can then use in their decision-making. The model is based on what has been presumed to have happened in the large private business sectors and in the modern military sector where 'R and D', research and development, prevail. The R and D approach calls for the use of science to translate concepts into products, to test these products for effectiveness, and to refine them continually until they come up to the needed standards. The 'hit-and-miss' of casual creativity and judgement is supplanted by systematic, hard-nosed, scientific procedures.

The social pilot/demonstration has this aura of the scientific/research model. This chapter argues that another model is closer to reality, that is a *political model*. The misunderstanding of the roles of the pilot blunts its effective use.

The Undependability of Technocratic Rationality

Pilot projects encounter problems of definition, deflection, operation, evaluation, inference and implementation. These problems, which we discuss below, make the product of the pilot effort something different from the simple application of a scientific approach to a social problem, the 'scientific model' of the pilot or demonstration project.

Definition

As every evaluator has learned the hard way, at least half the impetus of an evaluation depends on a definable, researchable set of objectives which is accetpable to the programme operators and the funders of the project. Since most pilots, especially broad-based ones, have multiple objectives, it is difficult to obtain and maintain agreement on what are the most important. For example, Operation Headstart, a pre-school programme for low-income children, wavered between the goal of identifying health problems of the children and pre-paring them for more effective performances in schools when they entered the first grade. The problem of identifying and specifying goals is not easily overcome and yet it is basic to the scientific model, for without specification, the measurement of outcomes cannot proceed. But the delineation of goals is a disturbing political and administrative act, bringing out latent and not-so-latent disagreements at funder (e.g. the govern-mental officials) and administrative (the operators of the pilot) levels. Often the evaluator leads funders or administrators into goal specification or does the job with limited contributions from the others.

The goals then frequently become distorted in order to meet the precision, and clarity which the evaluators require to move ahead in setting up their precedures and measures. After a pilot is evaluated, disagreements abound about what really were its goals. Sometimes, the dissent is disingenuous, as administrators contest unfavourable evaluation by disavowing the goals or objectives which were the standards employed by the eval-uators.

The dispute about goals is widespread for frequently the implicit purpose of the evaluation is to discover what is a useful or usable goal rather than the stated mission of testing the effectiveness of a particular means to achieve a sharply specified goal. In broad-scale pilot projects to deal with poverty in low-income communities, a goal of reducing poverty, as measured by income, is over-ambitious and inappropriate. Certainly sizable achievements could not be attained in three or five years, especially if forces external to the community determine its well-being. The implicit purpose is to discover what is worthwhile trying to do with a community-based approach, rather than measuring the short-run impact of that approach on the income levels of households in the area. *The forging of purpose* or objectives is what the pilot enterprise may be about — a discovery of a worthwhile aim — not the weighing of the effectiveness of means to foreordained goals. A pilot has to locate the right questions to try to discover.

The very form of a pilot may limit possibilities and prejudge conclusions. A community-based project to test out approaches to poverty may (and almost invariably does) mean that some basic factors in producing or maintaining poverty are ignored. For policy decisions at the national level which affect employment levels, regional or industrial development, and public transfer benefits are not evaluated. The narrowing of issues to those with a community-based pilot can deal with results in neglect of extra-community influences which may be more significant than the intra-community forces. One result is that basic decisions and structures are left unchallenged or, at least, unexamined in their national effects upon poverty. The pilot project can *encapsulate* a problem, limiting rather than deepening understanding.

A second result is the promotion of the 'blaming the victim' syndrome or diagnosis. Since the focus of the anti-poverty community pilot is restricted to local factors, the likelihood is that difficulties in reducing poverty will be ascribed to the wayward behaviour of residents, for that is what is studied, rather than to the inadequacies of national policies and structures. These latter influences are not in the purview of most community projects, while individual behaviour is much more likely to be the focus of evaluation. In Britian, the Intelligence Unit of the Community Development Projects detected a plot-like effort to blame the victim in the community projects. The more likely occurrence is a structural bias in the development of a pilot which encourages the unveiling of individual pathology rather than the depiction of bungling or premeditated failure at the policy and bureaucratic level.

The poor have been charged by Edward Banfield and others with producing their problems because of a short-run orientation, an inability to delay gratification. This short-run outlook may truly exist but may be more important among policy-makers whose narrow calculations and expectations of quick anti-poverty results often victimise the poor. A pilot project is unlikely to locate accurately where that inability to delay gratification resides because its structure does not lead to the collection of the relevant data.

Deflection

Some have defined a pilot project as a device for generating the maximun of publicity with the minimum of resources. Governments and agencies may deal with criticism and unrest by setting up a pilot project. This token of their interest in dealing with a problem carried with it the implication that much will be done later when firm knowledge emanates from the pilot. Latin America and other Third World countries are dotted with pilot projects that lead to no national programme. In the late 60s it was reported in the USA that not one of the twenty-five health demonstrations projects that had been judged 'successful' had moved on to become nationwide programme.

The pilot project can be a way of blunting or deflecting action rather than leading to it. The pilot can provide an aura of concern and commitment where little of either quality exists among policy-makers. It can be a way of 'cooling out' unrest by very small-scale, relatively inexpensive, activities in the presumption that something in the future much will be done if the demonstration proves itself. Since few pilots achieve fully the intentions ascribed to them it is always possible to say that more cannot and should not be done in this rational world because of the presumed failure of the pilot. Or, delay may reduce the fever of discontent which led to the offering of a pilot so that neglect may greet the final report without fear of political retaliation.

Some degree of cooptation may occur in pilots. Dissidents who cause trouble can be converted to staff members of a pilot and become enmeshed in the problems of operating it. With responsibility can come political quietude. Many believe that this happened in black communities in the USA which experienced many projects (pilot and more long-term) that provided employment for dissidents as well as others.

Operation

Since the pilot is a fresh, new activity, it starts from scratch. A board of directors, a chief administrator and staff have to be located; offices and stations have to be found; relations with funders and other important bodies have to be established; local residents and institutions have to be won over to acceptance; a programme has to be clarified and developed; financial arrangements solidified; a research operation put into place. But the pilot has to produce definitive results in a short period. Consequently, the pressure is to reduce start-up time as much as possible in order to maximise the time of actual operation. This haste to begin not only creates waste; more importantly, it leads to bad decisions and commitments from which it is difficult for a pilot to extricate itself.

At the other end, the pilot is not slowly phased out so that all involved can adjust to new conditions *sans* the pilot. Rather, as the pilot nears its appointed demise, its activities are in highest gear as the staff and residents now understand what they are about. Then, burial day suddenly looms, leaving many disappointed, disgruntled people, especially where the funder has dangled the possibility of continuance before the pilot. Furthermore, the greater the uncertainty about the future of the pilot, the more difficult it is to conduct reliable research. The slow start-up is overbalanced by fast finishes.

In between the beginning and the end, the pilot has more than the usual run of administrative difficulties. At every level of the pilot — from the (various levels of) funders, administrators, headquarters staff, field staff, researchers, to local people — a different motivation emerges.[1]

These concerns and interests often collide, producing acrimony and publicly noted discord. A frequent source of conflict is in relations between the governing board, or funder, and the project staff.

A new project is likely to attract and hire young people who are more interested than older persons in a new approach, despite the financial insecurity attached to a short-term venture. The generational, occupational and ideological differences between staff and funder-board may be sizable and result in tension, Or, established institutions may be offended by a pilot's staff attempting to fulfill its goal of institutional change, affecting the practices of established institutions. Mobilisation for Youth, a large and important demonstration project in New

256

York City which pioneered many programs later adapted into the war on poverty, faced both sets of problems as some of its original founders, established social service agencies, objected to the activist bias of the staff, as did the police, schools and other established agencies which did not welcome the pressure from the neighbourhood residents who were helped to organise by the project.

Meeting its goals (say, of institutional change) may endanger a pilot project. An effective pilot project is likely to swim in hot water, plagued by external stirring which worsens the internal conflict. The *political cost* of a project may be too high for the funder or governing board, and the pilot may be prematurely terminated or forced to dampen its disturbing actions.

The life of a pilot is not a simple administrative and scientific exercise. Poor communication, hidden agendas and suddenly revealed or unrealisable agendas (e.g. no bad publicity) affect the day-by-day operation of a pilot, interfering with the pursuit of 'scientific knowledge'.

Evaluation as a Social Process

The notion of evaluation is very attractive. Rigorously testing to what degree a concept or mode of action can fulfill its mission is a very sensible endeavour that should precede a decision to invest a good deal of public money. Unfortunately, the conditions for careful, reliable and broadly applicable evaluations seldom exist.

Evaluation research tends to be ritualised with set procedures and orientations. It is difficult to understand and act on the awareness that pilots differ in objectives, needs, uses, contexts and stages and therefore require different research strategies. Even where this is understood, it is not easy to pose the appropriate questions for research since there is disagreement about what they are. Since researchers tend to be married to a methodology, if not to a more narrow set of methods, they may not be flexible enough to adopt a set of procedures that are suitable to the question-and-action approach. Researchers are beset by their own politics of what is acceptable professional behaviour and may attempt to bend circumstance to inappropriate methods. In the 60s in the USA, for example, many broad-based community pilots were evaluated by psychological instruments with their individualising rather than institutional-changing bias, because these instruments were though to be reliable as well as immediately available and easy to score. The choice of methods corrupted the original purpose of the pilot which was the pursuit of institutional changes.

Choosing the right questions to seek to answer and the useful methods for getting those answers are not only questions of methodology. They are also questions of values. As Paul F. Lazarsfeld, a well-known theoretician and practitioner of social research, declared: methodological procedures affect substantive results. At every research stage of a complicated project like a broad-based community one, value issues are implicated. This is particularly true where a pitted, rocky, changing, terrain challenges the researcher pursuing a rigorous evaluation.

One example of the untoward circumstances for evaluation is that the administrators and field staff of a pilot want to improve its operations as they gain experience and understanding. This changing is troubling to the evaluator for what causes what effects comes increasingly cloudy as the interventions of the pilot are modified. What it is that is being evaluated is unsteady. But to keep to the original design may block the development of a more effective approach to the goals of the pilot. The desire for operational achievement usually overwhelms the evaluator's need for programme stability.

A second example is the difficulty about segregating control groups who do not receive the intervention and thereby provide a base line for measuring change resulting from the pilot's activities. The obstacles to obtaining a true control group are so great that many careful evaluators have discarded that well-established term and now substitute the phrase 'comparison group'. This replacement recognises the inability to constitute a true control group — one matched on important characteristics with the experimental group but not receiving the interventions that the latter experiences — and is an open declaration that the evaluator is dealing with some imperfections in research practice affecting the ability to draw conclusions. The broad-based community pilot does not provide comfortable circumstances for rigorous evaluation and has led American researchers to pursue much tighter and narrower experiments which they, rather than programme administrators, control.

Timing is another problem in evaluations. Many, if not most, evaluations are premature, beginning before a pilot has reached its stride and reaching a verdict on its effectiveness much too early. The evaluator, like the programme administrator, is faced with pressure to show results and seeks to use as long a time horizon as possible. The result may be to lump together ineffective beginnings with more effective latter-stage results.

On the other hand, the evaluation usually ends with the pilot so that the researcher not only does not have time for effective analysis of data but is unable to study the long-term and delayed impact of the pilot. Some projects inject a temporary stimulation which wears out soon; other projects do not have great impact in the short-run but have a significant impact on the longer-run. If evaluations are unable to follow-up the impact of a project over time, its effects may be over or under-estimated.

The expense of longer-time follow up may preclude that stage. This expense issue is endemic at all phases of a careful evaluation. Small funds for research impede the evaluation; sizable research funding reduces the amounts available for actual operations. The sums needed for a rigorous evaluation are surprisingly high. The consequence is that most evaluations are under-funded and unable to carry through the careful steps involved in a tight evaluation.

The competition for funds and attention leads to conflict between researchers and administrators and field staff. In addition, and usually more important, field staff is reluctant to be evaluated —for they see the research as a weighing of their personal effectiveness — and are unwilling to endanger their relations by letting a research team ask disquieting questions and upset the fragile activities which are developing.

While few researchers have encountered as much hostility as in the UK Community Development Projects, the experience is instructive. For here the various community-based pilots objected so vigorously to the research efforts that much of the evaluation had to be abandoned, the research centralised rather than decentralised, and a new intelligence unit dominated by the field teams established. Since the designers of CDP had been warned by Martin Rein and other Americans of the abiding tension between action and research, the intensity of the conflict testified to the difficulties in learning from the experience of others and the structural basis of the conflict between programme and evaluation.

Field teams see what they are doing as providing service or promoting mutual aid or action, not as part of a grand design in which evaluation plays a great role. They are involved in an action with a commitment to their communities. They are not committed to an experiment which they see as imposed from without, not generic to their activities. If they adopt a broader mantle and see themselves as part of a research endeavour primarily aimed at generating knowledge for faraway decisions, they believe that they will lose their motivation and effectiveness. They are probably right in this belief. As a result, they may regard research as an enemy or at least not an aid in carrying out their difficult role. Strained relations between field staff and researchers are endemic and affect the quality of the evaluation.

Researchers have their built-in biases as well. They tend to find fault with what exists. As Szarton writes on the basis of study of social science efforts to aid USA local governments:

> Since nothing works as well as it might, and since evaluators demonstrate their acuteness most readily by *finding fault*, programme evaluations are almost always critical. Even when they propose correctives, evaluations focus mainly on fault: questionable policies, probably inefficiencies, inadequate foresight, perhaps a taint of fraud.[2]

The orientation of many evaluations is to provide a yes-or-no answer, worthy or unworthy, with a bias to the negative result. Such responses may not only be ill-based but may misunderstand what is really needed. The question that an evaluation addresses is not whether a pilot 'works' but the more detailed set of questions about *what works with whom under what conditions and why*? Understanding rather than a satisfactory passing or failing grade on a pilot is what is usually desirable. The focus on failure usually obscures trying to learn from success. Some people are aided by a project even if many are not. In the effort to obtain an overall assessment (of failure), the opportunity to learn about processes and avenues to gains are lost. *The evaluation is miscast as a judging event rather than as a learning attempt.*

Assuming positive results, can the pilot be replicated elsewhere? How generally applicable are its results? Is there staff available for carrying through the pilot on a wide scale? Can political difficulties be overcome when many communities are experiencing the built-in conflicts of most policies and programmes? Or, could the pilot work better elsewhere? These questions are not in the purview of a rigorous evaluation.

Important information for making a policy decision is not provided by evaluations.

For these and other reasons, evaluations of pilots and demonstrations do not provide as confident and useful information as they are called upon to do and as their supporters frequently contend that they can. Some difficulties of evidence, standards and inference become apparent when evaluators seek to make their final reports.

Inference

Despite the careful efforts to pursue scientific guide-lines, evaluations like other research face many difficulties. Earlier, we mentioned the problem of imperfect control groups. Here, we shall refer to another difficulty: that of adequate statistical methodology. A prime example is the evaluation of Operation Headstart, the pre-school programme. When the Westinghouse research organisation evaluated Headstart, it concluded that the children in that programme did not do better in primary school than similar low-income children who were not in the programme. A change in methodological procedures in a later evaluation showed that the Westinghouse conclusion was wrong; the Headstart children did gain over non-Headstart children. The pursuit of reliable knowledge is racked by problems in design, statistical manipulation and simple error, as well as the imperfections of the basic data which are treated in the statistical exercises.

Assuming that one had reliable, valid results, what is a satisfactory level of performance? That, or course, is a value judgement which is usually obscured by the evaluator's report and the media/political interpretation of it. With drug addicts, an employment training programme may show only a 10 percent gain in steady work, while with women receiving welfare the gain may be much more substantial. But the first programme may have been a much greater 'success', since it is so difficult to improve addicts' work performance while welfare women easily move into work if they have any opportunity. The inference to draw from the results is not apparent. It depends on the standards that are employed. Since one cannot expect a pilot to eliminate all of a problem, what is a satisfactory level of performance? This standard is almost never (we know of no case) specified at the beginning of the pilot.

One way out is through the concept of cost effectiveness, or benefit/cost analysis. Do the benefits yield more in monetary units than the costs? This calculation requires, first, calculating everything in monetary units, which is no easy, certain task. Second, it assumes some clairvoyance about what will happen in the future in terms of benefits and costs. Third, an interest rate is deployed to discount future benefits since they are less attractive than current benefits. The level assigned to this rate weighs heavily in the final calculation of benefits relative to costs. Fourth, what is a benefit or cost is no obvious, sure item. In the USA 'benefit hunters' have emerged, who creatively dream up benefits which outweigh costs, thereby giving a pilot or proposal a more favourable rating than it would have in the absence of this neglected benefit. For example, pilot schemes aimed at juvenile delinquents are much more likely to appear cost effective when the cost of the prison stay that they might have in the absence of the programme is included as one of the savings (benefits) of the pilot. Creativity in evidence may tip the scales of judgment.

Broad-based pilots have a special problem. They do many things; they are the foxes of diverse actions compared to the more single-minded hedgehog of the one action of the experiment. Like Isaiah Berlin's foxes, the pilot knows many things since its activities are manifold, offering diverse social services, organising people, providing technical advice and information, advocating actions, connecting groups, making national relations. Which of its varied activities are important to its accomplishments, which peripheral? Which are worthy of spread, of adaptation elsewhere, and which are dross that should be abandoned? Few evaluations can provide a differential diagnosis of what determines performance. Consequently, the policy *inferences* for future action whether of simple replication or modification, are limited.

What persuades to further action?

Implementation

The assumption of pilot schemes is that the scientific elite is giving direction to a political elite. One tests for results; the other acts and utilises those results. Both parts of this assumption are ill-founded. By concentrating in this section on problems of implementation, what happens to results, we can see some of the faults in the second part.

The pilot or demonstration is premised on the belief that success on the small scale of the pilot will lead to replication and spread on a national scale. From the pilot acorn, the strong oak of national policy will grow. As we mentioned earlier, seldom is this case. The question that greets the pilot is: Is anybody listening? Is anyone paying positive attention to the pilot? Or is it being neglected even where it has positive results, or is it scapegoated so that its virtues are obscured by its conflicts and faults?

As pointed out earlier, the offering of a pilot may be a substitute for commitment and may serve to deflect attention and pressure from the need for action. No government agency may pay serious attention to the pilot, unless it causes trouble and its results may get very short shrift indeed. The pilot may have as its audience, itself — its board, staff and local participants — not national decision-makers. Reports are unread, filed in the musty catacombs of bureaucracies. They lurk in the social amnesia of a society or are caricatured and minimised by an often-inadequate label. The pilot has done its job, no new action must be undertaken; the death of action is the achievement of the pilot.

Inaction and inattention, or course, are not inevitably the experience of a target. But not infrequently that is the case. Where the party in power changes from that which inititated the pilot, as has occurred with Combat Poverty in Ireland and The Community Development Programme in the UK, then the pilot is killed, attenuated, paid little attention. A pilot that has influence usually has had the good fortune of continuity in office with the political party which permitted it to start. Electoral stability is an important condition for implementation of a pilot on a wider scale.[3]

Those elements of a pilot are most likely to be picked up and used which conform to the experience and prejudices of the decision-makers. As Szanton concludes: 'avoid originality'. If projected ways can be strengthened without generating conflict, a pilot is an attractive generation of solutions. But if a new path is indicated and/or conflict likely, a pilot may have little chance of use. If pilot projects clash too much with continuing practices and received, traditional wisdoms, then it is difficult to induce the changes that are desirable. But if the pilot does not offer a road to important changes, why engage in it in the first place? Thus, the pilot project by its very nature is likely to appear to be too controversial and unsettling in its questions and answers for its experience to be utilised as a guide to practice and policy.

When the findings and models of a pilot are deployed on a larger scale, they are likely to be diluted. Financially, the sums available for individual projects in a national programme are usually less than those available to the much smaller demonstration or pilot. With less funds in each activity, less can be accomplished. The diffusion of a pilot is likely to be accompanied by funding attenuation. Less money means not only less but a different programme. A somewhat similar practice occurs politically. Wider implementation of a pilot usually means that its more unsettling, disturbing ingredients — say, active and important citizen rather than elite determination and participation — are played down. The price of spread is the avoidance of controversy. What then is implemented or utilised of a pilot may be a faint reminder of it, a token obeisance to a mythicised experience.

We have been reviewing obstacles in the construction and utilisation of pilot projects in the development of public policies. Our conclusion is that the mantle of science is ill-worn by the pilot. A more realistic approach is needed.

The Political Pilot

Despite its many difficulties, the pilot project is a hardy form, frequently employed. Even those suspicious of the technocratic rationality/policy science orientation, see some value in it.[4]

Despite its use for deflection, the pilot can focus and maintain attention to a problem. Problems of poverty and inequality only occasionally and for a short period engage a society. Under particular circumstances, pilots can keep alive the interest in the deprived, the disadvantaged, the poor, the underprivileged, the unequal. By their existence as activities designed to respond to the needs, as defined by elites, of the usually neglected lower strata of a society, they can periodically bring back to attention that poverty and inequality still exist. They can serve as holding actions, until society is willing to respond more fully to the needs of those who have fallen or been pushed behind the rising standards of the nation. Or, pilot projects can serve as a foot-in-the-door, attempting to widen the concern for the disadvantaged and urging by their example the desirability of broader action. Or, in an especially neglectful time, they can provide needed services to a small section of the needy; not a great victory, but better than nothing.

Ideally, a pilot project should commence with a commitment to aid the poor. The pilot then is attempting to learn better ways of realising the pledge. Unfortunately, the commitment to national action seldom proceeds the small-scale pilot. Few pilots have in-built mechanisms planned for the continuation of successful projects'.[5] Commitment is needed because even if a pilot does not do well that does not mean that there is no problem and no actions that should be taken. Difficulty in a pilot should not lead to neglect of a problem and avoidance of responsibility for doing something more. A failed pilot does not mean that an unimportant or intractable problem exists. If, on the other hand, a pilot does do well, it is demoralising to all concerned for the small-scale project to terminate and no national programme to replace it.

One great value of a pilot is that it provides a 'social moratorium', where concepts and programme can be tried out without great costs. At least, that is how many hope it will operate — as a *learning context.* In this context, purposes can be clarified; means can be improved; To carry through this learning process, the emphasis should be on what works for whom, rather than overall assessments of the merits of the project. Particular attention should be paid to 'unanticipated consequences' of the pilot. For example, localities may pick up important components of the pilot itself. Scientific methodologies should be used not as definitive judgements, but as ways of understanding processes and problems, as aids to understanding rather than functioning as a Saint Peter, judging which shall enter the pearly gates of the heaven of successes. *Practical wisdom* as well as science are needed in understanding what is happening in a pilot, why it has the results that it does, and what might be useful elsewhere.

Instead of relying on a national commitment which is seldom there and a science which at best can play only a limited role, those conducting a pilot need to have a *strategic orientation.* They need to have an awareness and sensitivity to the political fields in which they roam and a keen understanding of what they seek to accomplish. The first goal is to maintain a national concern to aid the disadvantaged; the second is to put forward and push some ways of reducing poverty and inequality in which they have confidence. Scientific approaches can help in both activities, but certainly not alone nor completely nor without refinement.

The first task obviously is to develop an effective pilot, which usually involves some empowerment of the submerged. But that is not enough. A second task is to influence the way the media, the public and politics interpret that pilot. For the way that the pilot's experience is interpreted is crucial in reactions to it, the possibilities of its adoption and adaptation, the support it gains and the resistance built up against it. The pilot has to conduct an active campaign of interpretation and explanation, clarification and understanding, if it is not to be assigned unwelcome labels and be known only for its untoward incidents rather than for its major achievements.

The third task is to develop a basis for *persuasion.* If evaluations are difficult to develop and conduct in a scientific and useful manner, that does not mean that pilots can only rest with individual testimonials about their effectiveness. The effective pilot has an approach to convincing people about its achievements. Case-studies, first-hand field experiences of media people and decision-makers, focused evaluations on some segment of the larger pilot, public presentations by the affected residents — these are examples of ways of conducting a persuasive reporting on the pilot. If formal evaluations have their limitations, then other forms of persuasive evidence must be employed.

The fourth task is to develop constituencies for the furtherance of the pilot model. As Hayes says 'a good idea once demonstrated does not necessarily drive out a bad one.' A very positive pilot experience, as we noted earlier, seldom leads to a national programme. The spread of the pilot model requires building support for it in an intelligent effective way. Constitutiencies and support networks have to be built during as well as after the termination of the pilot period.

The first source of constitutencies is those who have been aided by the pilot. A second source is the staff of the pilot itself. But both sources are usually inadequate to press for a full-scale national programme. Other groups with a national base have to be won to support of the pilot approach. This orientation is difficult because the pilot model forces a limitation of outlooks. A focusing on a small geographic area is the usual concentration. But a pilot programme that seeks to have national impact must look beyond its small area. The pilot may have to link up with some national organisations or promote a new one; at the same time, it must be on its guard against being limited in what it does locally because of its national connections. But to have an exclusively local orientation reduces the chances of moving the pilot to a longer term and wider basis.

The underlying theme of these observations is that a strategy is needed: a strategy for learning rather than only a strategy for evaluating; a strategy for impact rather than relying on evaluations, reports and an unlikely commitment to lead to a national programme.

We do not suggest that a new model be born. It exists, but its form is inchoate, inadequate, for it is dimly understood. The scientific aura of evaluation has smothered the understanding of what pilots actually do. These remarks seek to promote the understanding that the now timid ventures of pilots in influencing responses to them are one of their major tasks, not a an after-thought or an unbecoming activity. To be unpolitical in a political world is to be naive (or saintly). Naivety frequently breeds cynicism and despair. The poor have experienced enough of all three qualities. The pilot offers the possibility of something different. The opportunity should not be missed.

REFERENCES

1. A useful discussion of this problem and many others that face pilots is found in Cheryl D. Hayes, 'Toward a Conceptualization of the Functions of Demonstrations', Study Project on Social Research and Development, May 1976.

2. Peter Szanton, *Not Well Advised* (New York 1981), p. 138.

3. A key administrator may be crucial. Some contend that the Community Development Programme would have had a different course if Derek Morrell, the civil servant who initiated it, had lived. The turnover in administrators and politicians who are the sponsors of pilot schemes is generally high. In small-scale pilot schemes to improve the qualityy-of-work-life in USA factories, even successful programmes are ended when the originating administrator is shifted to another plant.

4. For a short, useful critique of policy science positivism, see Brian Fay, *Social Theory and Political Practice* (Boston, 1975).

5. Nick Bailey, Ray Lees, Marjorie Mayo, *Resourcing Communities; Evaluating the Experience of Six Area Resource Centres*, 1980. Available from the authors at the Polytechnic of Central London, 76-78 Mortimer Street, London WI.

EITHNE FITZGERALD is an economist who has specialised in social policy. Educated at Scoil Chaitriona and University College, Dublin, she worked for a number of years in the Department of Finance. After her first child was born, she moved to a part-time job with the National Economic and Social Council. She has written three reports for the NESC — 'Statistics for Social Policy'; 'Universality and Selectivity'; 'Social Services in Ireland'; and, most recently, 'Alternative Strategies for Family Income Support'; She has contributed to a number of others. Aged thirty, she now cares at home for her three children, and does occasional lecturing and research. She is a Labour member of Dublin County Council, a member of the Dublin County Health Committee, and a member of the Joint Committee for the Settlement of Travelling Families.

A member of the Higher Education Authority, Dr. LIAM RYAN has been Professor of Sociology at University College, Maynooth since 1969. A priest of the diocese of Cashel, he was born in Cappamore, County Limerick and was educated at University College, Cork. He studied postgraduate theology at the Dunboyne Institute, Maynooth and sociology at St Louis University, Missouri, USA, where he obtained a Ph.D./on a thesis concerning Irish Emigrants in Britain.

BRIAN DILLON is a native of County Tyrone. He graduated from Queens University, Belfast, in 1979 with an honours degree in Social Studies. He also completed a Master's degree in Town and County Planning and is the author of a thesis on the role of sociology in town planning education and practice. He has worked on an inner-city development project in Belfast which was funded by the Northern Ireland Housing Executive, and on a rural development project funded by Roscommon

County Council. He has been Threshold's Research Officer since January 1980 and is editor of the Threshold reports 'The Present Crisis in Rent Controlled Accommodation' and 'Private Rented — The Forgotten Sector'.

LANCELOT O'BRIEN was born in Nenagh, County Tipperary. He was educated at University College, Dublin, where he obtained a Master's degree in Geography. He worked first as a research assistant in the Economic and Social Research Institute, Dublin and then as an administrative officer in the Department of Finance. He now works in the consultancy agency of the Agricultural Institute. He has contributed much to research in housing over the years and has taken a special interest in the housing needs of single people. He is co-author of 'The Irish Housing System — A Critical Overview' and has been a member of the Threshold board of management since its formation in 1978.

FATHER DONAL O'MAHONY, OFM Cap., founder of Threshold, was educated at Christian Brothers College and Rochestown College, Cork. His appointment as flat-dweller's chaplain in Dublin was an experience which prompted him to found Threshold, a housing research and advisory organisation. A peace activist, he is one of the twelve elected members of the International Executive Council of Pax Christi in Belgium, a member, by invitation, of the Emergency World Council in the Hague and national chaplain of the Irish section of Pax Christi. His special portfolio in the international movement is the promotion of non-violent alternatives in society and he has been invited to play mediating roles on many occasions.

JUSTIN O'BRIEN born in Arklow, County Wicklow, is a graduate of University College, Dublin. He holds a diploma in Child Care from the School of Social Education, Kilkenny and a diploma in Social Work from Glasgow University. He was a child-care worker for six years. He was a founder member of Trust, a socio-medical service for the single homeless in Dublin. He also worked for Dublin Simon Community both as a full-time worker and as committee chairman. He is currently a social worker in Strathclyde, Scotland.

JOHN CURRY is Director of the National Social Service Board. He was formerly Secretary to the Social Policy Committee of the National Economic and Social Council and Senior Research Officer in the Rural Sociology Department of the Agricultural Institute. He is author of *The Irish Social Services* (IPA, 1980) and of an NESC report entitled 'Rural Areas: Social Planning Problems'.

ROBBIE GILLIGAN was educated at Belvedere College and at Trinity College, Dublin. He graduated as a social worker in 1975. At present he is development officer with the Society of St Vincent de Paul and his responsibility for advising on and supporting the work carried out by 10,000 volunteers in the Republic of Ireland and in Northern Ireland. A member of the Council of CARE, he is a member of the management committees of three residential projects geared to the needs of young people at risk in inner Dublin. He is currently lecturing in the Department of Social Science, University College Dublin.

TONY BROWN, born in Dublin in 1940, is an economist and graduate of University College, Dublin. Employed as an economic advisor to an Irish semi-State Company, he is International Secretary of the Labour Party, a member of the Bureau of the Socialist International and vice-chairman of the Irish Council of the European Movement. A member of the board of the Dublin Institute of Adult Education, he is also on the management board of the European Centre for the Development of Vocational Training. A former Chairman of the Irish Commission for Justice and Peace, he was also a member of the National Committee on Pilot Schemes to Combat Poverty and served on the Pringle Committee on legal aid and advice 1974-77.

BISHOP PETER BIRCH was born in Jenkinstown, County Kilkenny, in September 1911. He was educated at St Kieran's College, Kilkenny, and at St Patrick's College, Maynooth, where he was ordained in 1937. With an M A. in English and a Ph.D. in education, he was appointed to the Chair of Education at St Patrick's College, Maynooth in 1953. He was appointed Bishop of Ossory in 1962 and, until his death in March 1981, he was closely involved with the growth of social services in Kilkenny and was well known in Ireland and elsewhere for his commitment to social justice.

Dublin-born WALTER WALSH is a law graduate of University College, Dublin. As a result of winning the 1978 Bank of Ireland Human Rights Scholarship with an essay on 'Human Rights in Prison', he attended the International Institute of Human Rights in Strasbourg. He is a member of FLAC (Free Legal Advice Centres), a voluntary organisation which campaigned for the introduction of a State-sponsored legal aid scheme and has provided free legal aid and advice to approximately 40,000 clients since its foundation in 1969. He was responsible for founding and is currently editor of NEW DEAL, a current legal and social affairs magazine.

Born in Dublin, NOREEN KEARNEY was educated at University College, Dublin, and at Edinburgh University. She qualified as a psychiatric social worker in 1962 and worked both in Northern Ireland and in the Republic of Ireland. A member of the Eastern Health Board and of the WHO Expert Advisory Panel on Health Manpower she has been on the staff of the Department of Social Studies in Trinity College, Dublin, since 1973.

Oregon-born DR A. DALE TUSSING was educated at San Francisco and at Berkeley, California. He was awarded a doctorate in Economics at Syracuse University, New York, in 1964. Presently Professor of Economics at Syracuse University he was until recently Research Professor at the Economic and Social Research Institute, Dublin. Author of *Poverty in a Dual Economy* (New Tork, 1972) he was also responsible for the 1978 ESRI, Report 'Irish Educational Expenditures in Past, Present and Future'.

MICHAEL MERNAGH, a native of Kilkenny, is a member of the Augustinian Order. Formerly a director of a cathetical centre in Northern Nigeria he was until recently director of the National Committee on Pilot Schemes to Combat Poverty. He studied at Collegio Santa Monica, Rome, Ecole des Hautes Etudes, Sorbonne, and at Manchester University, England. A member of the board of Congood, the Association of non-governmental organisations promoting overseas development, he is also a member of the executive of the International Association for Community Development at Marcinelle Belgium, where his task is the promotion of community development in overseas countries.

MICHAEL MILLER is Professor of Sociology in Boston University. He was formerly Professor of Education and Sociology at New York University, Professor of Sociology at Maxwell Graduate School and Senior Research Associate, Youth Development Centre, Syracuse University. He was a consultant to the US Government on poverty and social change and is the author of many publications on these topics.

SISTER STANISLAUS KENNEDY is a member of the Irish Sisters of Charity and a professional social worker. She was chairperson of the National Committee on Pilot Schemes to Combat Poverty, from 1974 to 1980. She has been on the staff of Kilkenny Social Services since its inception and is now co-ordinator of its services. Born in Dingle, County Kerry, in 1940, Sister Stanislaus is a graduate of University College, Dublin (M. Soc. Sc.), and of the University of Manchester (Diploma in Applied Social Studies). She is the author of *Who Should Care, The Development of Kilkenny Social Services* (1981).

272